I0793566

POSTCARD HISTORY SERIES

# *Great Sodus Bay*

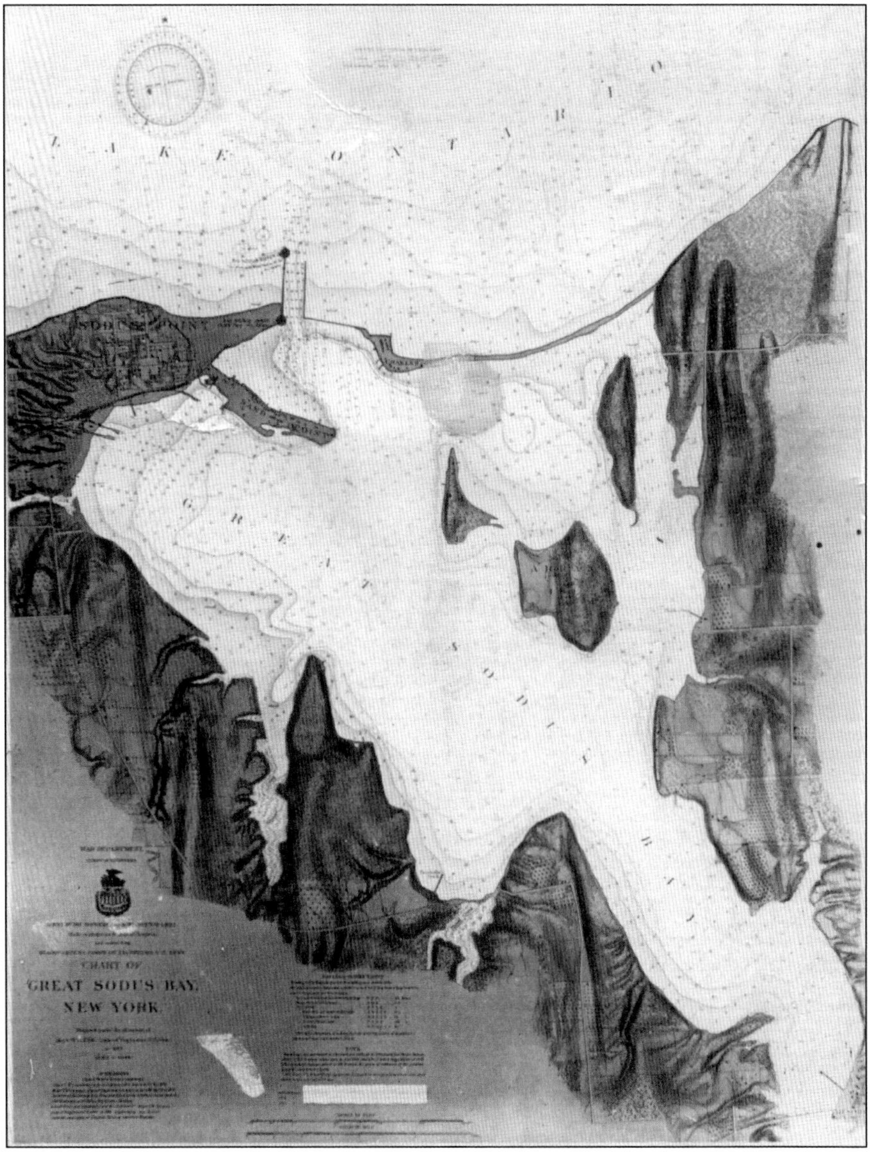


Postmarked July 1911, this postcard shows an Army Corps of Engineers chart for Great Sodus Bay. An important tool for sailors, charts help to enable safe passage as well as in locating important sites and landmarks. As H. Jackson Brown Jr. writes in *P.S. I Love You*: "Throw off the bowlines. Sail away from safe harbor. Catch the trade winds in your sails. Explore. Dream. Discover." Set course for Great Sodus Bay! (Author's collection.)

**On the Front Cover:** The well-known steamer *Sunbeam* passes the Sodus Bay Yacht Club on its way to deliver passengers to their destination on Great Sodus Bay. (Author's collection.)

**On the Back Cover:** Only a few postcards highlight winter views of Sodus Bay. Wind and wave action freezes the mounds of snow and ice over the pier and catwalk, making for a very difficult journey. This image of the west pier, lighthouse, and catwalk reminds readers of the danger lighthouse keepers faced as they did their job each day in all kinds of weather. (Author's collection.)

POSTCARD HISTORY SERIES

# *Great Sodus Bay*

*Rosa Fox*

ARCADIA PUBLISHING

ISBN 978-1-4671-1661-9

Published by Arcadia Publishing
Charleston, South Carolina

Printed in the United States of America

Library of Congress Control Number: 2015957320

For all general information contact Arcadia Publishing at:
Telephone 843-853-2070
Fax 843-853-0044
E-mail sales@arcadiapublishing.com
For customer service and orders:
Toll-Free 1-888-313-2665

Visit us on the Internet at www.arcadiapublishing.com

*Great Sodus Bay is dedicated to David and Lizzie.*
*This book would not have been accomplished*
*without their love and support.*

# Contents

# Acknowledgments

This book is possible thanks to the photographers who captured images of Great Sodus Bay. Bruce Schipper, my eager proofreader, provided brilliant suggestions for improving the flow of this book. Joe O'Toole, curator of the Sodus Bay Lighthouse Museum, was so very welcoming and enthusiastic as I descended upon him to dig through the museum's image files. I am grateful to Gilbert Burgess and John Boogaard for their unwavering interest and encouragement. Fellow postcard collector and Sodus Bay historian John Powell provided inspiration and amazing tips to rare postcard finds. Sodus Point historians Bruce and Edith Farrington and Bill Huff shared lively discussions about Sodus Point. Wayne County historian Peter Evans and his clerk, Jane Milem, assisted my beginning research.

Many thanks go to Nancy Doubleday, Steve and Janet Garfield, Jim Kunkel, and Rob Cunningham from the Seneca Waterways Boy Scout Council; Scott Price, US Coast Guard historian; and Rosemary Willette, Sodus Bay Yacht Club historian, for digging into their collections to share images. Amazing Sodus Bay history buffs on Facebook keep the old photographs and history alive—especially Ned Ludd and Cathy Contant.

Arcadia's best—Sharon McAllister and Henry Clougherty—journeyed with me through various stages of this writing process. My good friend Tim Pauldine planted the seed for this book a few seasons ago, and he has regularly watered this seedling with encouragement, wisdom, and good humor.

My daughter Lizzie provided nutrition for the table as well as for my mind and heart throughout this journey. David, my Sodus Bay soul mate, traveled to countless postcard shows, searched for postcards online, studied postcards to determine locations (especially since so much has changed over the past 100 years), navigated boat rides to better understand the views of particular postcards, and remained the most loyal supporter of this endeavor.

Unless otherwise noted, the images in this Postcard History Series book are from the Foxes' private collection. Additional images from the Town of Huron (TOH) and Sodus Bay Historical Society (SBHS) have greatly enhanced the content of this book. Other individual and organizational contributions are noted with great appreciation.

# Introduction

*Great Sodus Bay* pays tribute to a period beginning in the late 1800s and ending around 1930, when industry, travel, and leisure time expanded so as to evolve a different kind of explorer. During this period, Sodus Bay became a favored location for the development of commerce with the shipping of coal and other goods through the port of Sodus Point. Sodus Bay also became a destination resort for people from local communities, as well as distant places like New York City and Philadelphia. People seeking water recreation, fresh air, and the beauty of nature came to Sodus Bay. The mission of this book is to convey through images and stories the growth of and affection for Great Sodus Bay.

The history of Great Sodus Bay is unique and diverse. A number of interesting communities around Sodus Bay developed during this period of expansion and most continue to thrive today. The stories of these rising communities comprise chapters 1 through 7. Chapter 8 is dedicated to the lighthouses that have served as beacons to ships great and small. Chapter 9 highlights the different boats that have found their way around the bay.

Making a distinction between Great, Blind, and Little Sodus Bays is appropriate here. Little Sodus Bay is about 14 miles east of Great Sodus Bay, on the south shore of Lake Ontario where the village of Fair Haven is located. Blind Sodus Bay lies 12 miles east of Great Sodus Bay and is nearly landlocked, with a very small channel that must be dredged every season by local residents. Great Sodus Bay is referred to in this volume as Sodus Bay.

There are numerous writings and varied sources for historical information on Sodus Bay. I have listed several books in the bibliography that should be on every Sodus Bay history buff's library shelf. Walter Henry Green's *Great Sodus Bay: History, Reminiscences, Anecdotes, and Legends*, published in 1947, provides a detailed account of the early history of the area. Several unpublished local writings by authors with summer residences in Sodus Bay communities provided material pertinent to particular locations. Notable unpublished works are *Hills Tumble Into Ontario* (1989), which goes through the history of Lake Bluff, by John C. Becker and *Point Charles Sketch* (1902), which follows the story of Charles Point, by James C. Sheffield.

The bibliography includes several websites that provide continually developing historical information about Sodus Bay. Of particular note is Historicsoduspoint.com, administered by Village of Sodus Point historian Bruce Farrington. Farrington provides a wealth of information on this website, pertinent to not only Sodus Point, but also to other parts of the bay, making Historicsoduspoint.com a researcher's and layperson's playground. For much of this book, old newspaper articles became a chief research tool, providing information and historical tales for many captions contained within. The website Nyshistoricnewspapers.org offers an extensive library of publications.

The use and study of maps is critical to understanding the history of an area. Knowing the location of various points of interest provides clarity to better understand the geographic, commercial, and recreational components impacting the development of Sodus Bay. Close-up sections from *The 1904 New Century Atlas of Wayne County, New York* that show Sodus Point Village and the towns of Sodus and Huron are used to help the reader better envision location details.

Postcards and photographs are tremendously useful tools to tell the story of a person, place, or thing. The popular use of postcards began in the 1860s. Before 1907, the so-called undivided back postcard was used. These postcards allowed an address only on the back of the postcard. Any message was restricted to the front side, which often featured a photograph. Beginning in 1907, the Post Office Department allowed senders to place a message on the address side of the postcard. The divided back postcard remains in use today. The majority of the postcards and photographs in this book are from between 1905–1920, but later postcards and images are used in certain instances to help tell a story pertinent to the history of a particular topic.

During the latter half of the 19th century and into the mid-20th century, the commercial expansion of Sodus Bay grew hand in hand with recreational development. The course of time at Sodus Bay, however, has allowed that instead of embodying the highly desired and anticipated commercial and industrial landscape envisioned by some of the early settlers and explorers, this scenic bay has been able to retain an abundance of its natural beauty and grace. Sodus Bay developed into a resort that continues to draw upon the gifts of nature, allowing both the resident and the visitor an opportunity to enjoy recreation and relaxation on its beautiful shores and waters.

Before closing, I must recognize the invitation to history provided by some special people who were the original historic facilitators for this book. In 1981, my mom and dad, Frances and Bruce May, took me to a Genesee Valley Bottle Show where I found my first Sodus Bay postcard. It was a postcard of Lake Bluff—where my husband, David, spent summers growing up, where four generations of the Fox family have enjoyed the gifts of this unique spot on Sodus Bay, and where we now call home. As an extra special treat, the back side of that first postcard had a Lake Bluff postmark. Ever since, we have been hooked on collecting Sodus Bay postcards.

My father-in-law, Paul Fox, passed on a collection of Sodus Bay historical materials that facilitate much reading and family discussion. Vastly more treasured than the bountiful resource materials was the love and passion for Sodus Bay Paul so graciously shared. This closing notation would not be complete without remarking about Paul's sister, Harriet Fox Blow. Harriet's love of Sodus Bay, Lake Ontario, Crescent Beach, Lake Bluff, nature, and reading provided a model for living a good life. Harriet was blessed to live 101 wonderful years, likely because of the good air and community found at Lake Bluff!

Now, let us begin our cruise around Great Sodus Bay.

# *One*

# Resort

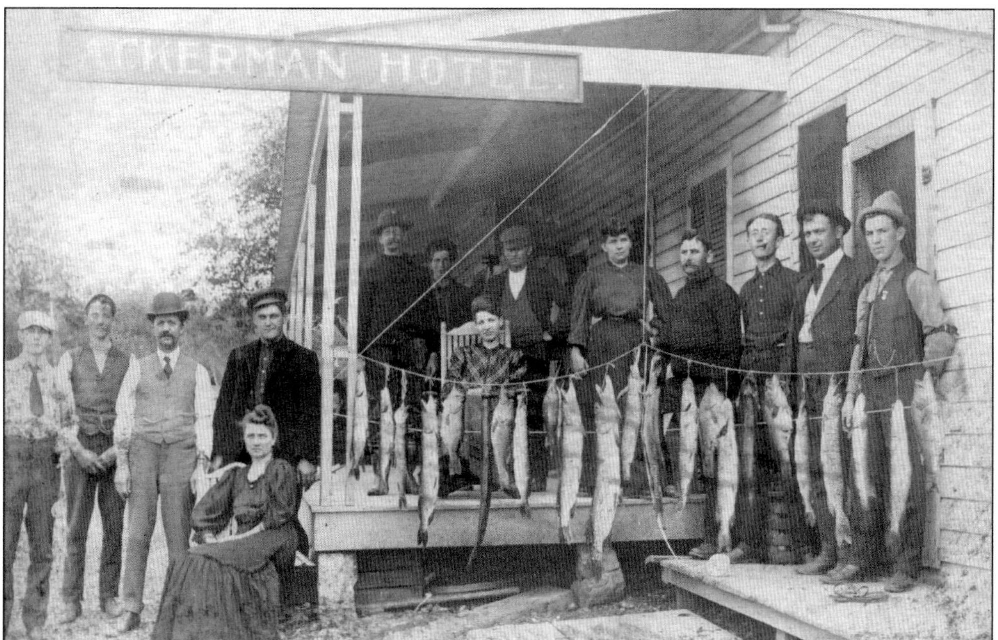


The caption for this image could read "All in a day's catch." The hamlet of Resort became a haven for fishermen and hunters. Proudly displaying their catch of the day on the back porch of the Ackerman Hotel, these stern-looking men and women viewing the photographer seem to be thinking "and the fish that got away was way bigger than any of these!" (TOH.)

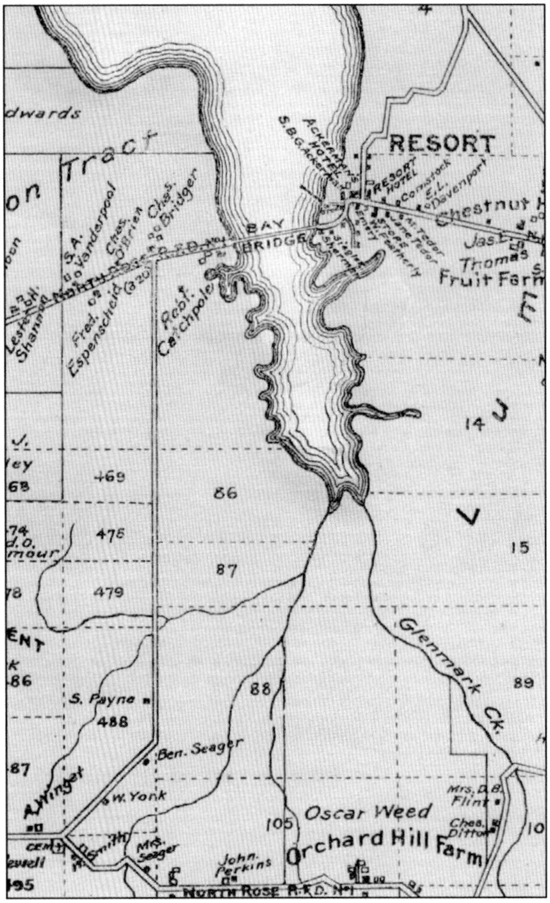


The headwaters of Sodus Bay, Sodus Bay Bridge, and the hamlet of Resort, formerly known as Port Glasgow, are shown in this close-up section of the map of the town of Huron from the *1904 New Century Atlas of Wayne County.* This map locates the hotels, stores, and residents of Resort at the turn of the 20th century. Some residents' names from that time are still familiar in the Sodus Bay area today. (TOH.)

In this bay-side shot, the photographer has captured a gathering of hardy, and maybe a little rowdy, musicians and friends posing on the bay-side porch of the Ackerman Hotel. The planking on the lawn leads to the dock at the water's edge. Resort's low terrain and seasonal high water made the planking necessary for guests to keep their feet dry. (TOH.)

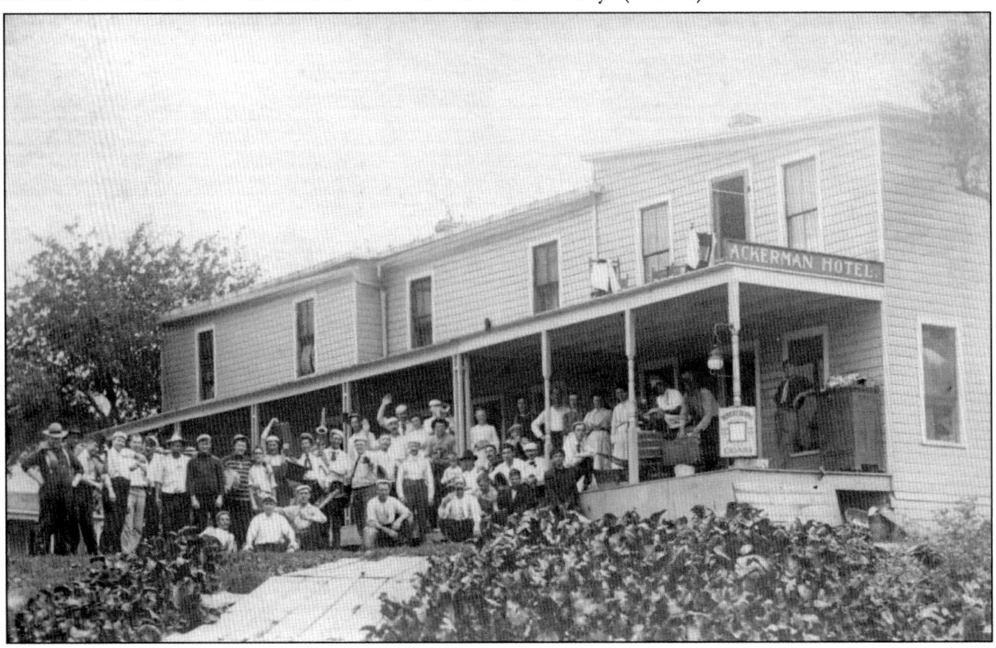

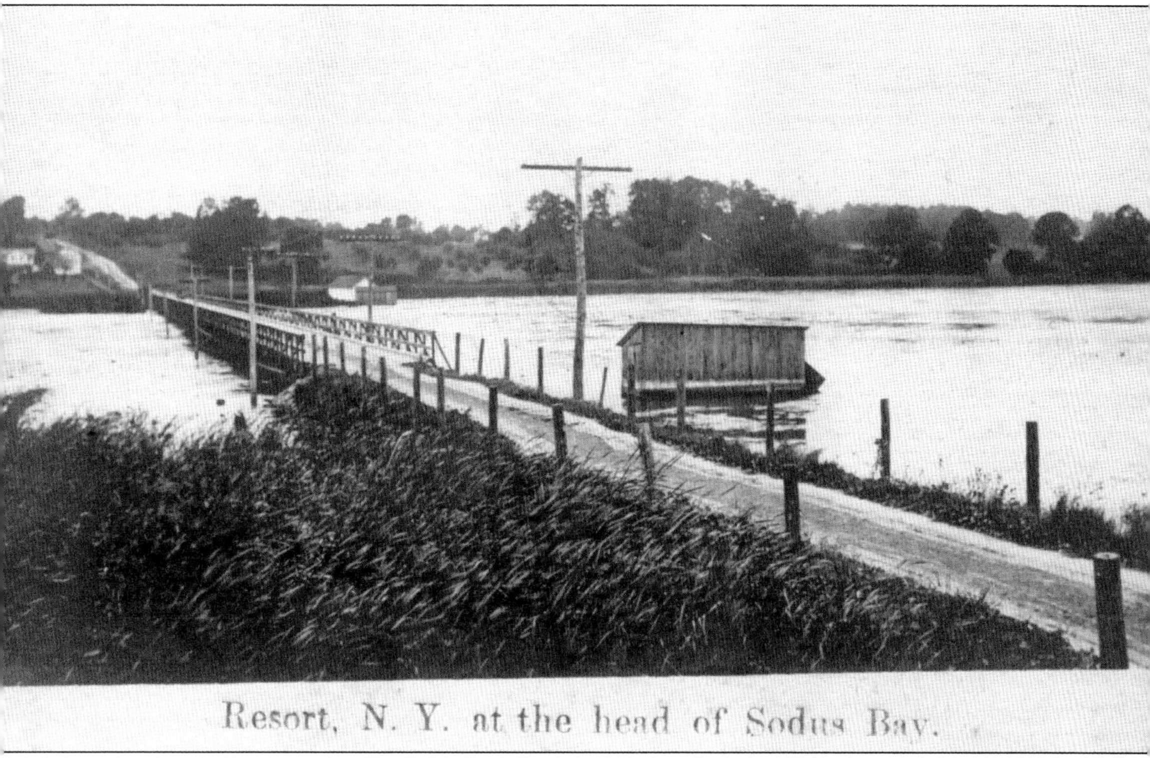


Ridge Road was once a trail for the Iroquois. In the early 1800s, the trail became a dirt road for mail and passenger stagecoaches traveling between Oswego and Lewiston. Several different methods were used to cross Sodus Bay. Initially, a bridge of floating logs was constructed. Storms and high water caused the floating bridges to wash out, so a log ferry with a rope tied to both sides of the bay was used to allow travelers transport from one side of the bay to the other. During the late 1800s, New York State devised several plans to provide a more substantial crossing structure. Efforts to improve this crossing in 1903 revealed a "false bottom." Beneath the upper two-to-three-foot layer of crust, workers discovered a bottom layer of silt over 70 feet deep. In 1904, an improved plan was created to provide a more stable footing for the new bridge. Looking west, this view from Resort shows the Sodus Bay Bridge connecting the east and west shores at the head of Sodus Bay. (TOH.)

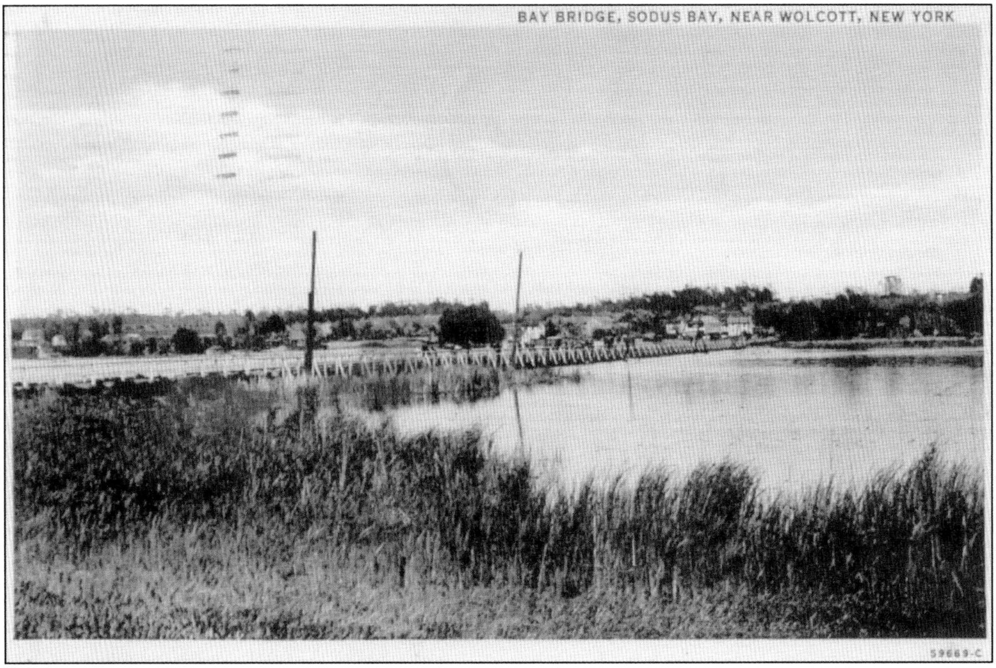


In these views looking east across Sodus Bay Bridge, sometime between 1905 and 1921, is the hamlet of Resort on the southeast shore of Sodus Bay. Once a hopeful commercial shipping port in the early 1800s, this little community has seen many transitions. Its first name was Floating Bridge, because of the structure used to cross the bay at the time. Then, in 1822, Joseph Fellows and Andrew McNab renamed the hamlet Port Glasgow after the city in their homeland, Scotland. By the turn of the 20th century, as use of the hamlet changed from the commercial dreams of the past to a small community sought out for recreation, it became known as Resort and has held that name ever since.

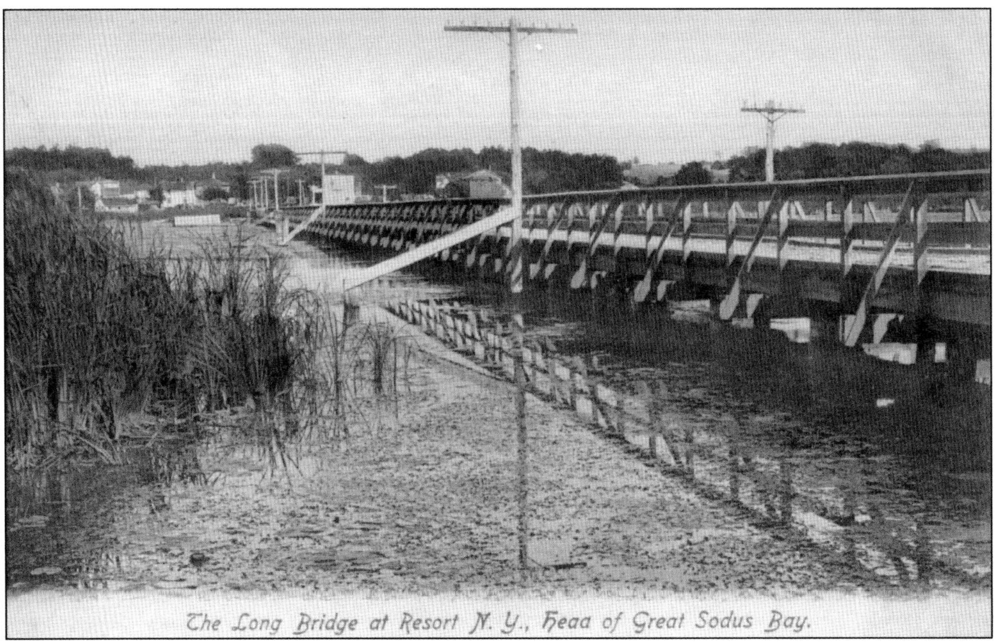

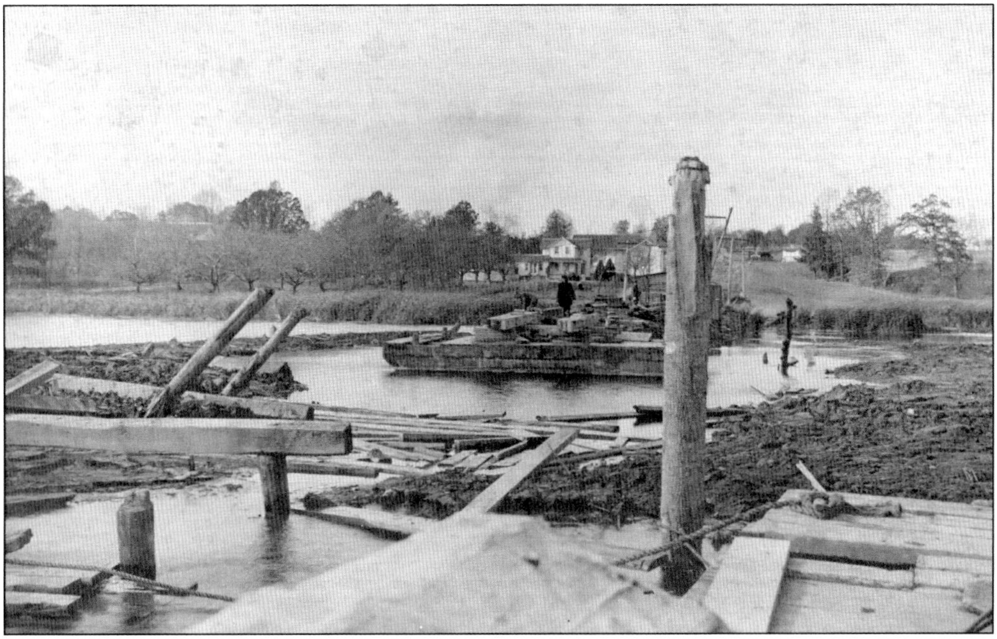

The photograph above provides a view looking toward the western shore across the construction site of the Sodus Bay Bridge around 1904. It is a wonder how these bridge builders ever managed such a feat with the obstacles they faced, such as the need for footers going down over 70 feet into the silt. The photograph below was taken around the late 1950s from just about the same vantage point (on the east shore looking west). This is another Sodus Bay Bridge, built in 1921. The walkway was added in 1938. (Both, TOH.)

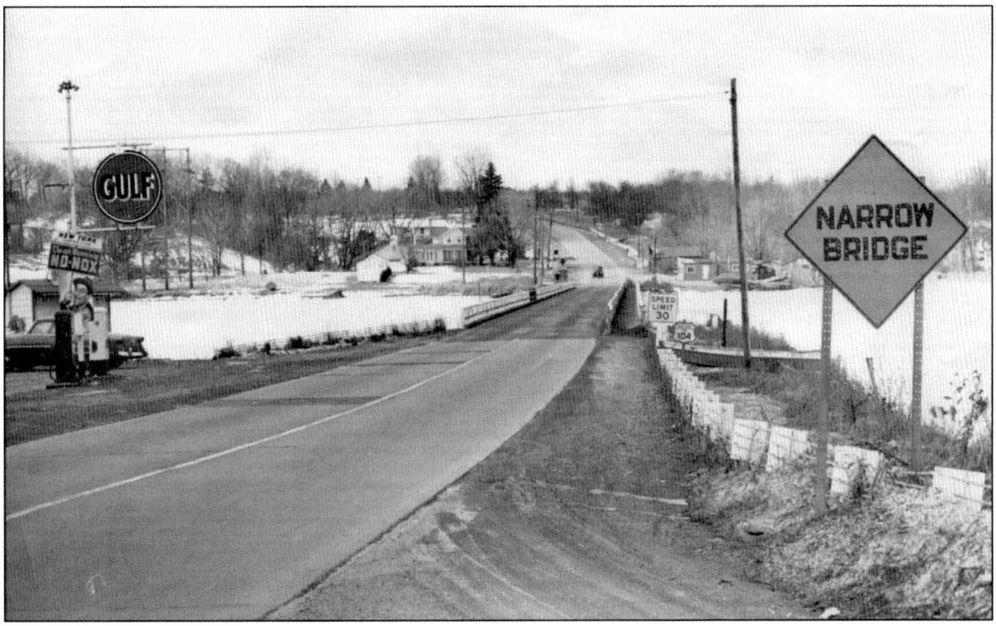

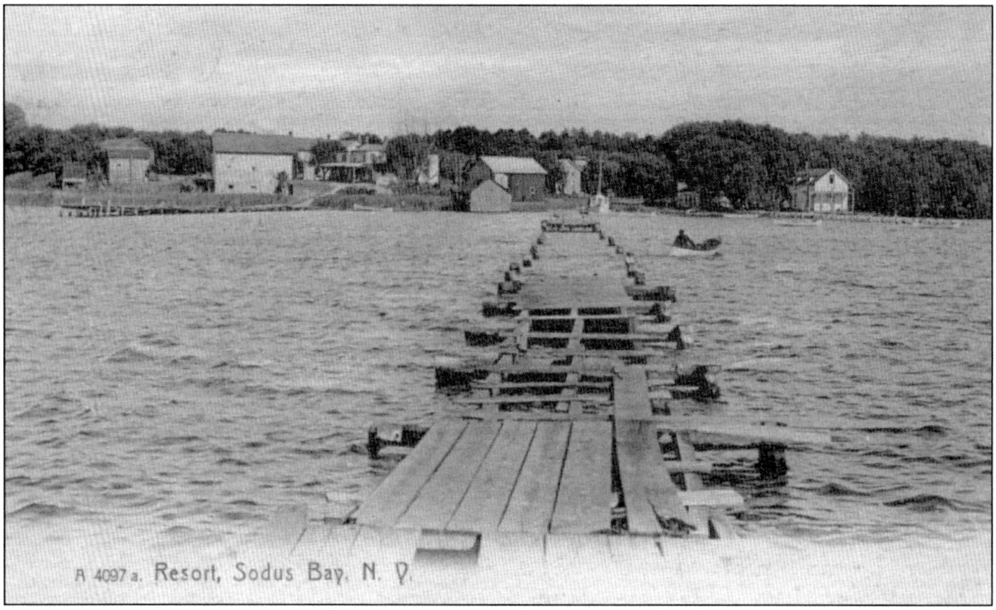


Looking like a bridge crossing the bay, this is really a long pier that was at Resort during the late 1800s and early 1900s. The view looks east toward Resort. The pier is north of the Sodus Bay Bridge. The approach to the bridge from the east can be seen to the right of the pier. The warehouse on the left is the site of the former Lotus Lodge.

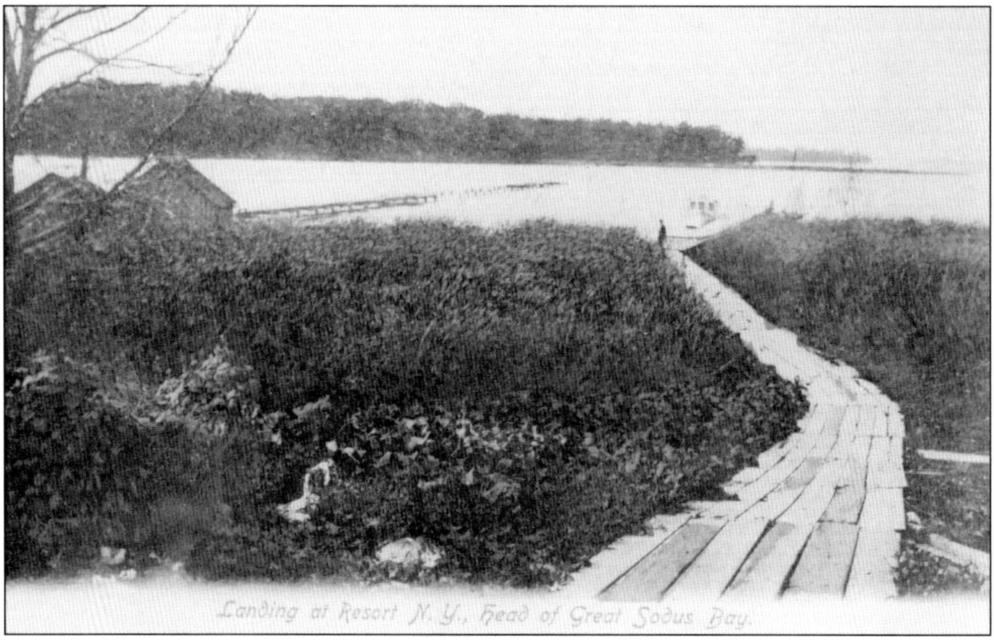


Viewed from the east shore at Resort, looking northwest toward Grassy Point, with Nicholas (Hunter's) Point in the distance, is one of the boat landings at Resort. Resort was on lowland and was frequently hampered by high water, which caused a need for raised planking for people to get to the docks at the water's edge. This photograph was likely taken at Ackerman's Hotel.

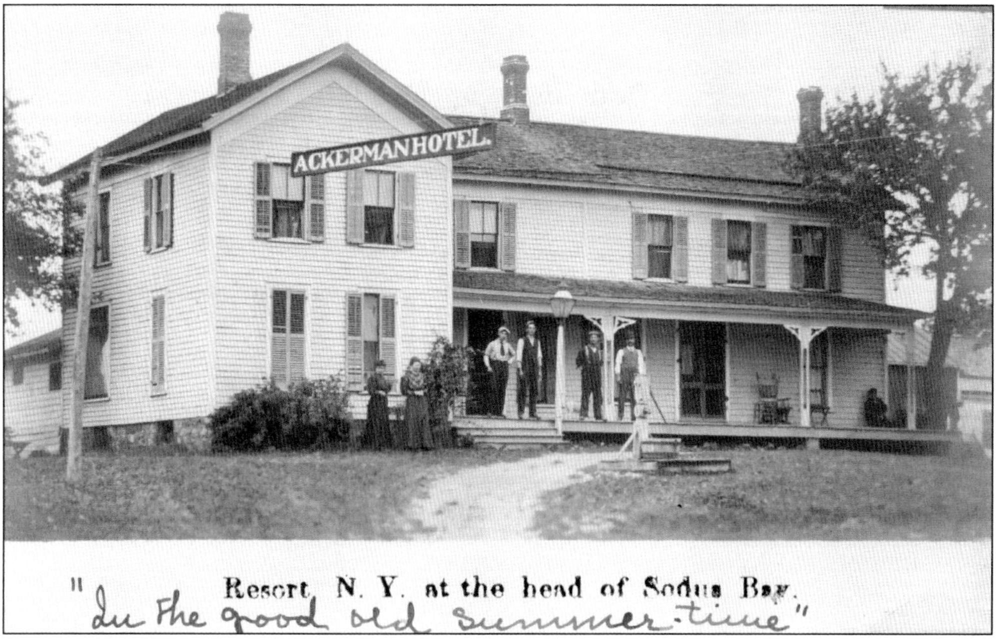


From the beginning of the development of Resort (Port Glasgow) in the early 1800s, there was a need for accommodations for travelers along Ridge Road between Rochester and Oswego. Sailors were also able to enjoy some time onshore at the hotels. By the late 1800s, Resort became a destination for those who enjoyed fishing and boating on the bay in the summertime. In the fall, hunters gathered at Resort to enjoy the pleasures of the local harvests of ducks, geese, and deer. The Ackerman Hotel was one of two hotels at Resort where visitors enjoyed good food and housing during their visits to Sodus Bay. The postcards of the Ackerman reveal some expansions made as business grew, as seen by the addition on the left in the image below.

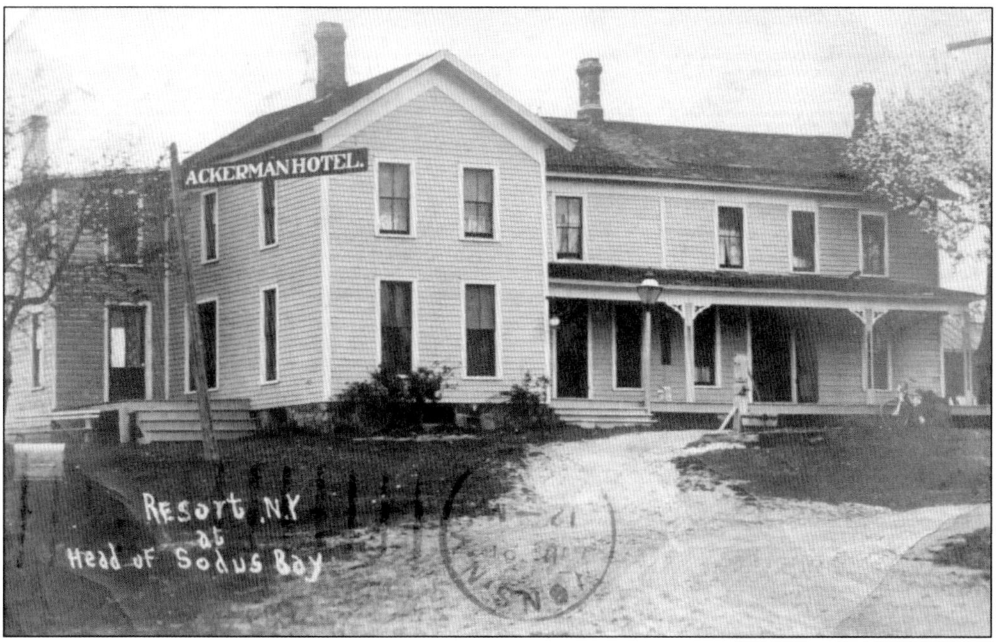

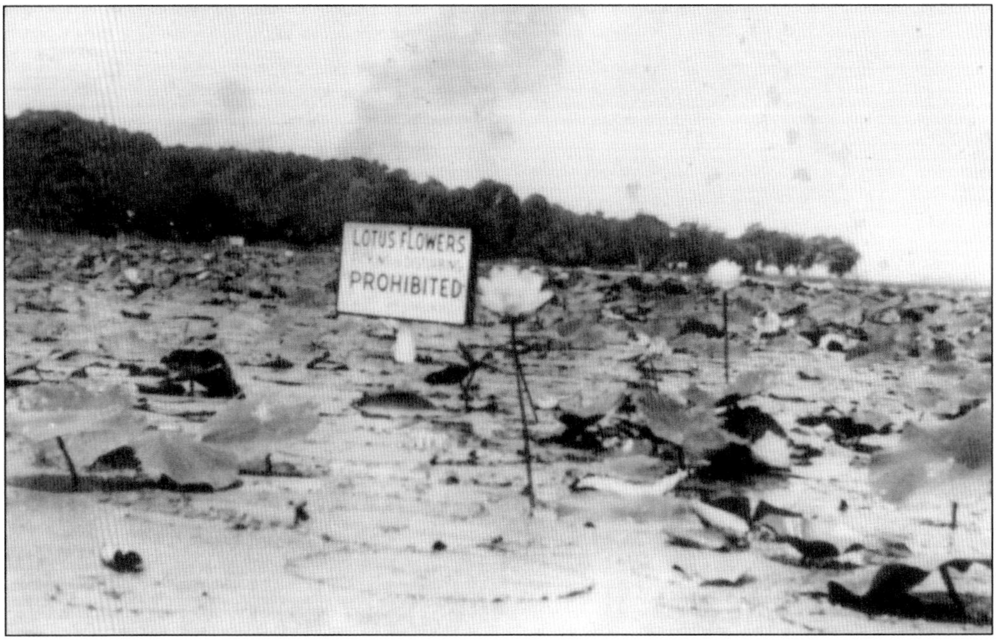


The American lotus is a water plant found in wetlands. Growing at the head of the bay at Resort, the lotus was thought to be native to Sodus Bay. A *Popular Science* magazine from 1888 states that the American lotus may have been planted by Native Americans, as they used the nuts (seeds of the pods) and the underground rhizomes for food. Over time, human interaction with the plant caused its demise on Sodus Bay by the mid-1960s. While the American lotus was only found in a few locations in New York State and Lake Erie in the north, it is found in areas of the southern United States and Mexico. The beautiful plant's rounded peltate leaves measure up to 15 inches in diameter, and its pale yellow-white flowers often reach a size of 12 inches across. (Above, TOH.)

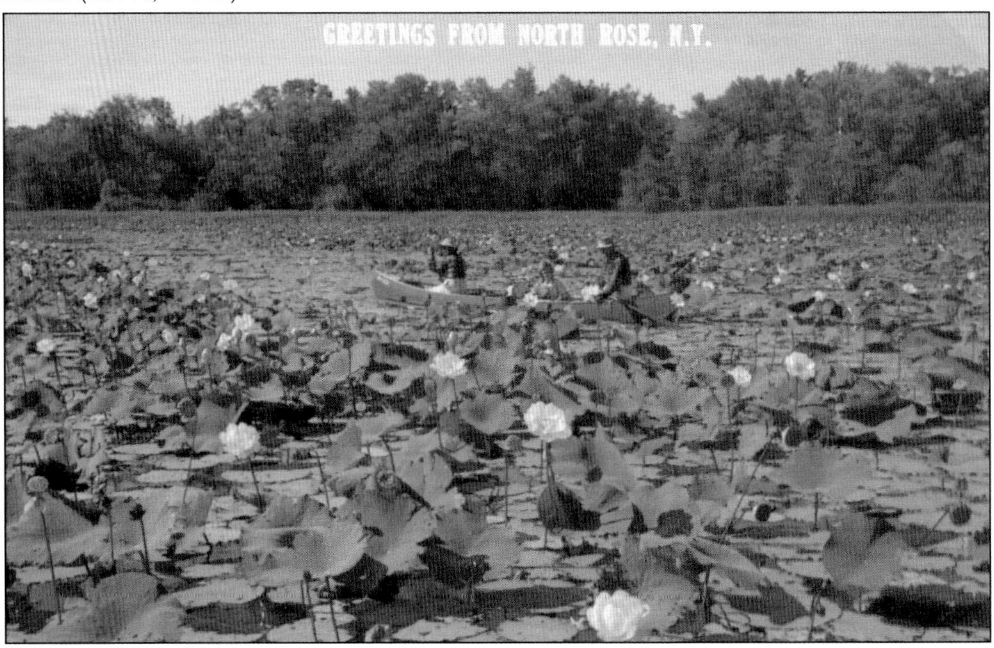

# *Two*

# Bonnie Castle

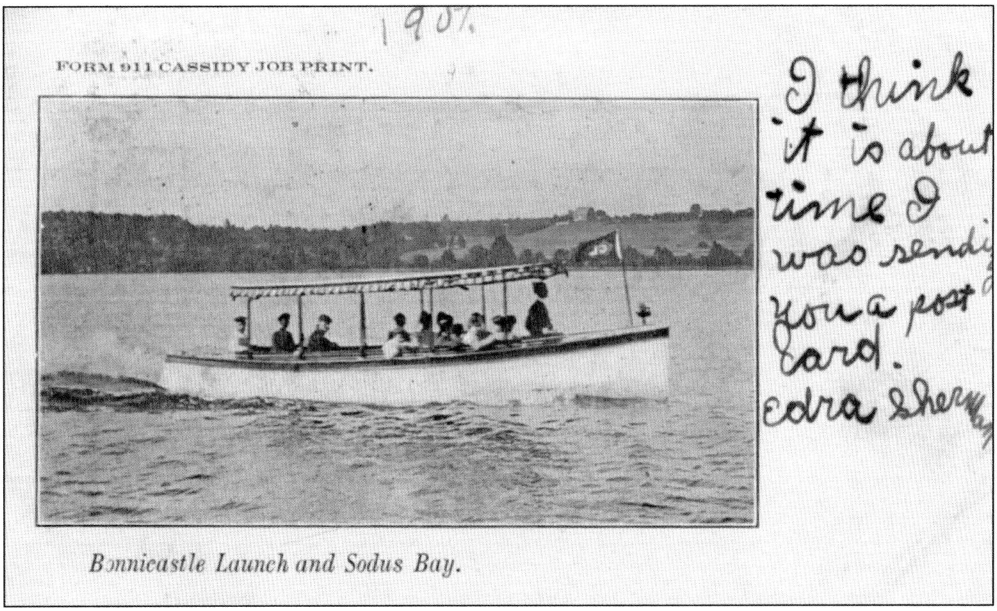


Many steam launches and other vessels made their way from the west shore of Sodus Bay at Sodus Point to "Bonnicastle" on Sodus Bay's east shore, crossing sometimes very choppy water to deliver visitors to this popular resort. Some guests would stay a day for a family picnic or church gathering. Others would stay a week for extended vacations or special events like the Wayne County Soldiers' and Sailors' Encampments.

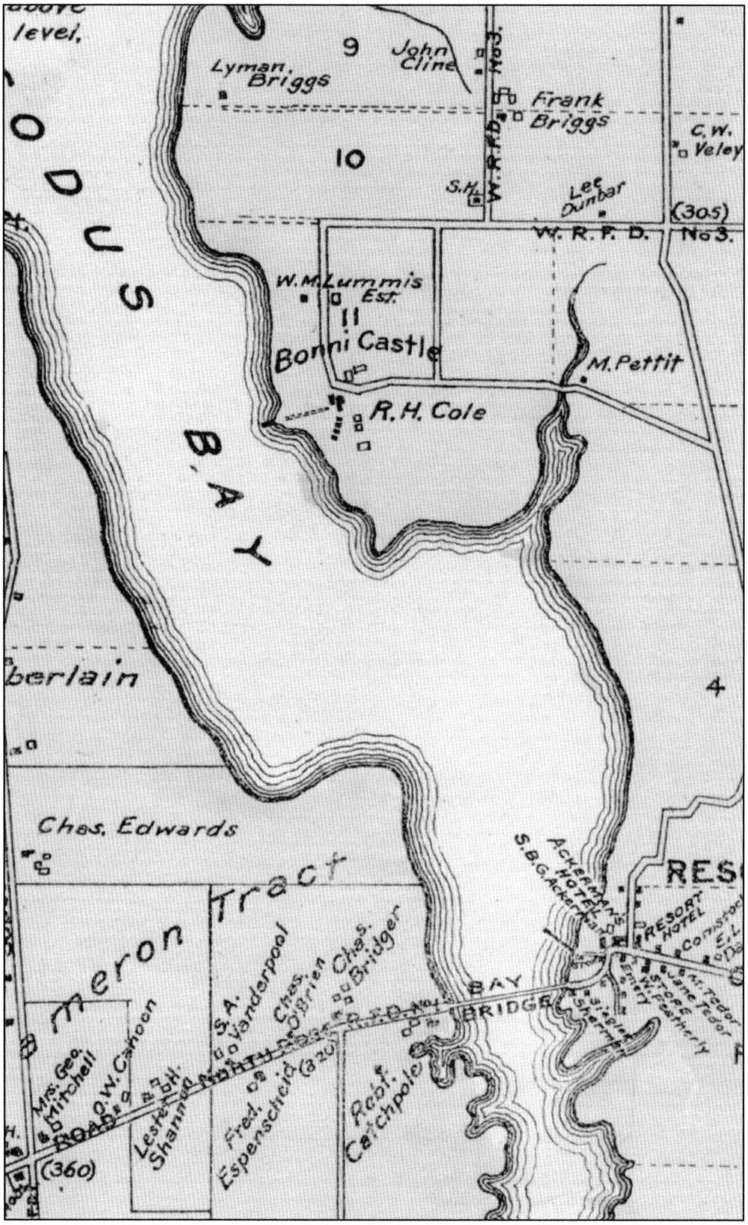


Recent review of historical documents places the location of the early-19th-century shipping port known as "Sloop Landing" along the eastern shores of Sodus Bay north of Resort. Around 1801, the Lummis family settled at Sodus Point (then Troupville), where they retained year-round residences. Two generations of Lummis folk, however, found a strong connection to the eastern shores of Sodus Bay. They cut and sold lumber and farmed here. By 1887, most of the Lummis Tract, consisting of several thousand acres extending along the east side of Sodus Bay from Resort to nearly the lakeshore, including the islands, had been sold. A small parcel of the Lummis estate remained at the time of this 1904 map, but this was soon sold, ending the Lummis era on Sodus Bay. The Bonnicastle resort era began in the mid-1880s. Though the resort community has seen several transitions over time, including various spellings of the name, Bonnie Castle continues to draw vacationers to Sodus Bay. (TOH.)

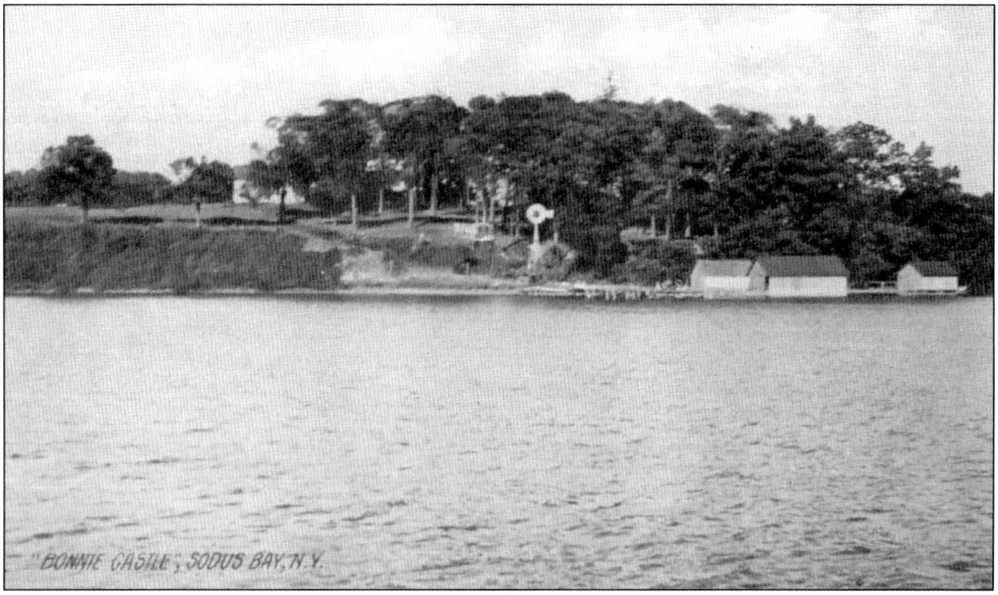


These postcards show the views visitors traveling to Bonnicastle by boat from Sodus Point would see while approaching the resort's dock (above) and stepping off the boat (below). The message on the back of the above postcard, written on August 10, 1910, states, "We have been to the S. S. (Soldiers' and Sailors') picnic at Bonnie Castle today. This is a good view of the place as you pass. We are having a very pleasant time. Expect to be home Saturday, or Monday, possibly later." Regional newspaper reports from this period between 1890 and 1920 about Bonnicastle depict a busy and entertaining resort colony. All was not so rosy for Bonnicastle during the early days of the resort. One newspaper offered the resort free advertising if the owners would improve upon the severe lack of proper toilet facilities. Note the spelling "Bonni Castle" on the postcard below.

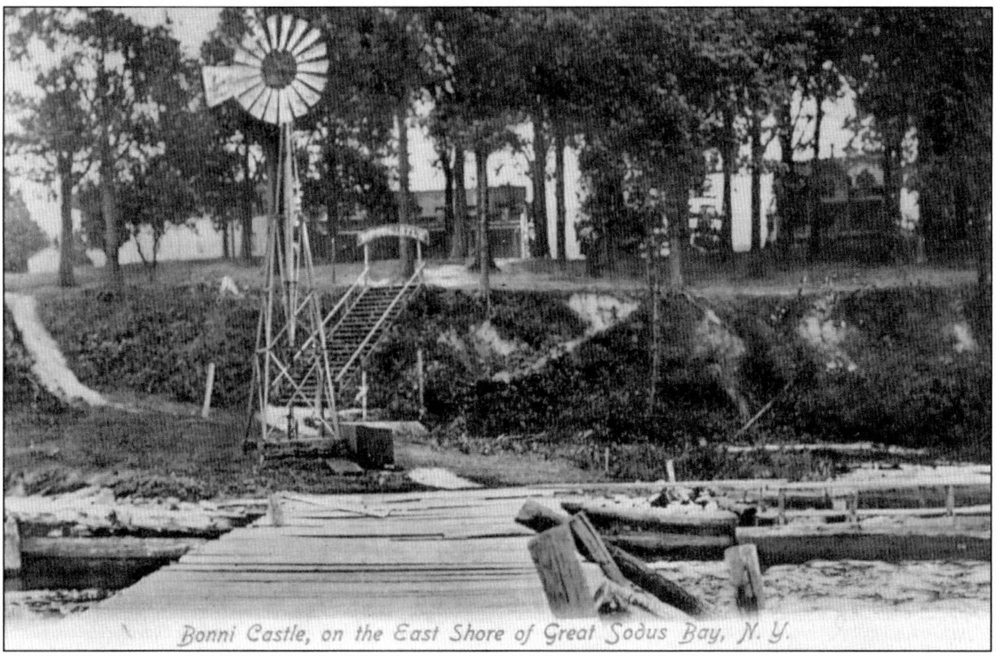

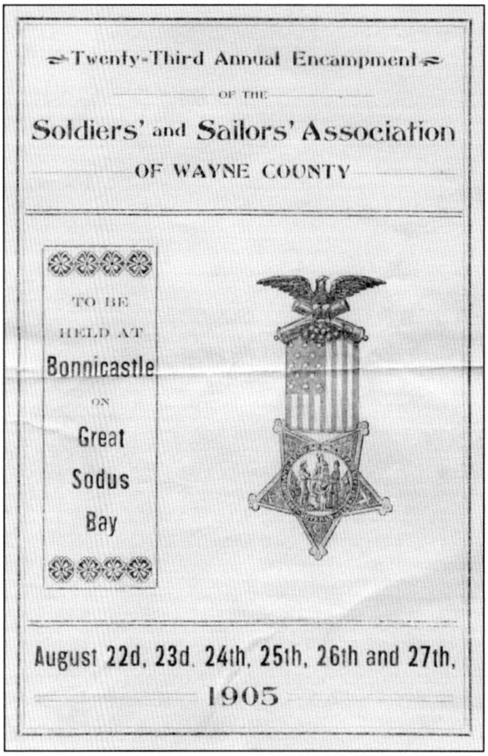


The Soldiers' and Sailors' Association of Wayne County annual encampment was held at Bonnicastle for many years from around 1894. A program cover (left) for the events of the 1905 encampment provides a listing of events during the reunion's six days—guest speakers, musical entertainment, evening campfires, socializing, and reminiscing. Each day's talk promised to be better than any previous. Young people played a special role in events such as School Day and Grange Day. Souvenir ribbons (below) were given to attendees of the Soldiers and Sailors Encampments. *"Grips" Historical Souvenir of Wolcott, N.Y. of 1905* provides details about Bonnicastle and says of the encampments that "one of these reunions numbered as high as 5000 in attendance and 180 tents were put up." (Both, TOH.)

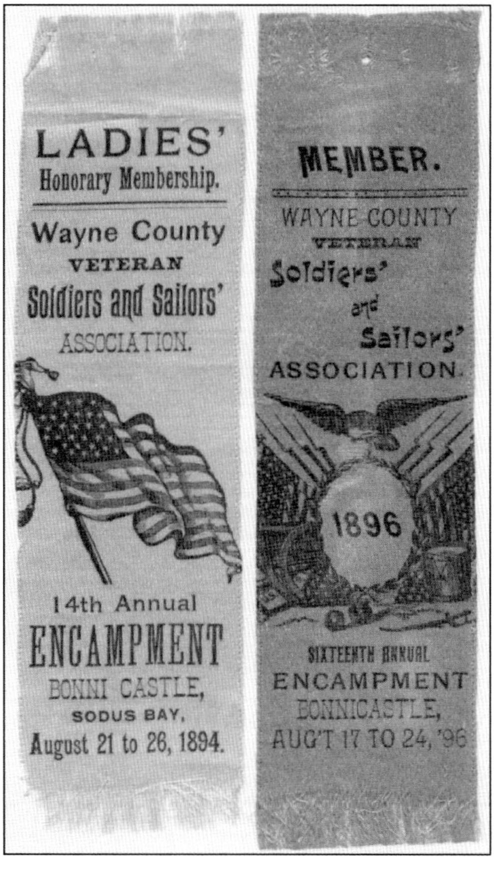

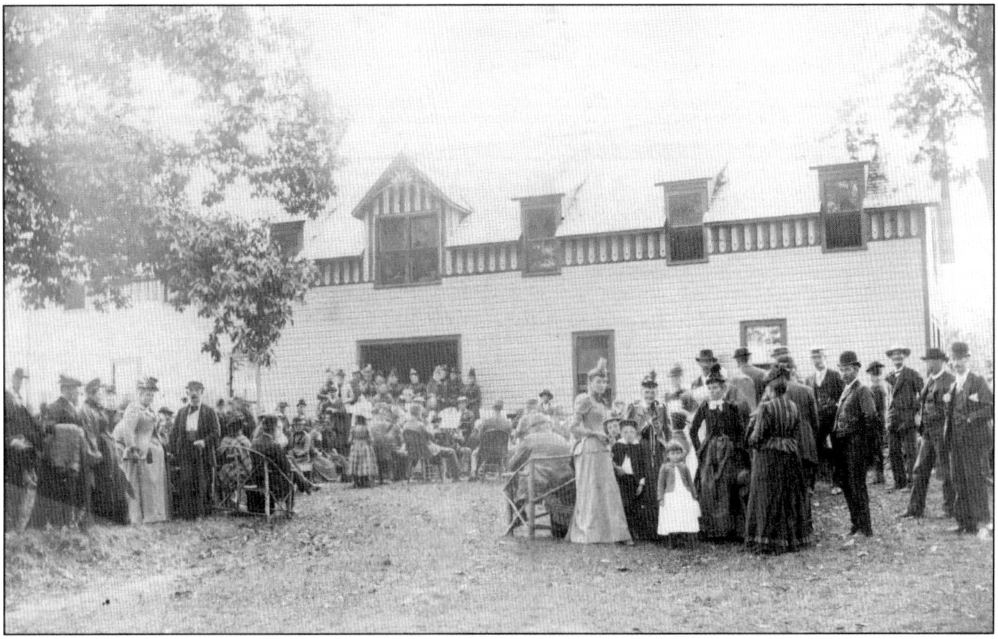

According to Jolene Seeger Jackson's 1977 Wayne County Hoffman essay "Homespun Fun," family reunions, church picnics, and other special get-togethers were held at Bonnicastle over the years when Cole and Catchpole ran the resort. The image above shows the pavilion with a sizable congregation of visitors enjoying some form of entertainment on a summer afternoon. The first floor of the pavilion housed a kitchen, dining hall, and a large dance hall with a screened porch. There were a number of guest rooms on the second floor of the pavilion. Some of the outdoor furniture pictured here was made from rough-cut branches. The pavilion was torn down in 1930. The lumber was reused in the building of some of the cottages still in use at Bonnie Castle, as shown in the photograph at right. (Both, TOH.)

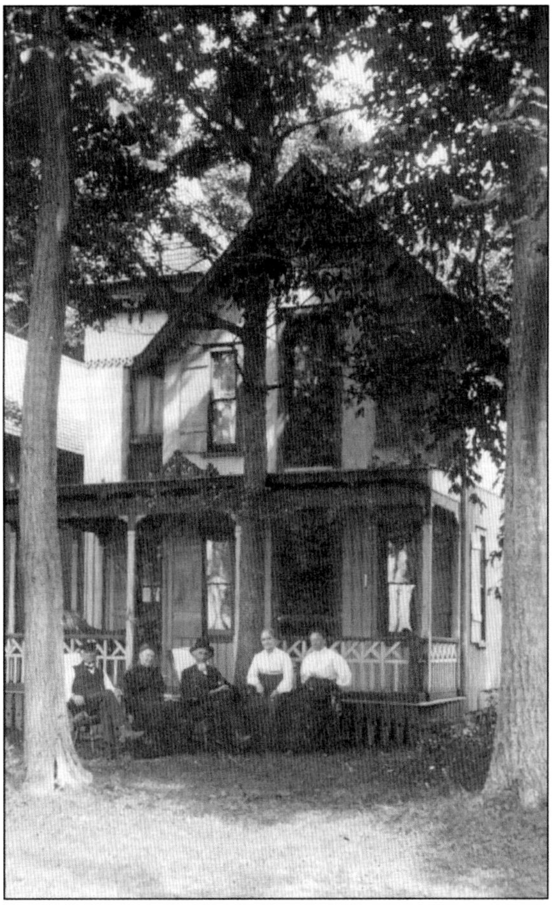

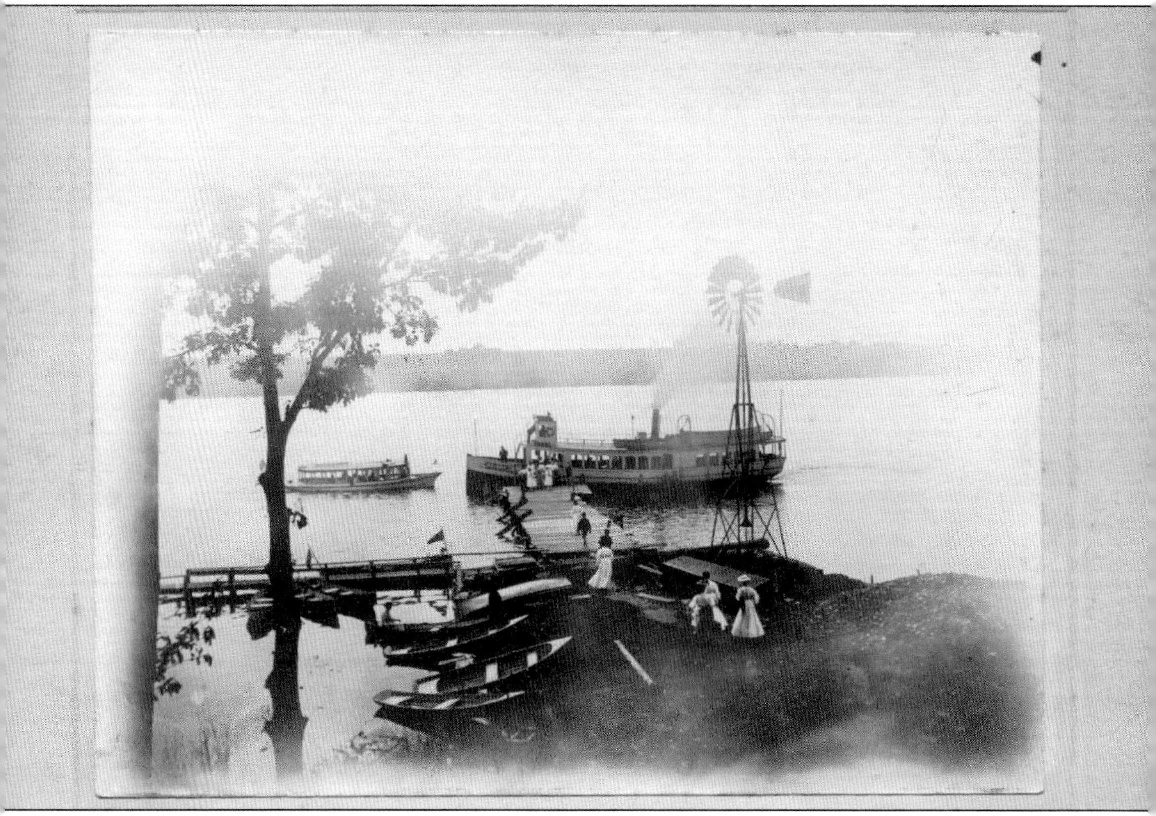

In this view looking from the pavilion, down the hill toward the bay, the *H.C. LeRoy* sits dockside, with passengers boarding for their return to Sodus Point or maybe a tour of the bay. A smaller gasoline launch approaching the dock reveals the great differences in size among tourist-transport vessels on the bay in this era. A Mr. Cole, owner of Bonnicastle, had a small gasoline launch for his family and guests that was built to hold 25 passengers. In the lower left corner of the photograph, wooden canoes and rowboats await vacationers who might like to go fishing or courting. Standing tall in the right of the image is the Bonnicastle windmill. Windmills were used to generate power to pump water up the hill to the pavilion for the kitchen and lavatory facilities. This image dates from around 1905. (TOH.)

# *Three*

# Shaker Tract, Point Lookout, and South Shore

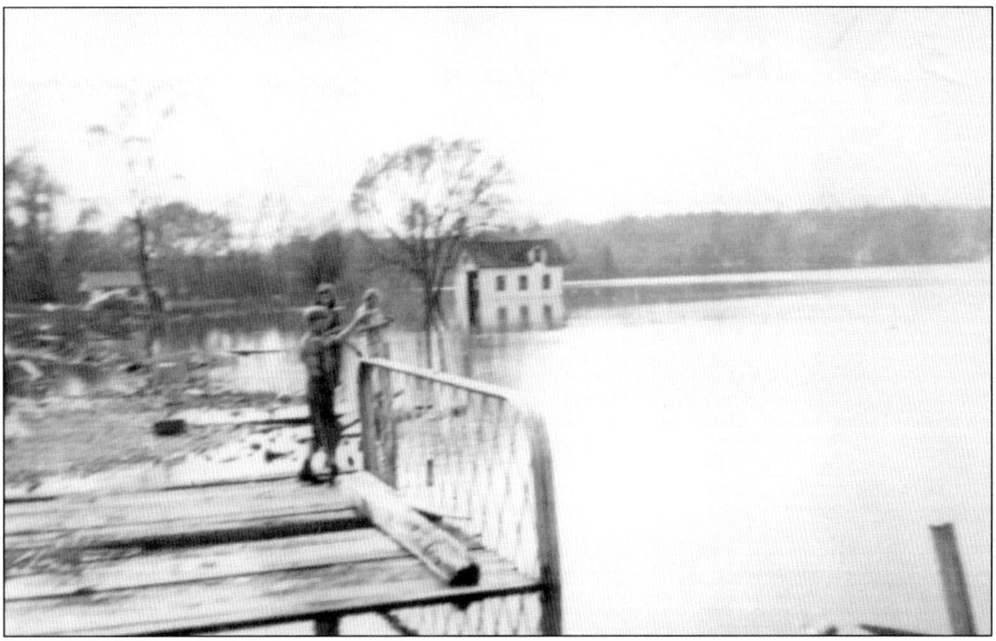

The Alasa Farm boathouse near Third Creek is seen here presiding over high water around 1924. The Sodus Bay Shakers lived on and farmed the land above the shores around Third and Second Creeks from 1826 to 1838. The Shakers' departure brought several transfers of the property to various owners over the years. Parshall and Chamberlain owned the Shaker Tract and built the boathouse around 1900. (Cracker Box Palace.)

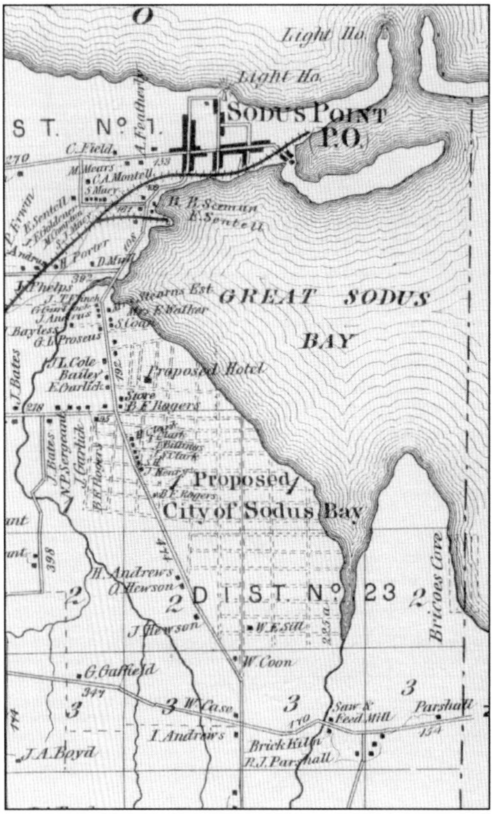


Both maps on this page are from the *1874 Atlas of Wayne County*. The map on the left shows a proposed plan for a "City of Sodus Bay" to be located where the present-day South Shore and Sodus Bay Heights Golf Club are located. The vertical dotted line on the map's right is the border between the towns of Sodus and Huron. The map below shows the town of Huron's portion of the Shaker Tract. The vertical dotted line on the left is the border between Huron and Sodus. Areas noted as D.W. Parshall and the surrounding land was the Shaker Tract. By 1904, the Parshall property was comprised of over 1,600 acres. Known for a short time as the Chamberlain Farm, it became known as Alasa Farm in 1924. (Both,TOH.)

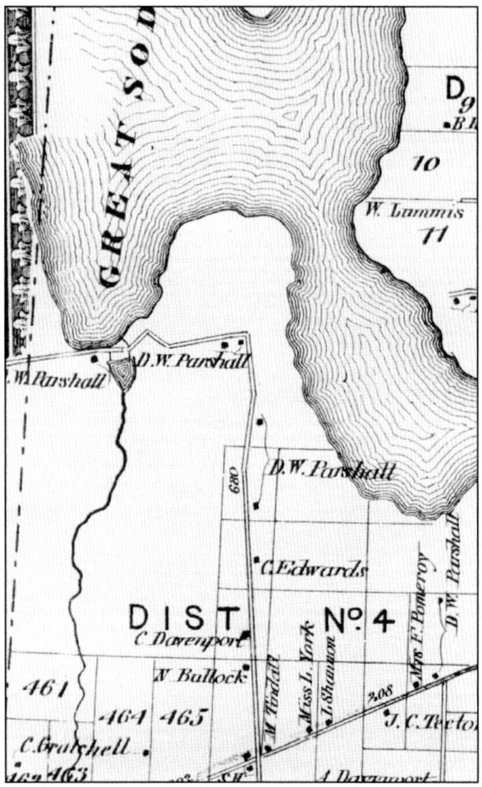

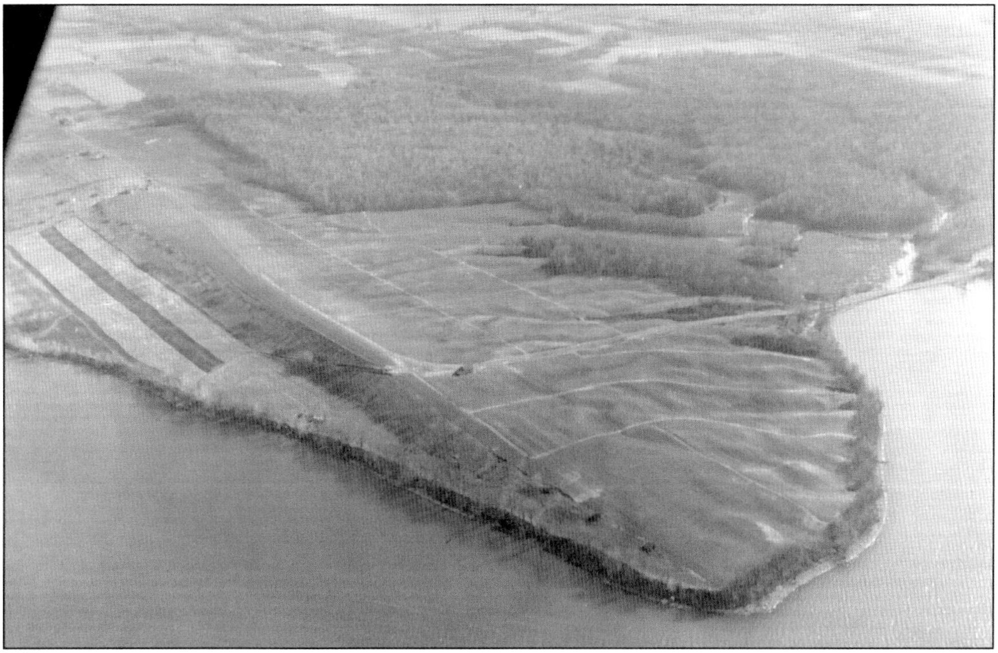

Photographed between 1950 and 1960, this aerial image captures what are known today as Shaker Heights, Hunter's Point (Nicholas Point), Sawmill Cove, and Third Creek—just prior to the purchase of this section of Alasa Farm by Henner and Graves in 1960. Farmland, woodland, and undeveloped shoreline are all part of Alasa Farm. Area residents still honor the local Shaker history with road names like Shaker Heights, Ann Lee Drive, and Shaker Tract. Much of the terrain commands spectacular views of Sodus Bay, Sodus Point, Charles Point, the islands, and the outer pier lighthouse. Third Creek flows into the bay in the center right of the photograph. There is a building located left of the creek before it flows into the bay. This structure, no longer standing, may be what was left of the old sawmill on Third Creek and reason for naming this cove Sawmill Cove. (Above, TOH.)

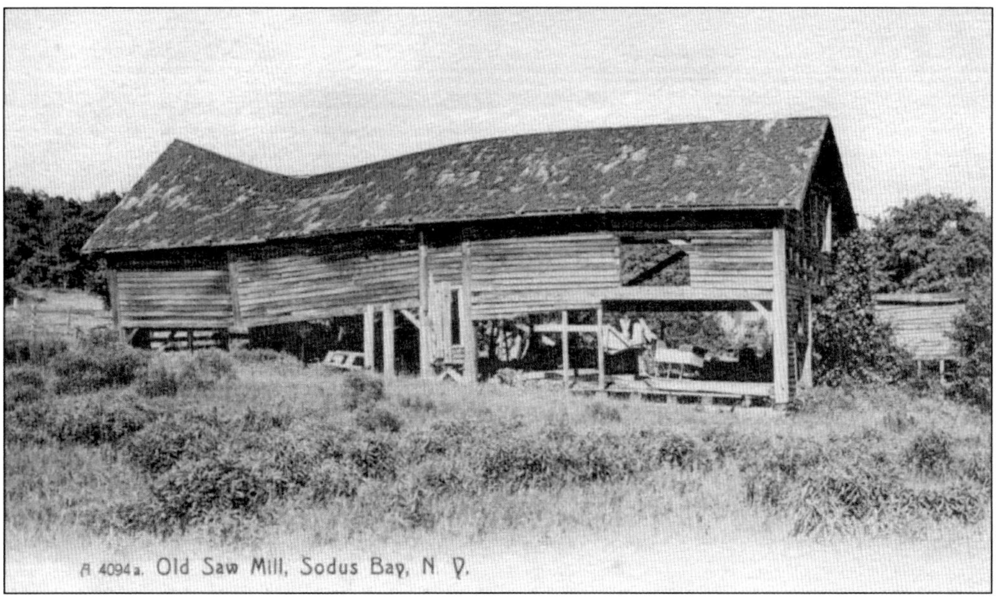

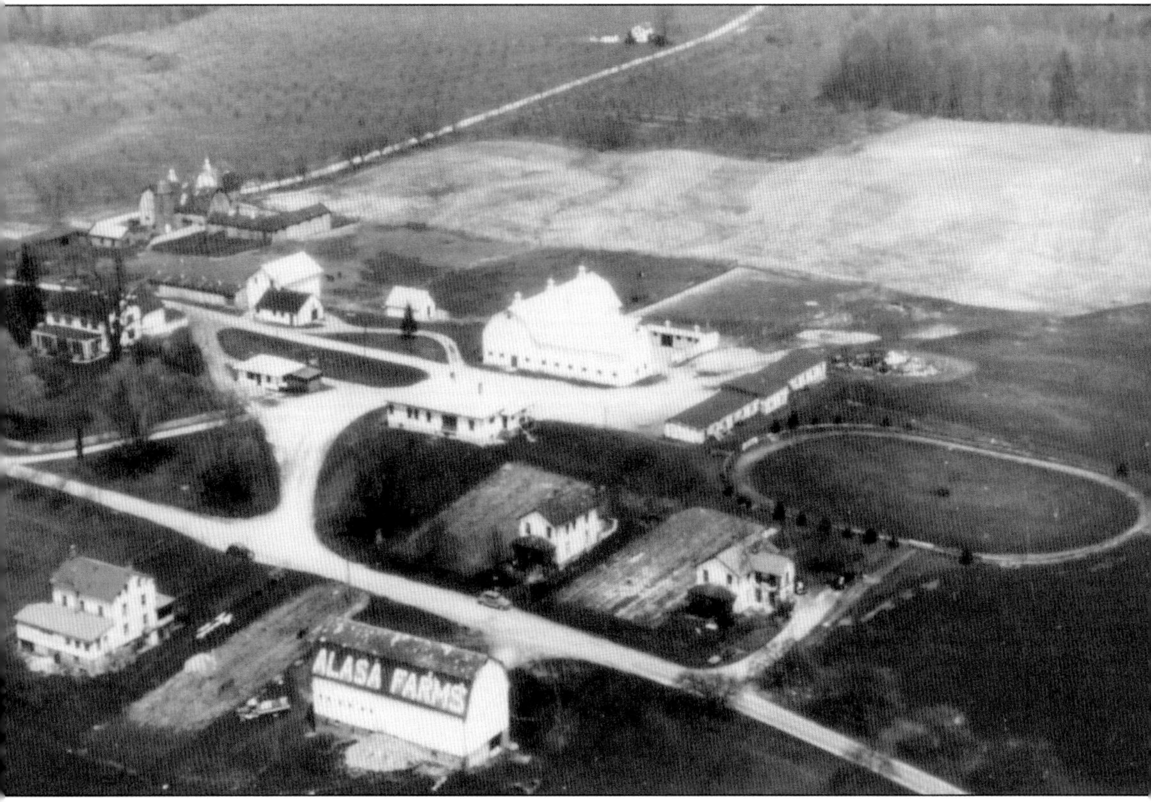


On February 23, 1826, Anne Nicholas, widow of Geneva judge John Nicholas, sold 1,400 acres of pristine woodland on the western shores of Sodus Bay to a small group of Shakers from Lebanon, New York. Known over the years as the Shaker Tract, the property originally was located within both of the Wayne County towns of Sodus and Huron. Between 1841 and 1858, Gen. William H. Adams made several failed attempts to construct a canal from the Erie Canal to Sodus Bay. The land was eventually purchased by Dewitt Parshall, president of the Lyons National Bank. Parshall and his heirs owned the Shaker Tract from 1868 to 1905. The tract grew over these years to over 1,600 acres. Alvah G. Strong purchased the property in 1924. This aerial view shows a horse-racing track on the right, horse barn in the center, and main house at center left. Over the years, a few buildings were destroyed by fire. The main house was severely damaged by fire in 2009. (Cracker Box Palace.)

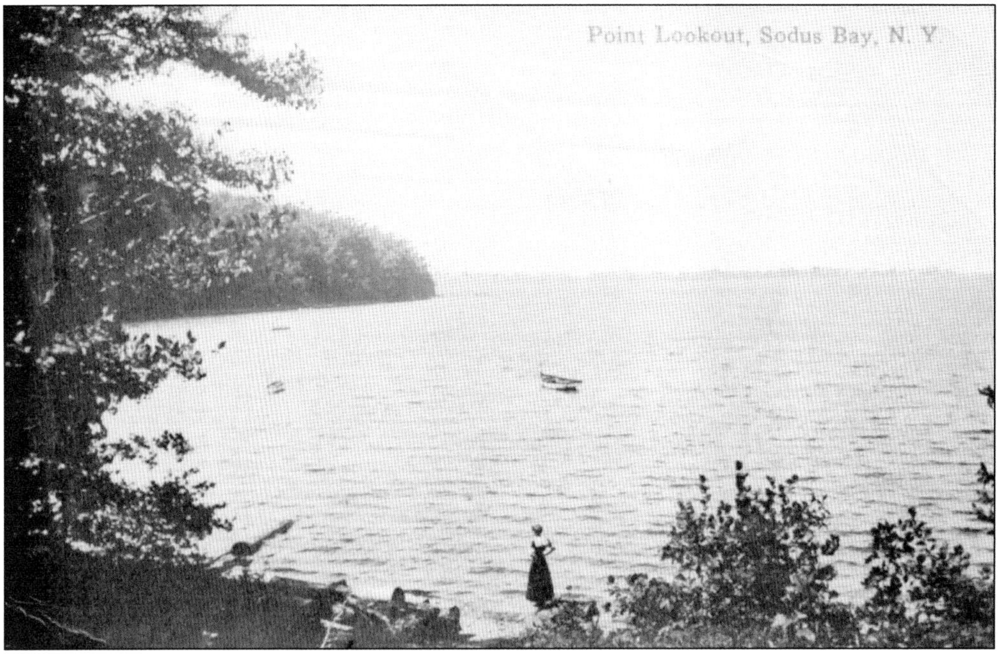


Point Lookout, also known over time as Thornton Point, was home to Aldice G. Warren's Summer School for Boys. Established in 1900, Camp Fitzhugh operated at Point Lookout until 1922, at which time it moved to Eagle Island where it continued until 1932. Fifty boys, ages 10 to 18, were offered a summer academic tutoring program as well as outdoor education through Camp Fitzhugh. Swimming, sailing, motorboating, canoeing, rowing, and fishing, land sports, music, and indoor games balanced out the summer recreation. Sessions ran from July 1 to August 31. The above postcard has a view of Point Lookout from Briscoe's Cove. The cove was named after a surveyor for the Pre-Emption Line who died and was buried here. A gravestone was discovered here in the early 1900s reading "A.N. Briscoe, died May 22, 1791."

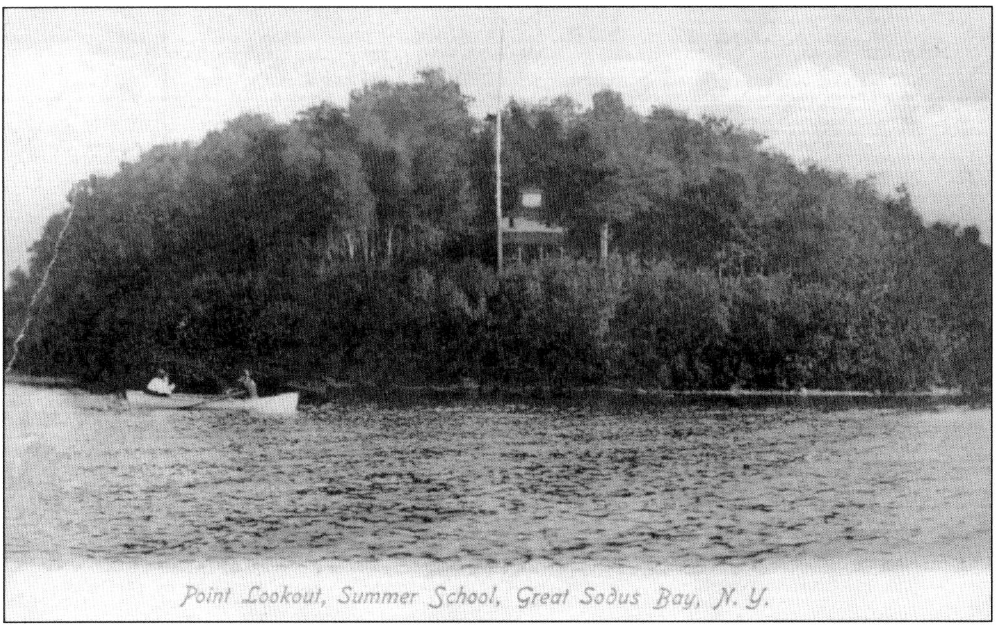

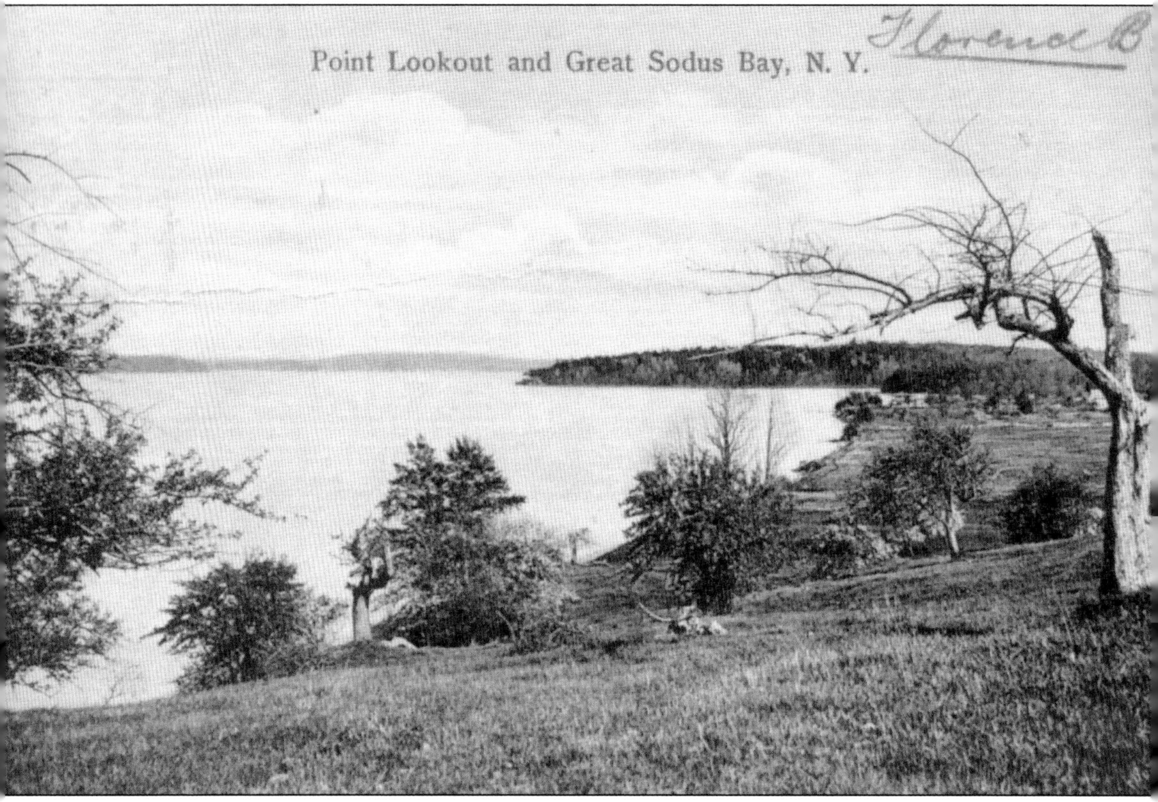


The view on this undivided back, pre-1907 postcard captures South Shore to Point Lookout (Thornton Point). This popular Sodus Bay view was enlarged and reproduced in several tourist publications during the early 1900s. Col. Peregrine Fitzhugh first settled on this stretch of Sodus Bay shoreline with 35 enslaved workers in 1803. The Fitzhugh family held the property until the mid-1850s, after Elizabeth Fitzhugh, Peregrine's widow, died. William Eaton Sill purchased this property around 1855. An article appearing in the *Arcadian Weekly Gazette* of August 1, 1894, titled "A New Breathing Place," describes property between First and Second Creeks that was christened "South Shore" by William Eaton Sill. Sill made extensive improvements to his farm tract including roads, an icehouse, a barn for horses, and a well providing drinking water. Approximately 70 lots were laid out on this tract for purchase and development. A number of shade trees were planted, and a solid riprap wall was built to protect the bay bluff from erosion. The article ends with "to see it, is to want it."

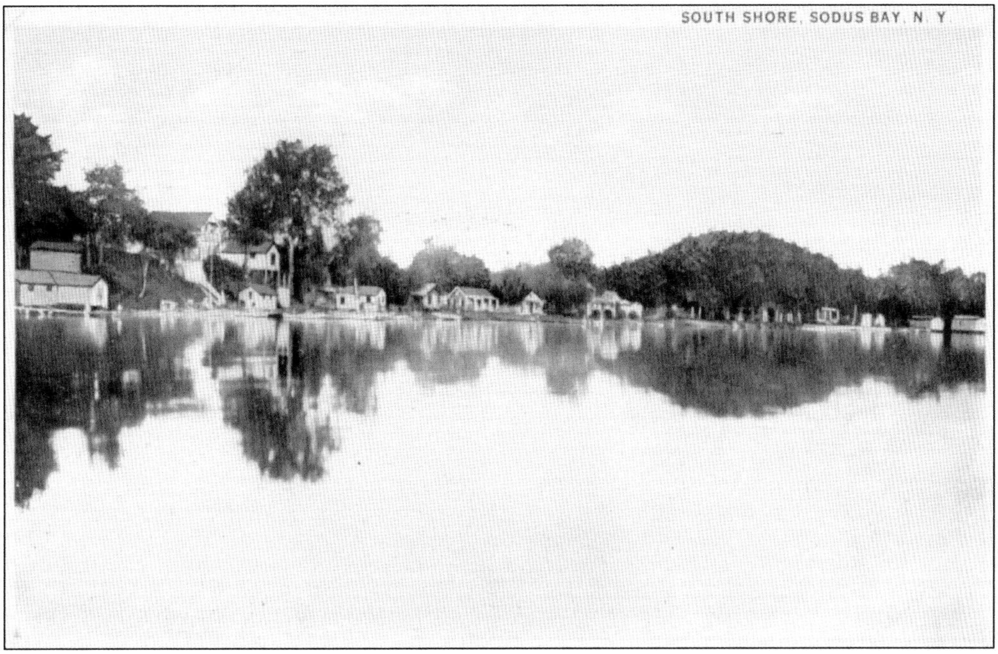


After Sill's 1894 invitation, the development of South Shore progressed at a rapid rate. Located close to Sodus Point, South Shore was easily reached by train from Rochester or Newark. The Alton-Lyons Road provided access from points south, east, and west. Sill assured privacy, beautiful views, and good fishing—with "the best pickerel grounds on the whole bay" near Sill's bluff. William Eaton Sill died in 1898 at the age of 56. His eldest son, Arthur Gavin Sill, acted as representative for his father in the sales of the properties, and, as heir to the estate, continued to further the expansion of Sill's "South Shore." Sill is one of the oldest family names on Sodus Bay, dating back to 1794. Several generations after William Eaton, Sill family members continued to engage in commercial and recreational activities on Sodus Bay.

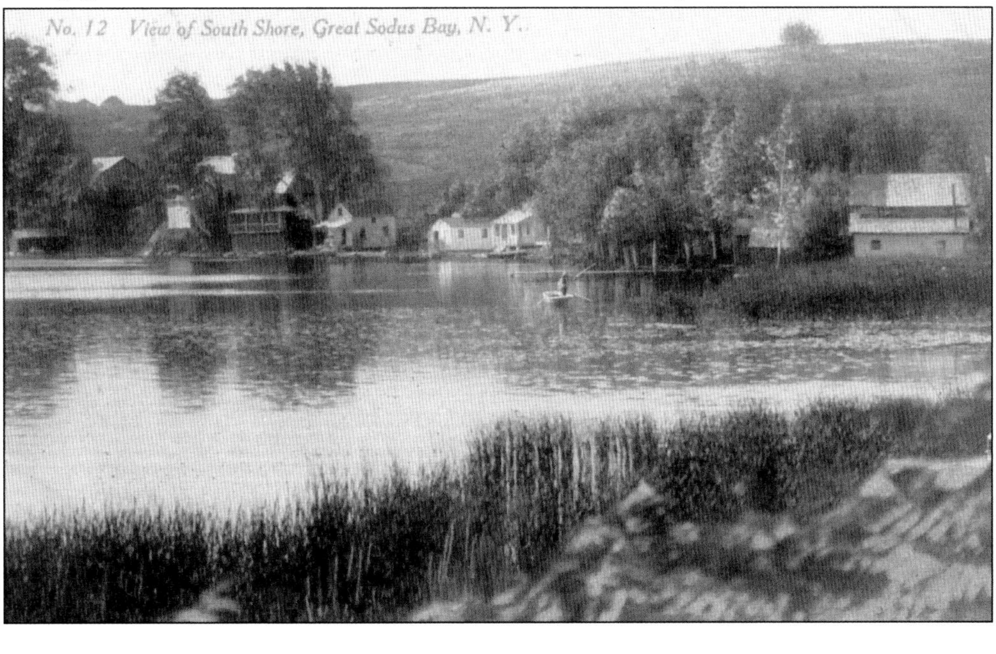

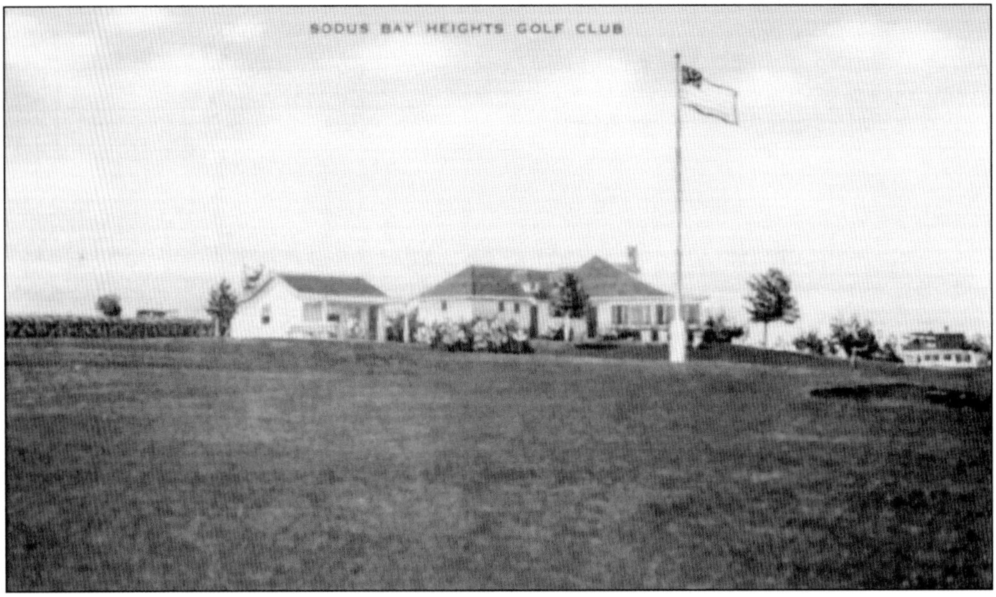


In 1880, Benjamin F. Rogers created plans for a "City of Sodus Bay," to include a large hotel, for which only the foundation was laid. Having financial difficulties, Rogers abandoned the project. Dr. Anthony Walton Evans acquired the property, and left it to his daughter, Countess Anna E. von Hemert. The property became known as the Blackmar Farm. During the early 1900s, the Lyons and Sodus Point Railway Company tried to secure a right-of-way through the Blackmar Farm to construct a rail line, steamboat dock, and coal trestle. The railway company was unsuccessful, however, in securing right-of-way easements from the countess. It was not until after her death that Blackmar Farm was sold. In 1922, the incorporation of the Sodus Bay Heights Land Company became the genesis for what was to become a great housing and recreational expansion on Sodus Bay.

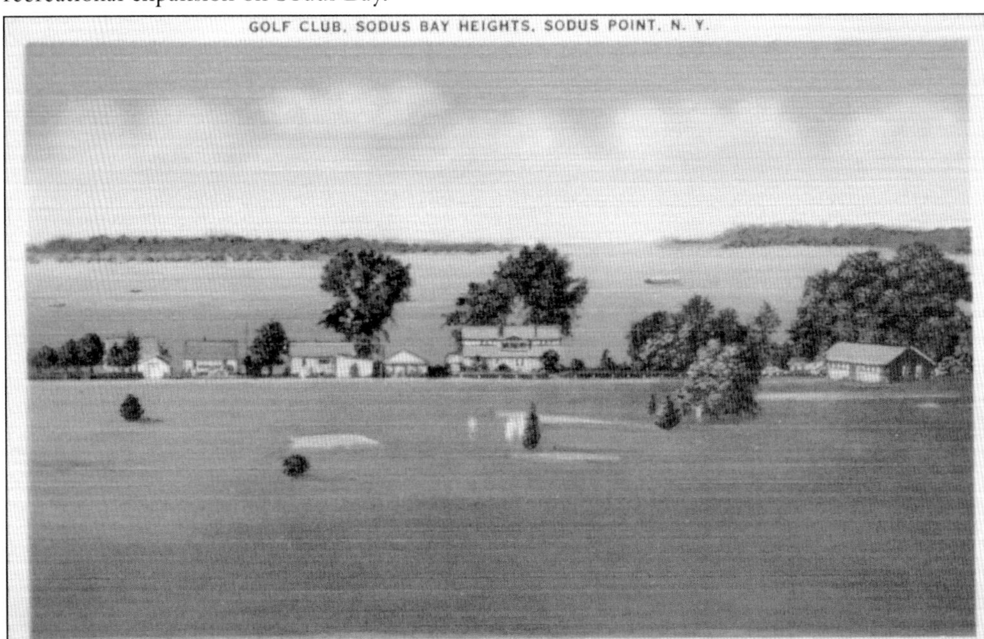

# *Four*

# THE ISLANDS

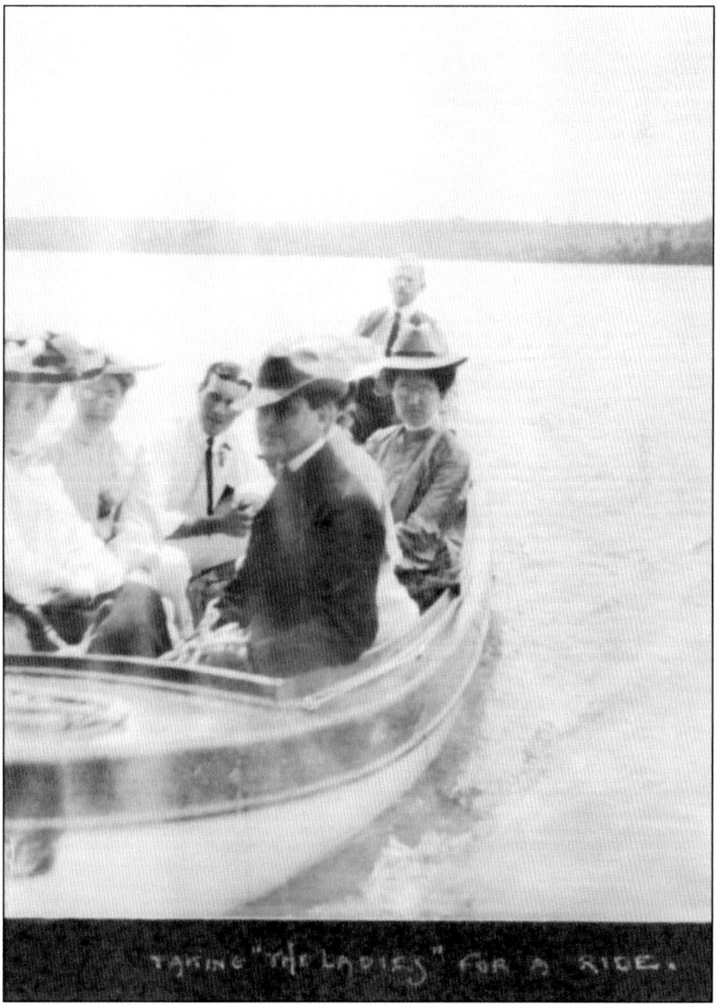


Summer residents and visitors traveling to Eagle and Newark Islands on Sodus Bay have always had to make the trip by boat, plane, or ice. Arriving at Eagle Island by motor launch is a party of guests for Charles Fowler Garfield. The woman on the right is Garfield's wife, Myra Avalene Shipley Garfield. The Garfield family owned Eagle Island from 1907 to 1919. (Stephen E. Garfield.)

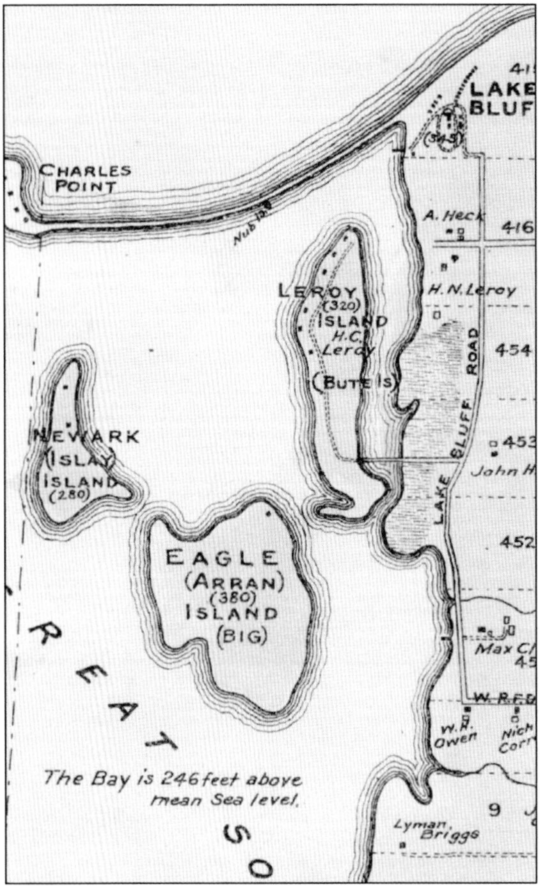


Sodus Bay's islands—Newark, Eagle, and LeRoy—are shown on this map from the *1904 New Century Atlas*. Nub (Knob) Island is seen near the barrier bar. Charles Point, only partially shown, was once an island. Not labeled on this map, Hog (or Hodge) Island is east of LeRoy Island on the east side of the bridge and surrounded by swamp. Tiny Duck Island at the foot of LeRoy was too small to be included. The postcard below provides a view of Eagle Island (left) and Newark Island (right) as seen from the southwest end of Leroy Island. This image is included in a 1901 book by Ellen Sergeant Rude titled *Two Legends: A Souvenir of Sodus Bay*, with the caption "Loga, Neoga, and Kenoga Islands," the Cayuga and Seneca Indian names for the three main islands. (Left, TOH.)

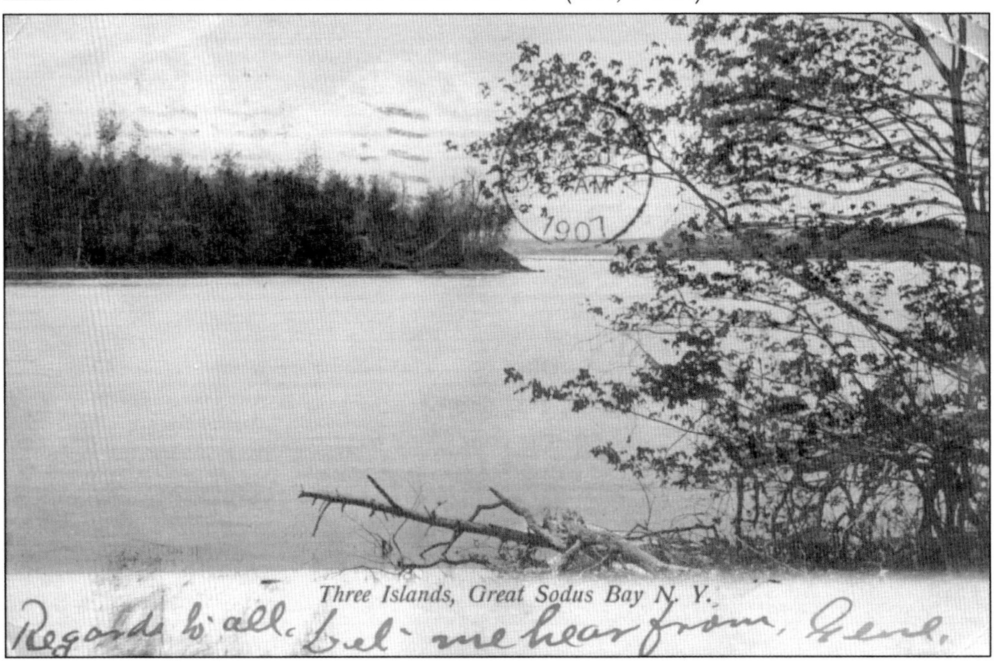

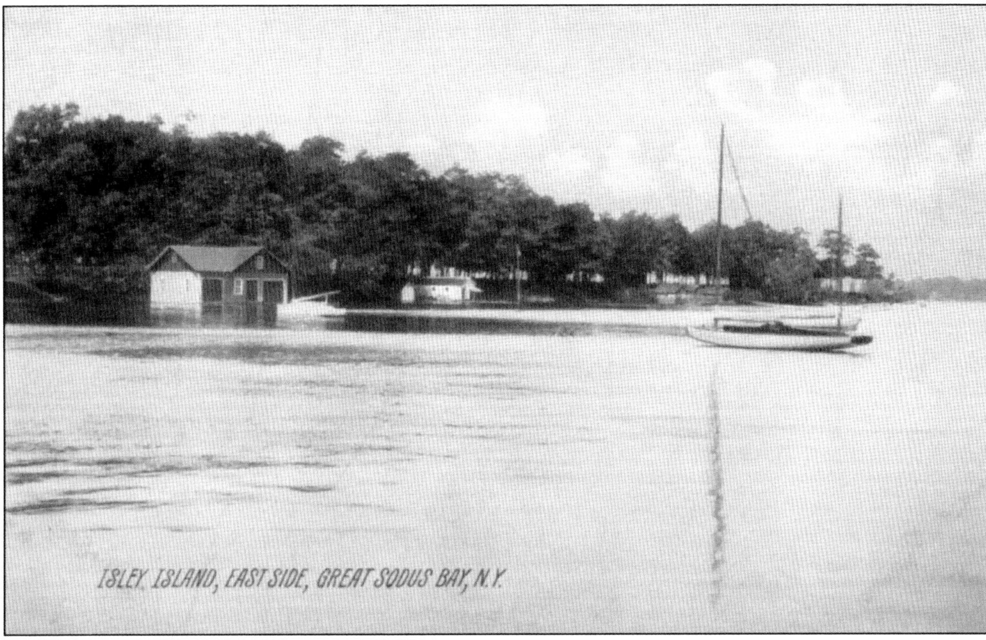


Newark Island is the smallest of the three remaining islands on Sodus Bay. It is a quiet island, and there are just a few summer cottages on Newark. The name of the island was given as the early property owners on this summer resort were from Newark, New York. The sailboat in the foreground looks like a small yawl. A closer shows two masts from two sailboats.

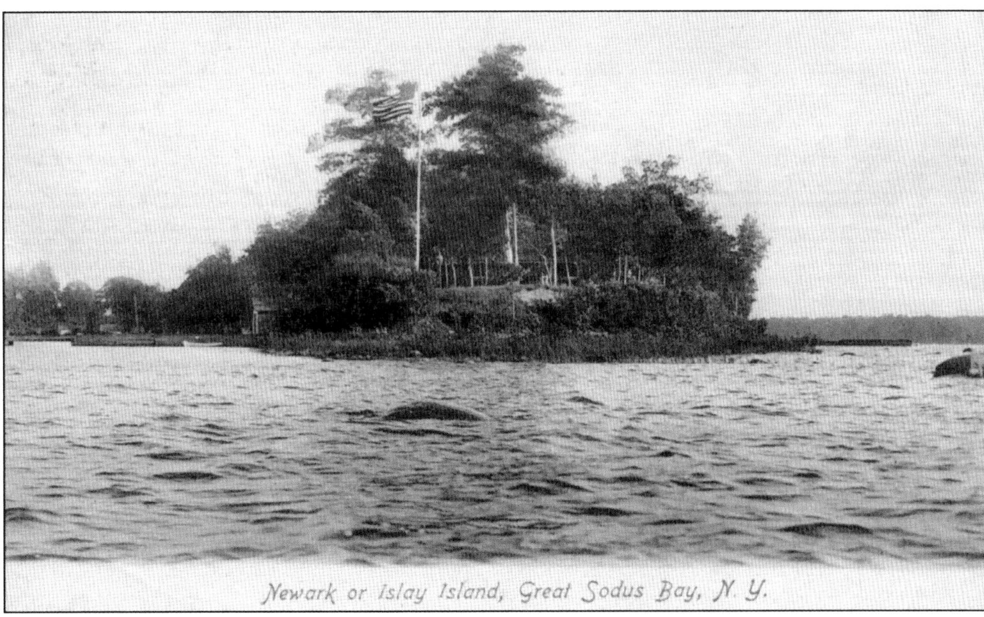


A rocky shoal extends from the north end of Newark Island into the bay, creating a navigation hazard. A Coast Guard buoy with a flashing light has been in place for many years to warn boaters to stay away from this spot so as to avoid going aground on the rocks or ruining a motor's lower unit. This point has been a popular area for hunters and fishermen over the years.

Located on the south end of Newark Island, the Bungalow was owned by Zenas F. Westervelt. Principal of the Rochester School for the Deaf, Westervelt brought students here to enjoy the bay. The cottage is reported to have burned in the 1930s. Postmarked in 1907, this postcard shares a message about a sailing trip to Canada with "Dr. W."—likely Dr. F.L. Wilson on his yawl *Lotus*. (TOH.)

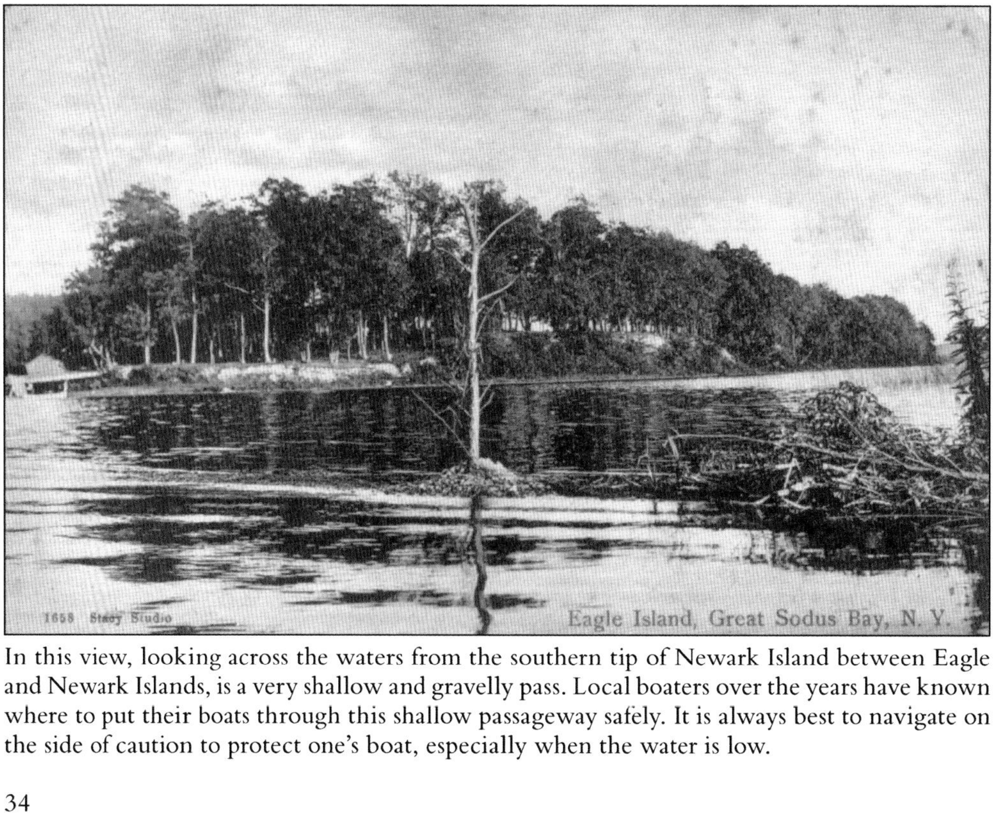


In this view, looking across the waters from the southern tip of Newark Island between Eagle and Newark Islands, is a very shallow and gravelly pass. Local boaters over the years have known where to put their boats through this shallow passageway safely. It is always best to navigate on the side of caution to protect one's boat, especially when the water is low.

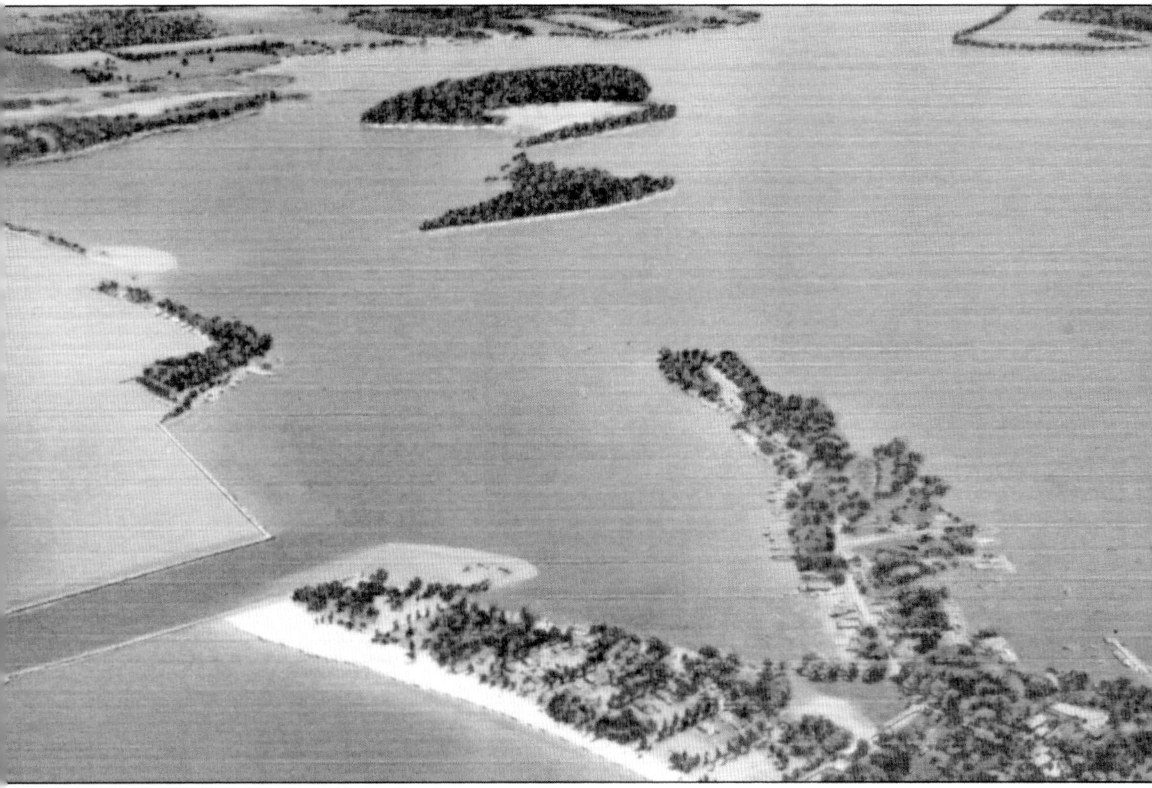

Eagle Island is favored with the most unusual history of the bay's islands. The Lummis family, and several other owners following Lummis, farmed Eagle from the early 1800s to 1919. In 1919, Donald Woodward, son of Jell-O millionaire Orator Woodward, purchased Eagle Island. From 1922 to 1932, while owned by Woodward, Eagle Island became home to A.C. Warren's summer school and camp for boys, formerly located at Point Lookout. In 1932, Woodward deeded Eagle Island to his younger sister, Helen Woodward Rivas, a prominent philanthropist. Rivas donated Eagle Island to the Otetiana Boy Scout Council in 1942. In 1954, the Otetiana Council sold Eagle Island to surveyor and engineer George E. Lookup and lumber dealer J. Walter Caves for $30,000. This aerial view postcard shows Eagle Island at the top center. The light area is farmland. Other noted spots are LeRoy Island on the left, Newark Island just below Eagle Island, a break in the sandbar on the left, and Sodus Point at the bottom of the postcard.

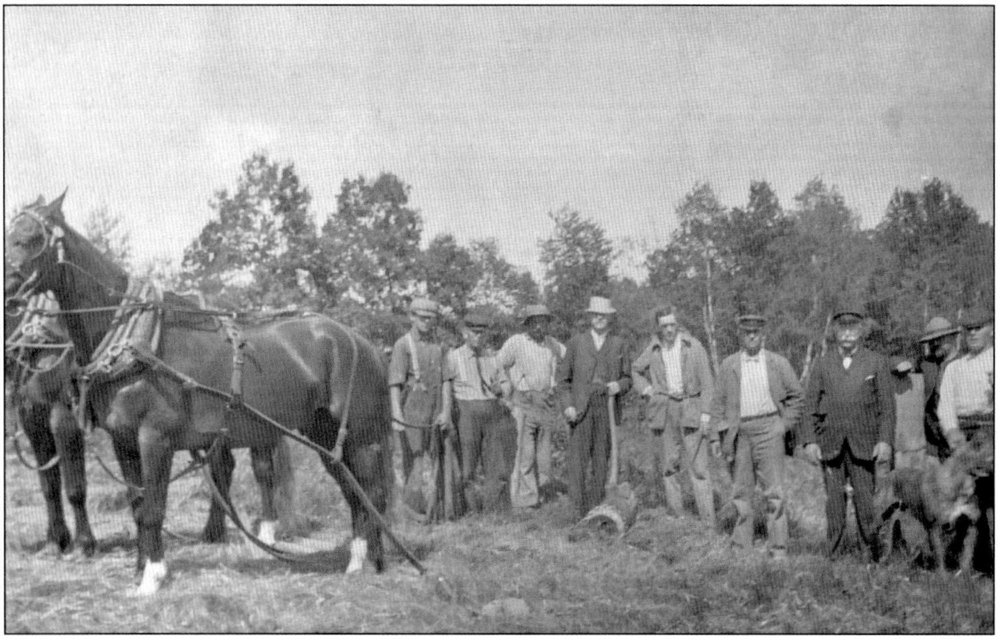

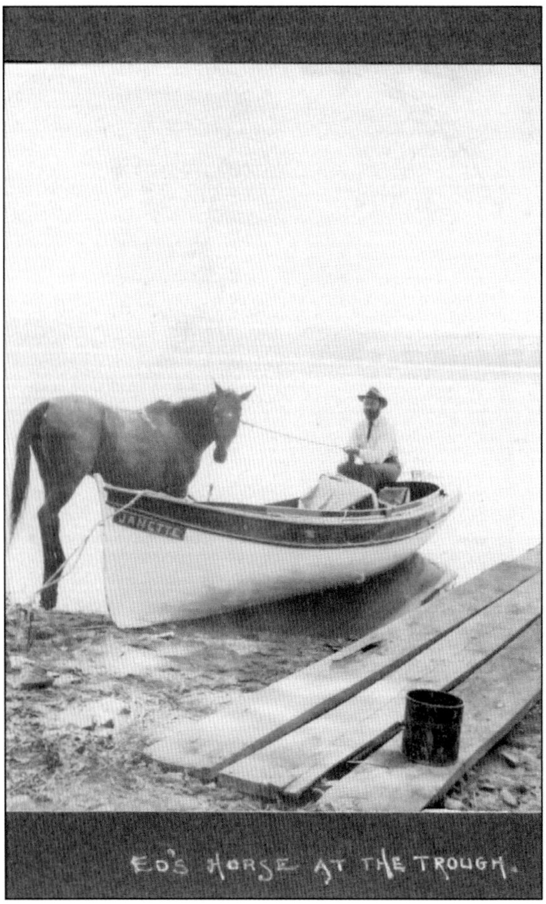


Charles Fowler Garfield was a third-generation descendant of Pres. James Garfield. C.F. Garfield purchased Eagle Island in 1907 from E.B. Parsons's widow. Upon acquiring the property, Garfield set out to tame "Garfield's Island." He made many improvements to the structures on the island built by previous owners. Above, a team of horses and men helps clear the land to make way for apple, cherry, quince, prune, and apricot orchards. At the far right of this photograph is Rex, Garfield's large Great Dane, who made several daily surveillance trips around the island's perimeter. At left, a photograph shows one of the workhorses enjoying a drink out of the bay after a day's work. Garfield sold the island in 1919 to Jell-O heir Donald Woodward. (Both, Stephen E. Garfield.)

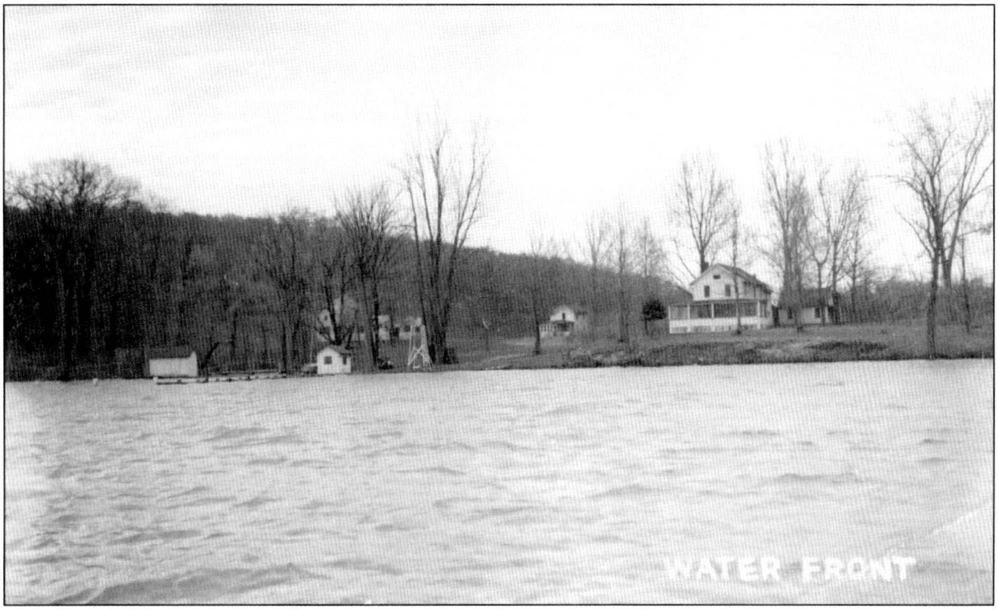


Donated to the Otetiana Boy Scouts in 1942 by Helen Woodward Rivas, Eagle Island became the summer and winter camping home for the Scouts from 1943 to 1951. The Scouts came across the bay from Sodus Point by motorboat supplied by Helfer's Boat Livery. Two hundred Scouts at one time could be accommodated by the island's facilities. An automobile is near the dock. (Seneca Waterways Council Boy Scouts.)

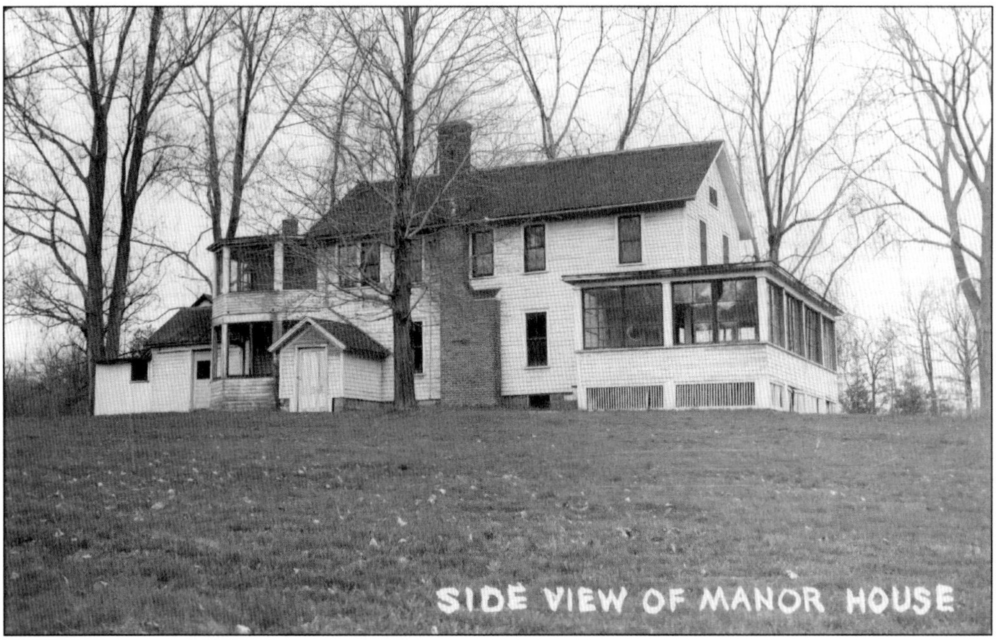


The manor house, built around 1875 by owner at that time, Benjamin R. Lummis, became a residence for the Scout leaders and for teaching crafts. Eventually, the Scouts outgrew the island's facilities and moved their new camp to Massawepie in the Adirondack Mountains. The Scouts sold Eagle Island in 1954 to engineer George Lookup and lumber dealer J. Walker Caves, both of Newark. (Seneca Waterways Council Boy Scouts.)

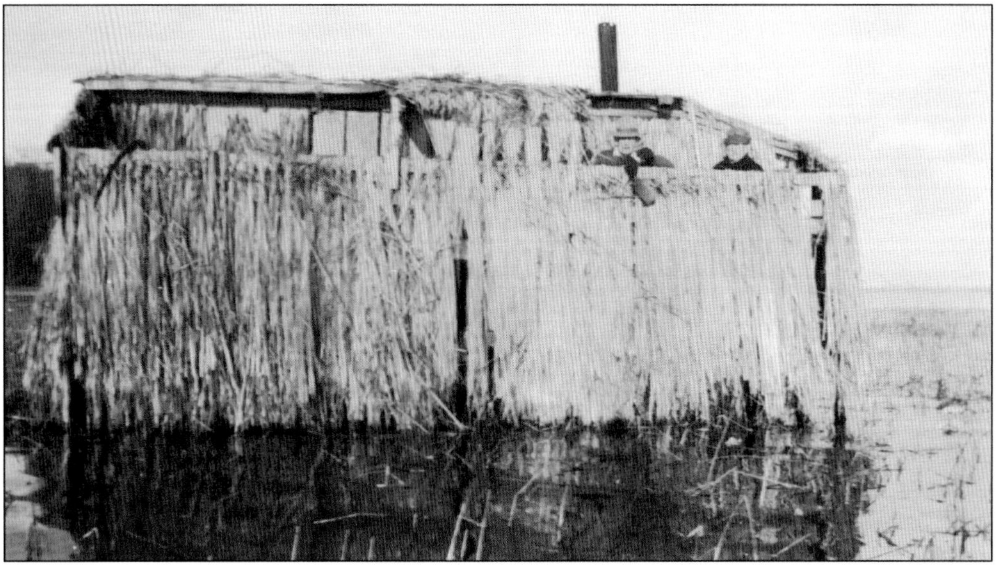

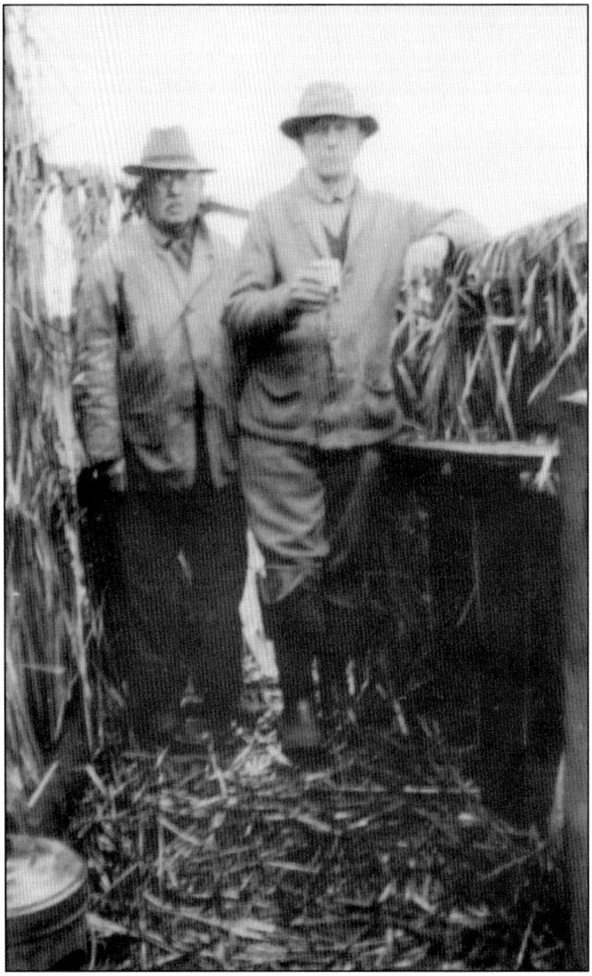

According to a 1939 Town of Huron Field Assessor's Book, George Gale from Sodus Point owned a tiny island off the southern tip of LeRoy Island that was known as Duck Island. Gale had a small sleeping cottage on this island with a cast-iron woodstove. His porch on the east side was a duck blind. Gale motored across the bay from Sodus Point, bringing friends to the island for a day's hunt. Pictured here are the duck blind (above) and a close-up (left) of Gale, on right, and his friend Henry Whitney, posing for a photograph taken by Whitney's grandson Bruce. The duck blind and island are now gone; the woodstove, however, still lies at the bottom of the bay at the site of old Duck Island. (Both, Nancy Huston Doubleday.)

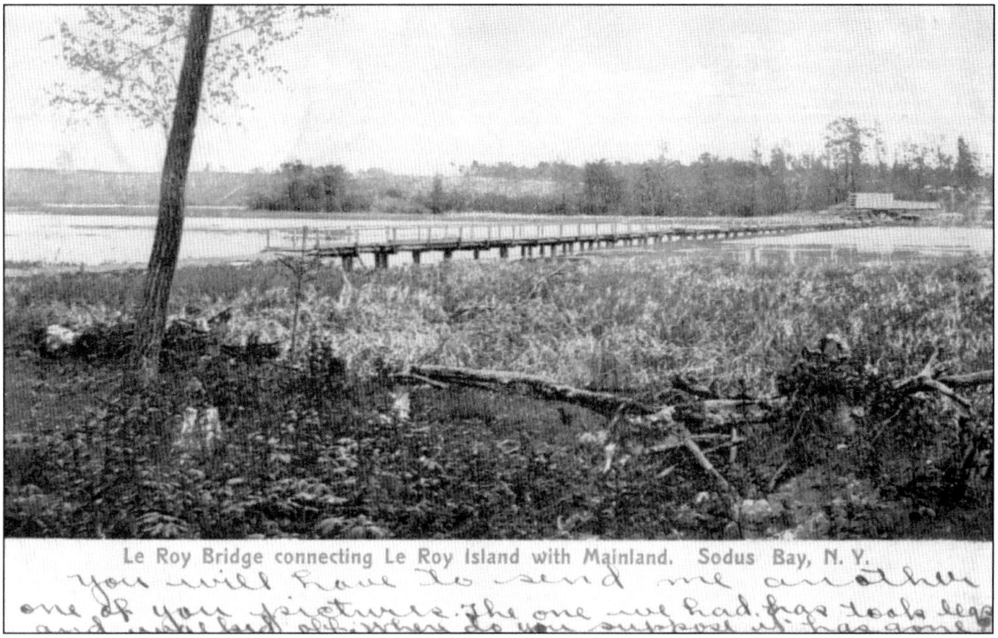


LeRoy Island is the only island connected to the mainland by a bridge. The original span was a footbridge, but cottagers now enjoy a two-lane wood/steel structure with an ample walkway for pedestrians and fishermen. The view in this 1907 postcard looks east from the island toward Hog Island and the mainland. The building in the right corner, located on Hog Island, is a sawmill owned by Harlow C. LeRoy, after whom LeRoy Island is named.

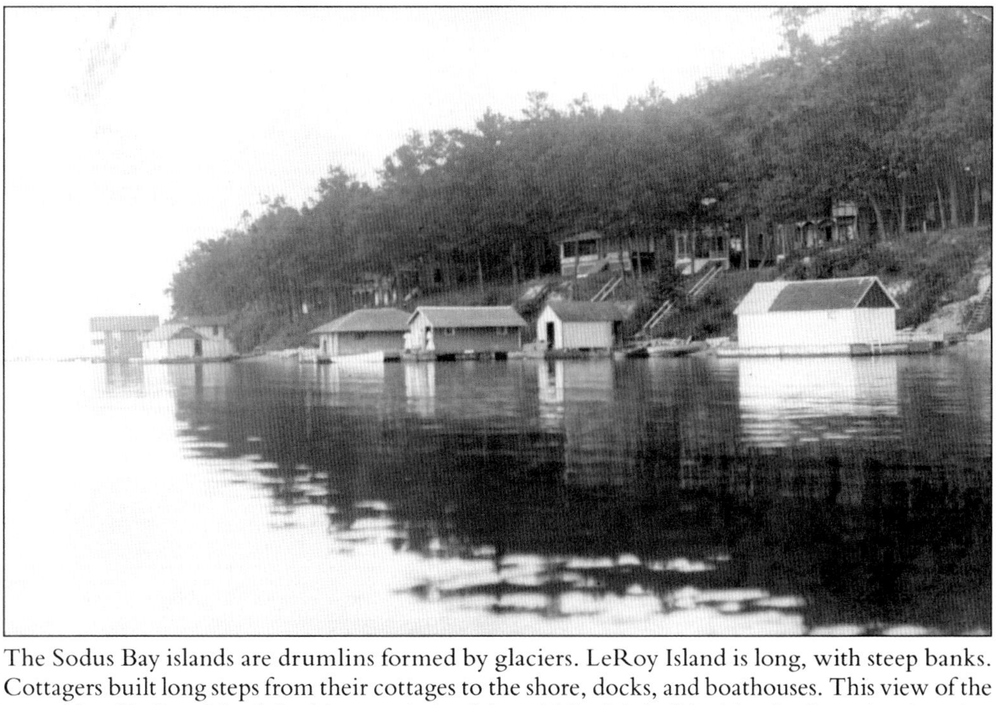

The Sodus Bay islands are drumlins formed by glaciers. LeRoy Island is long, with steep banks. Cottagers built long steps from their cottages to the shore, docks, and boathouses. This view of the west side of LeRoy Island, looking north, is of the middle third of the island, where the elevation is highest. Many of these cottages and boathouses on the west side are still used today.

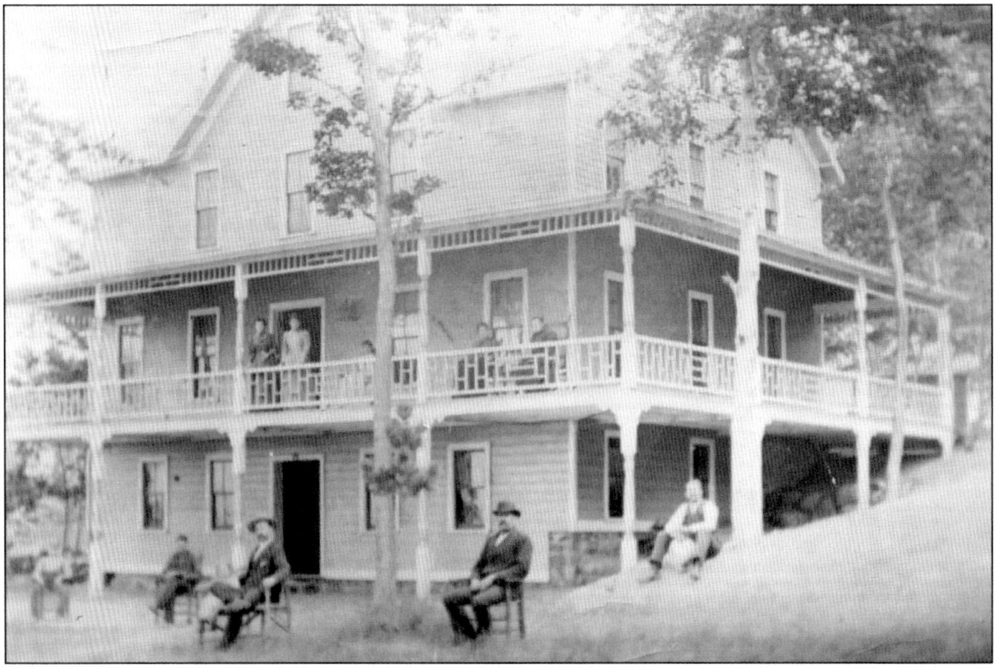

A hotel at the northern end of LeRoy Island was built, owned, and operated by Harlow C. LeRoy, a lumber dealer from Oswego, New York. LeRoy owned the entire island, then known as Long Island, as well as Hog Island where LeRoy's sawmill was located. A local newspaper, the *Lake Shore News*, reported that H.C. LeRoy's hotel burned in February 1901.

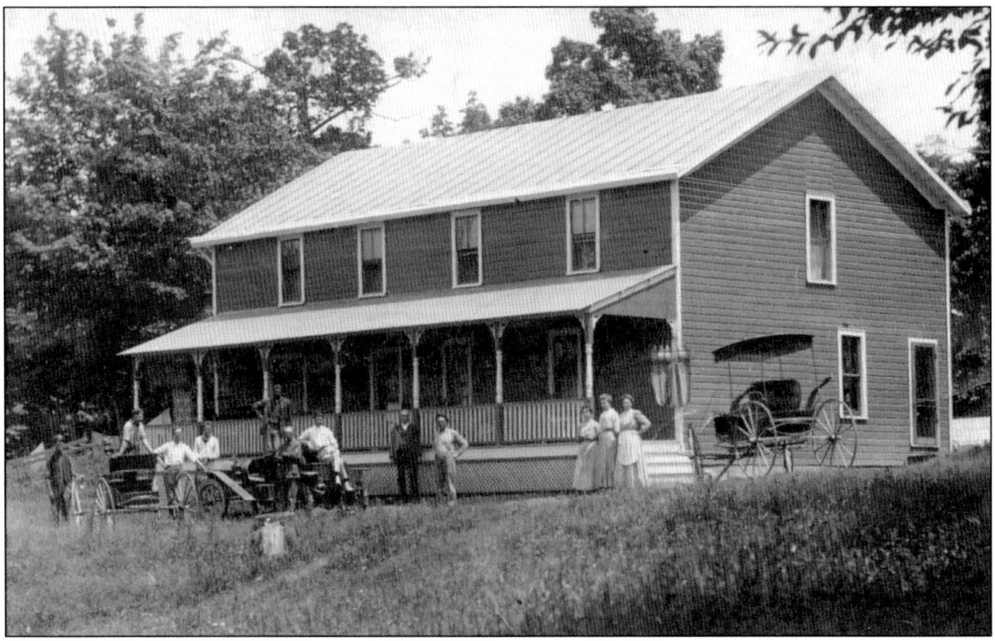

LeRoy built this second hotel after the first burned so he could continue serving guests on the island. There was a racetrack on LeRoy Island in the center, at the high point where it was most level. Horses were kept in a barn across the road from the hotel. It is likely the carriages seen here may have been used in some of the horse-racing events.

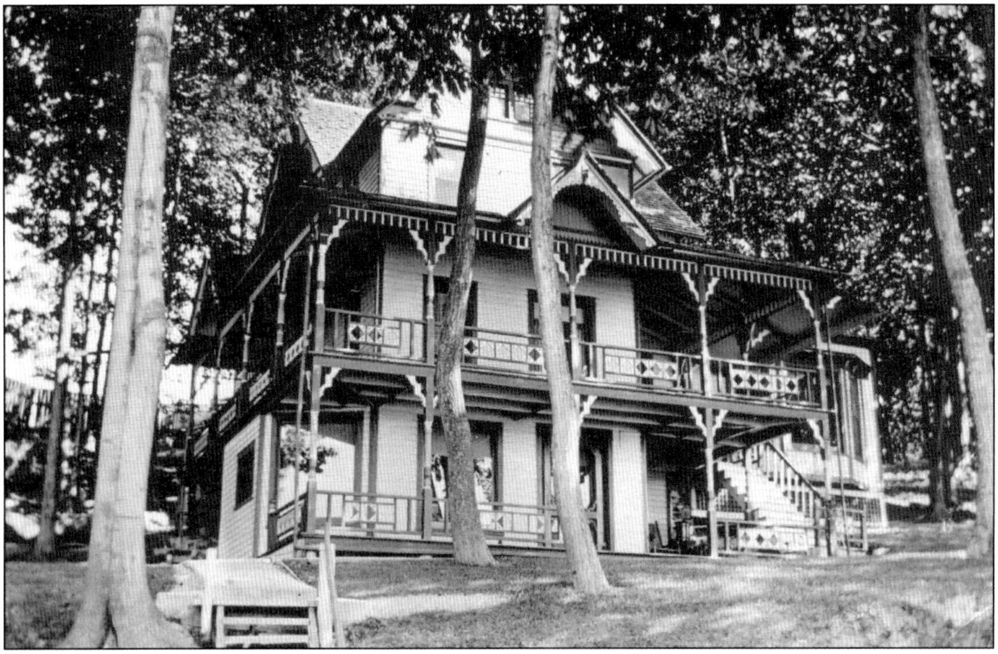

Information accompanying this photograph relates that Eben Newberry from Huron constructed this ornate Victorian cottage on LeRoy Island. James Decker owned the cottage from around 1900 to 1929. The family lived at the cottage well into the winter, as revealed by newspaper reports telling of their visits to friends in town and a report of their moving to California in January for the rest of the winter. (TOH.)

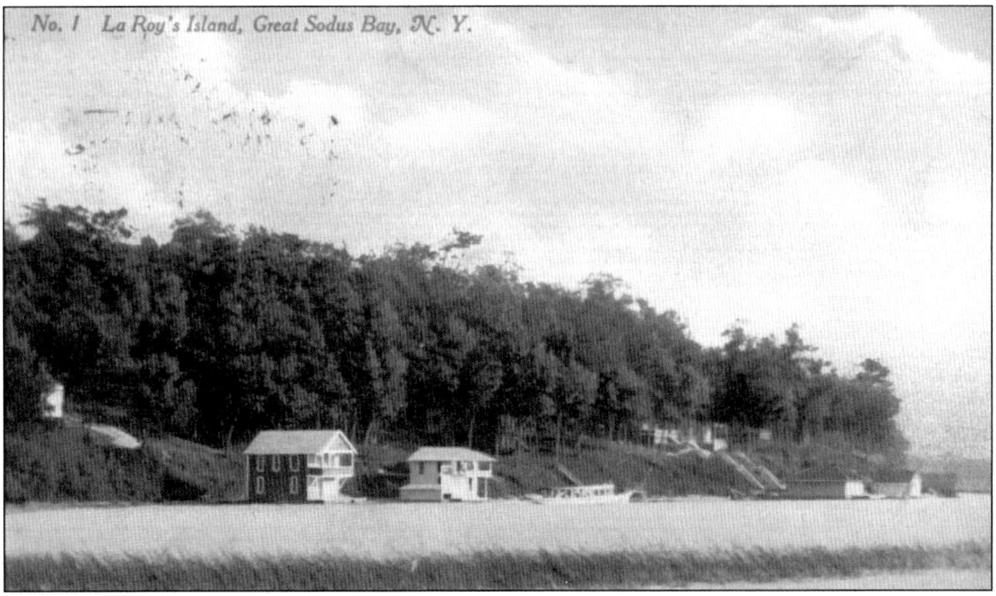


The Decker cottage is located near the center in this postcard. A small bay launch, possibly the *Seabird*, heads south along the west side of LeRoy Island. The tall reed grass in the foreground was once found growing on an underwater sandbar between Crescent Beach and LeRoy Island. This photograph may have been taken from a boat or possibly from Knob Island off Crescent Beach.

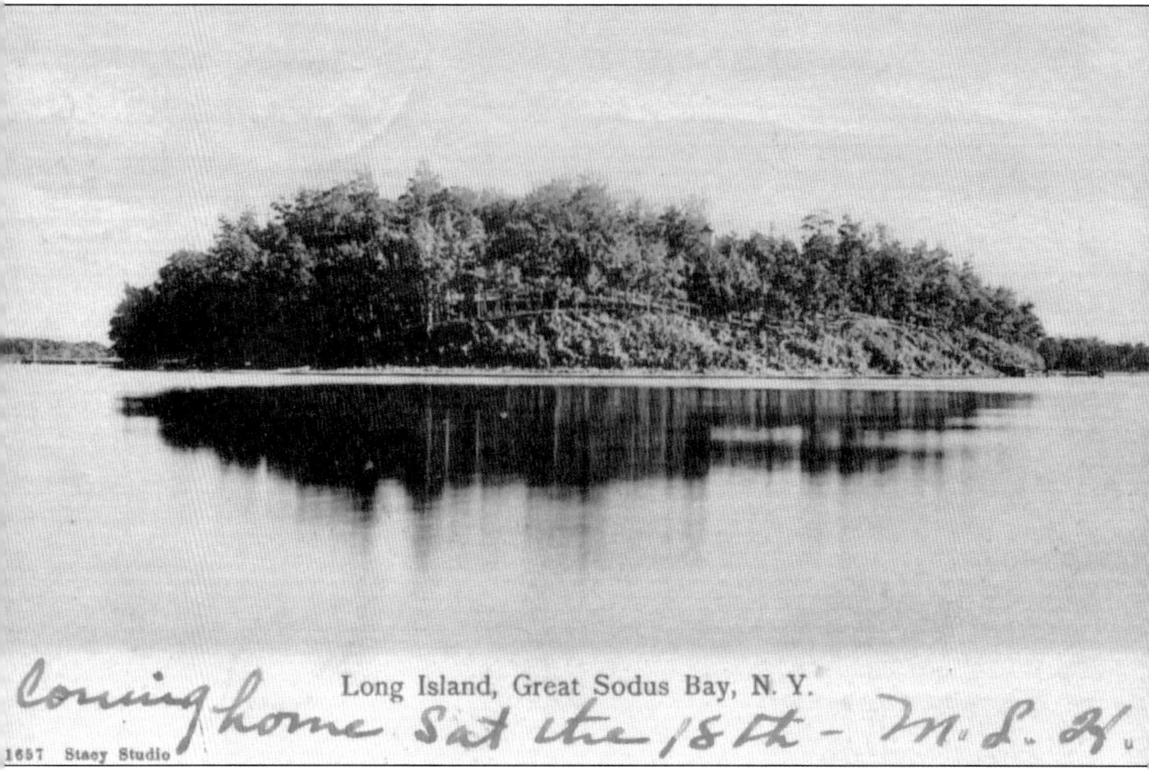


In this c. 1900 view looking south at the northern tip of LeRoy Island, considerably more wooded area is visible than may be seen on this island today. However, by the time of this photograph, H.C. LeRoy had harvested much of the timber on the island for his lumber business, hotel, several cottages, horse barn, and boat landing on the island. Though not exactly as the Cayuga Indians would have seen, this picturesque view is similar to what they may have seen at Kenoga Island.

# *Five*

# Lake Bluff

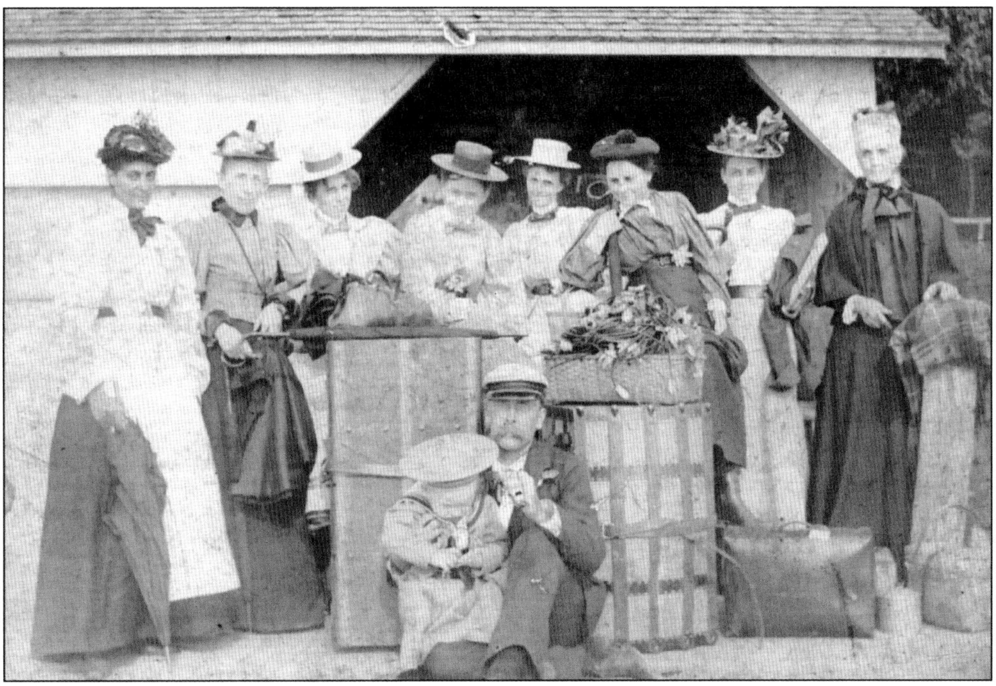

This gentleman and child, surrounded by a happy group of ladies with flowery hats, a basketful of water lilies, and steamer trunks loaded with lake stones, await the arrival of the steamers *Sunbeam* or *Willie Poucher* at the Lake Bluff steamboat landing. As these travelers ready themselves to board the steamer to leave Lake Bluff, another group will arrive with, instead of lake stones, a trunk filled with potatoes. (TOH.)

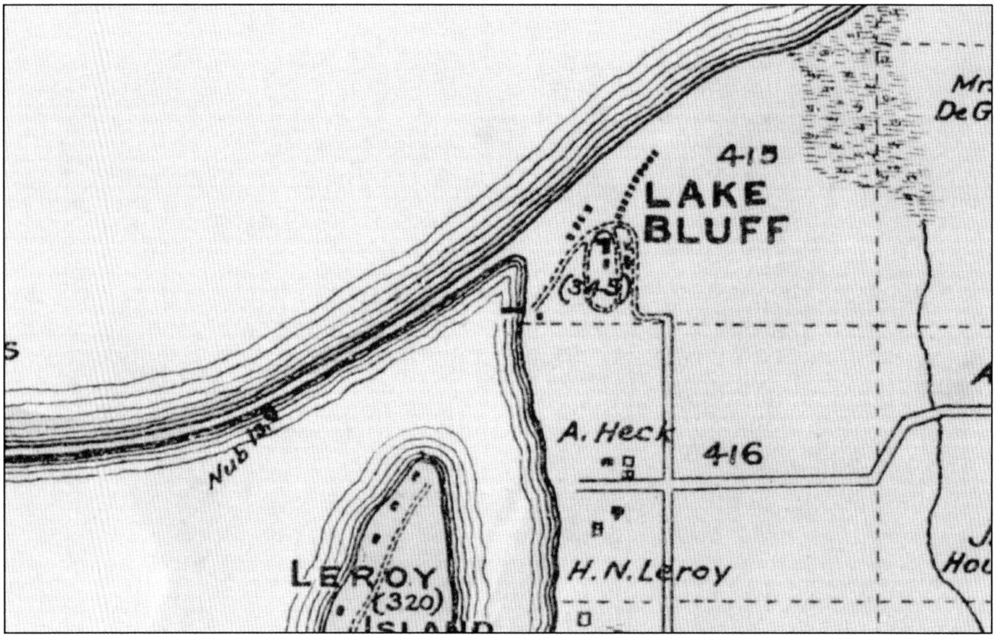


This map from the *1904 New Century Atlas* provides a good representation of what the northeastern corner of Sodus Bay looked like at the turn of the 20th century. Differences today include the disappearance of Nub (more commonly known as Knob) Island, the row of cottages extending above the loop at Lake Bluff, and the road leading to the bay from atop Lake Bluff. Below, the view looks south from the Lake Bluff cove to the northern tip of LeRoy Island. The Lake Bluff Steamboat Landing is on the left. From 1874 to around 1910, many Lake Bluff visitors traveled to this popular resort by boat. Visitors arrived at Sodus Point by train from Rochester or Newark or by passenger steamer from Rochester, Oswego, or the Thousand Islands and transferred to one of the bay's steamers like *Willie Poucher*, *Sunbeam*, or *Lizzie*. (Above, TOH.)

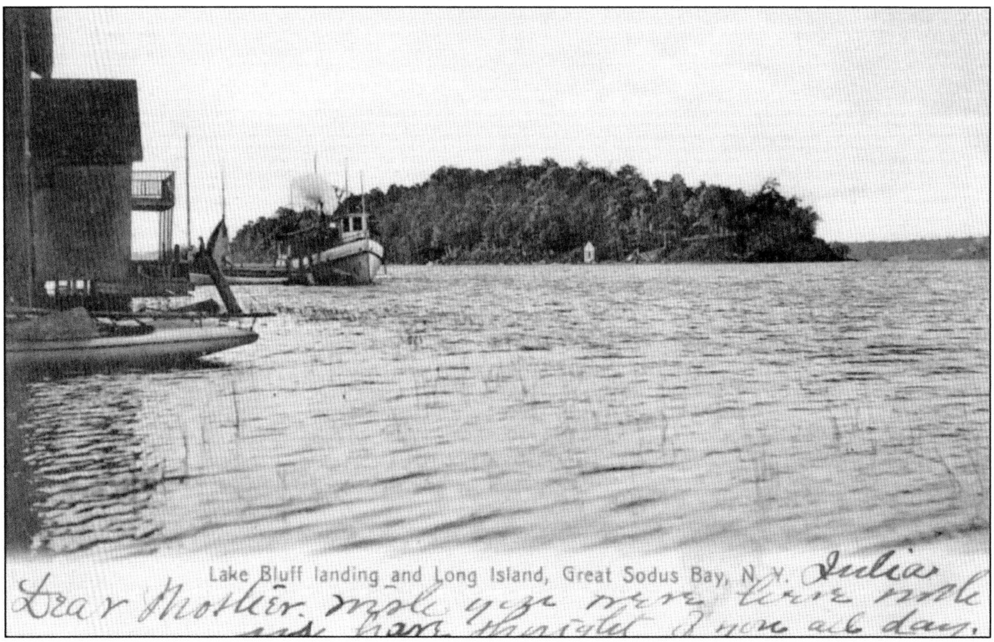

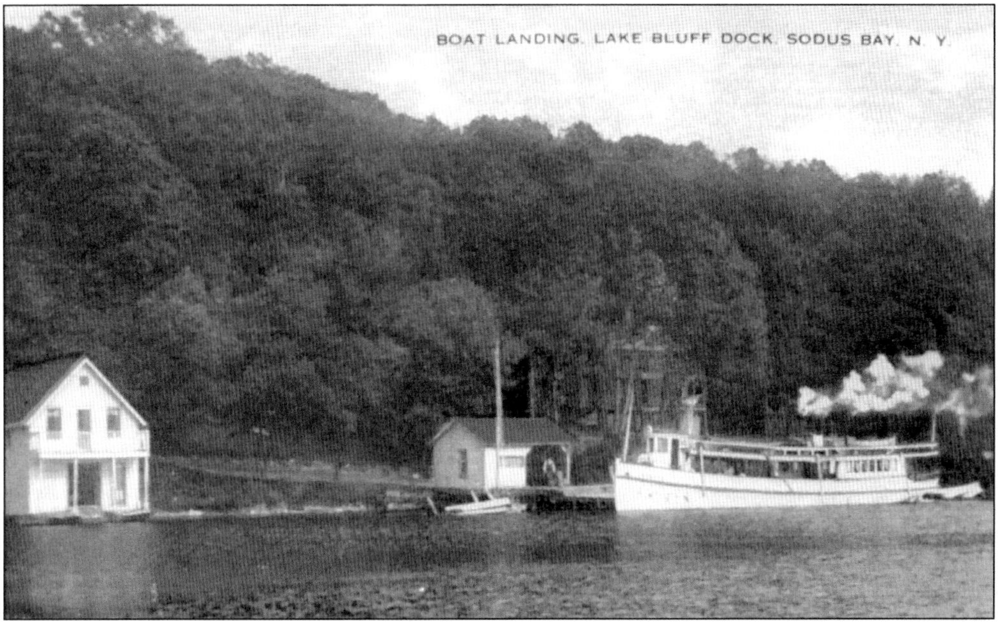


Above the boat landing, to the right, is the lower Lake Bluff hotel, known as the Lake View (or Cottis) Hotel. To the left of the boat landing runs Bay Avenue. Beginning at the top of the bluff, Bay Avenue came down along the side, with cottages on both sides, and turned at the base of the bluff to follow the shore to the boat landing. At the dock, *Sunbeam* awaits passengers.

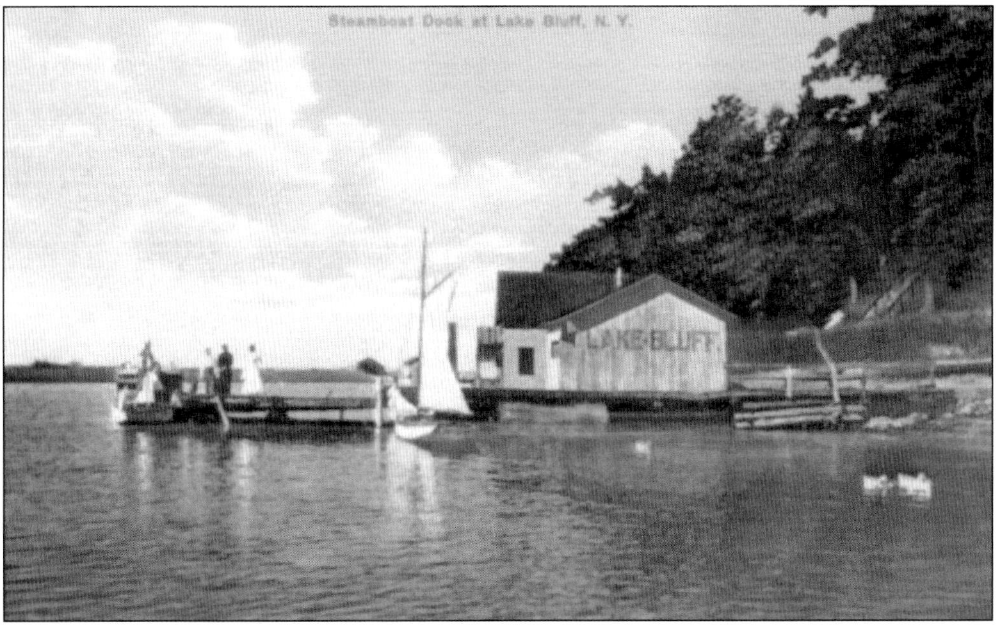


In this view looking north, the viewer gets a sense of what passengers coming by steamer or other water vessel may have seen as they arrived for a visit at Lake Bluff. A horse and wagon would transport the guests and their luggage from the Lake Bluff Steamer Landing to the upper hotel and cottages at the summit of the bluff community. In the distance is Crescent Beach. Beyond the beach is Lake Ontario.

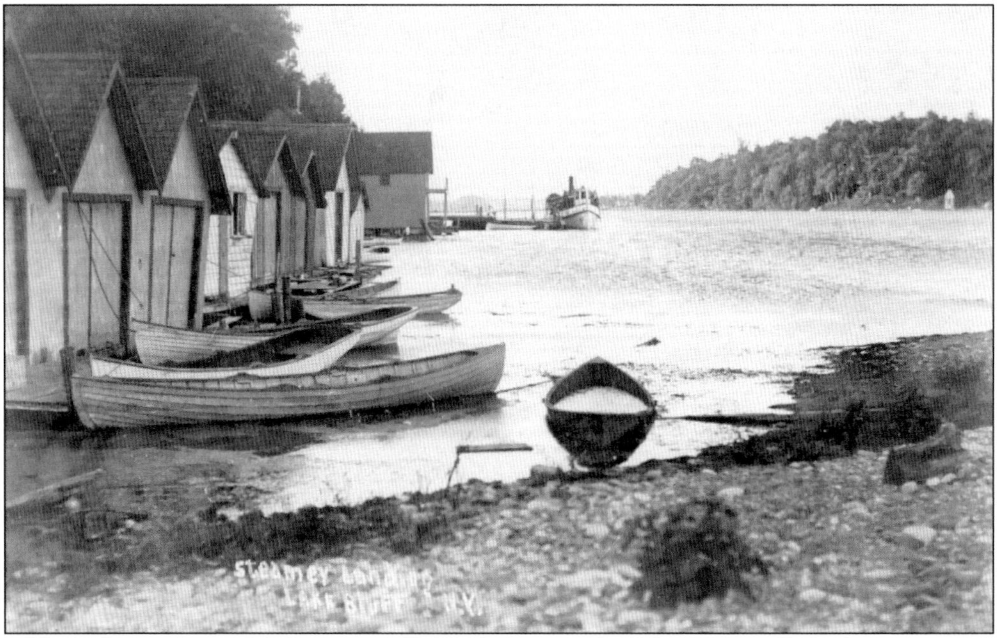


This view of the Lake Bluff steamboat landing and boathouses is from Sodus Bay's sandbar, called Crescent Beach. The eight boathouses in the foreground are no longer standing. If these boathouses were still present, they would now be found in Lake Ontario. Crescent Beach has moved back into the bay to the point of the last boathouse just before the steamer dock.

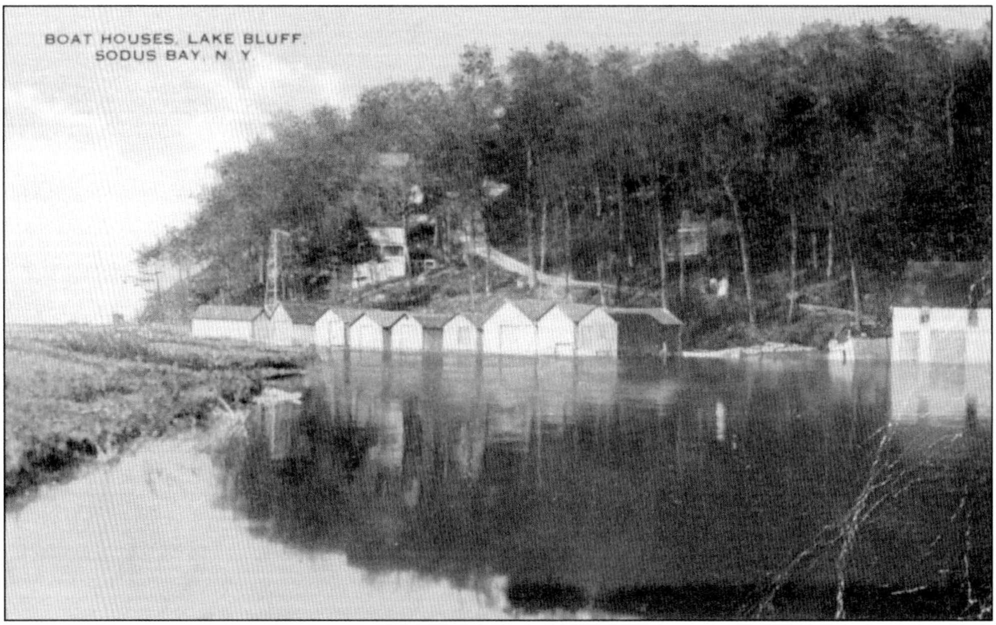


With a view facing northeast toward Lake Bluff from Crescent Beach, this image shows a different look at the boathouses along the bay. Bay Avenue can be seen coming down the hill. The row cottages and boathouses on the left and Bay Avenue are now gone. Crescent Beach and the lakeshore have moved back to the clearing to the left of the solitary boathouse on the right side of this photograph.

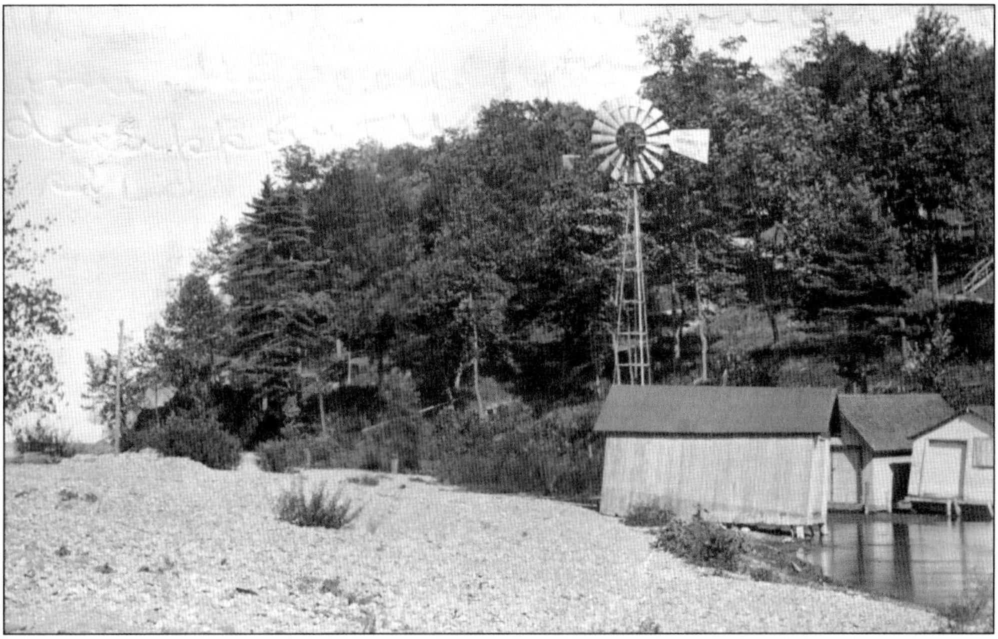

The windmill that powered the transport of water to a tower tank at the top of the bluff stands tall in this view looking east from Crescent Beach. Wind and wave action gradually moved the bar back into the bay and eroded the toe of the bluff, putting an end to the windmill. Eventually, gas and, later, electricity allowed for a motorized pump to service water to the summer guests.

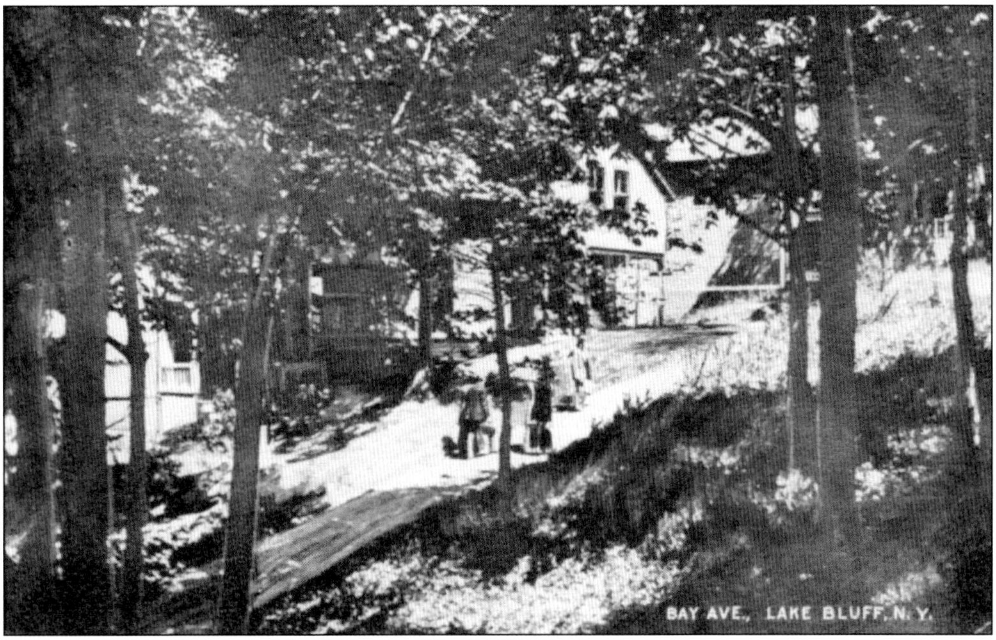


Leaving the shores of Great Sodus Bay, visitors to Lake Bluff would ride a horse and wagon to their destination atop the bluff or walk up the steep Bay Avenue. This image, postmarked at Lake Bluff in 1912, shows the cottages along Bay Avenue's precipitous ascent. The cottages along the edge of Lake Bluff had a panoramic view overlooking Lake Ontario. Bluff erosion caused the demise of these cottages.

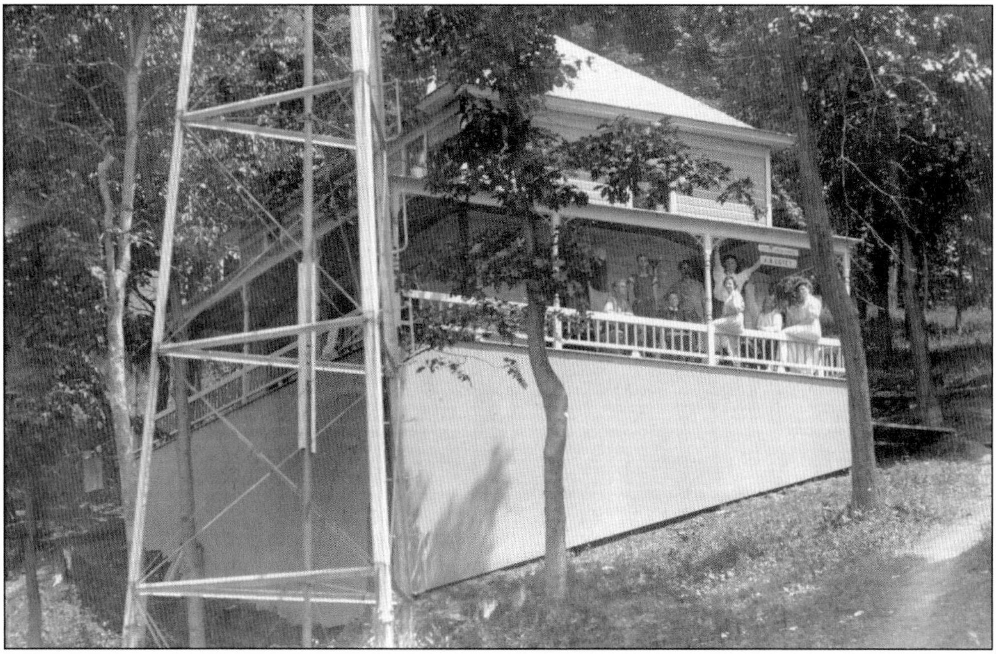

"*Pour Mes Amis*" (French for "for my friends") reads the sign on the A.B. Estey cottage at the foot of the bluff on Bay Avenue. This card reflects the camaraderie of the Lake Bluff community. Families and friends enjoyed sharing time and relaxation together during the short weeks of summer vacations. In the foreground is the windmill.

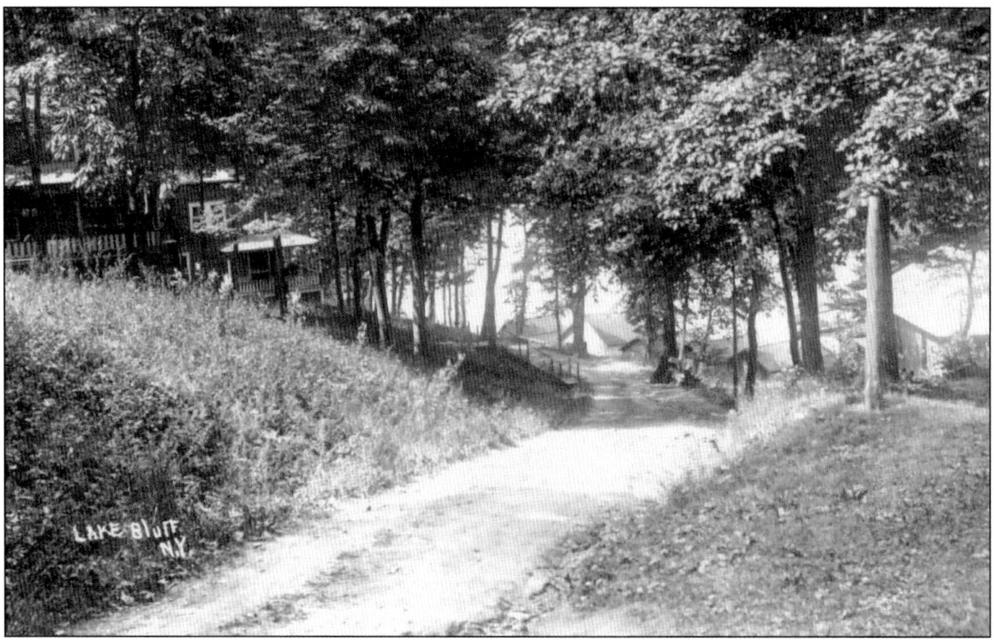


In this view looking down the slope of Bay Avenue toward the shore of Sodus Bay, the boathouse row can be seen beyond the trees. The portion of Bay Avenue depicted in this picture has been lost to erosion due to the force of wind and waves from Lake Ontario tearing away at the face and toe of the bluff. The lower cottage on the left still remains.

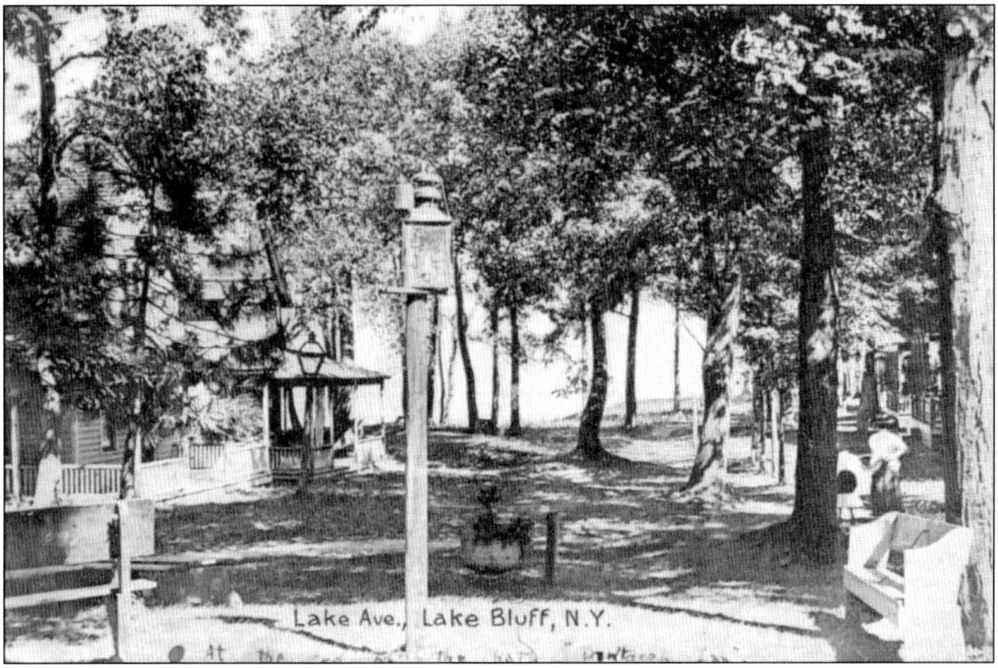


Bay Avenue merged with Lake Avenue. A number of quaint Victorian summer cottages, several of which still survive today, were located atop the bluff beyond Lake Avenue. These cottages had to be moved over time to save them from being torn down or falling over the bluff as it eroded. The two women on the right are looking toward the bluff's edge and Lake Ontario.

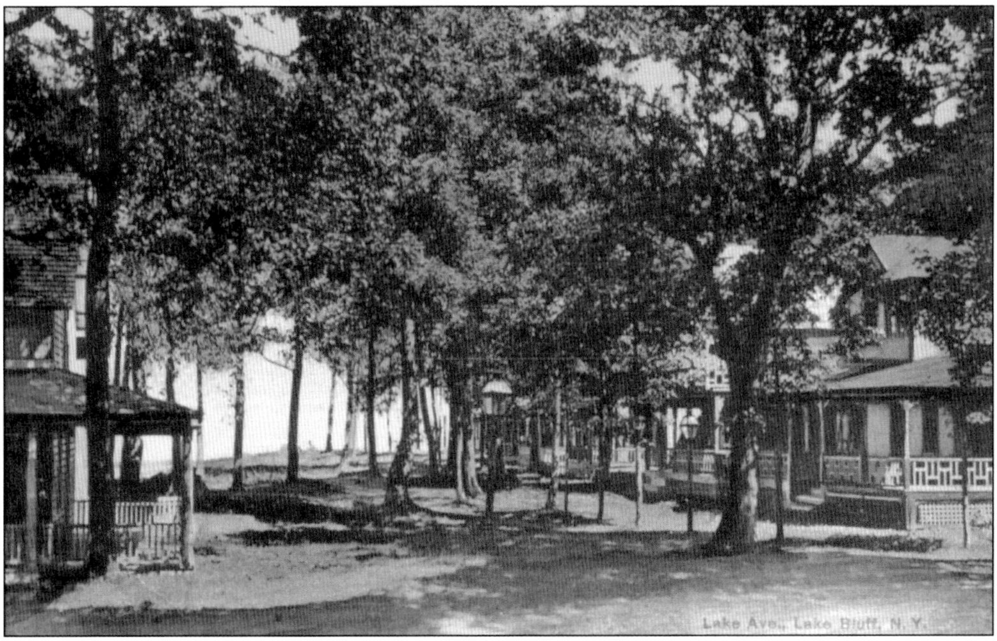


This cottage cluster was located north of Lake Avenue. The grove is likely American chestnut trees that were destroyed in the blight of 1925. The path leads toward the bluff's edge and a spectacular view of Lake Ontario beyond. This land and the trees are now gone. Only a few cottages were torn down; most were moved to safer ground.

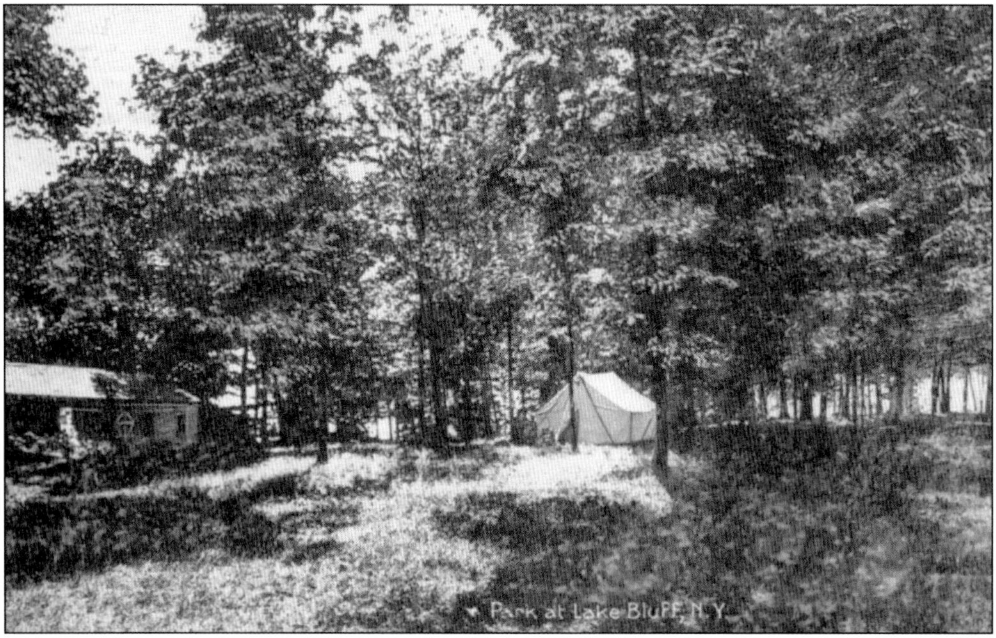


Lake Bluff began as a summer retreat campground for members of the Huron Methodist Episcopal Church around 1875. Families and individuals would pitch tents and enjoy recreation, nature, family, and friends in a serene wooded environment with beautiful vistas from the bluff. Refreshing swimming in the lake and limitless boating and fishing on the bay and lake were great attractions. It is said that hay fever was "cured" with a visit to Lake Bluff. The air was clean, and the lake breezes kept all the pollen away. It did not take long for the popularity to spread and for Lake Bluff to become a premier destination. This rise in popularity required more than a tent or cottage could provide, so a grand hotel was built to accommodate more guests.

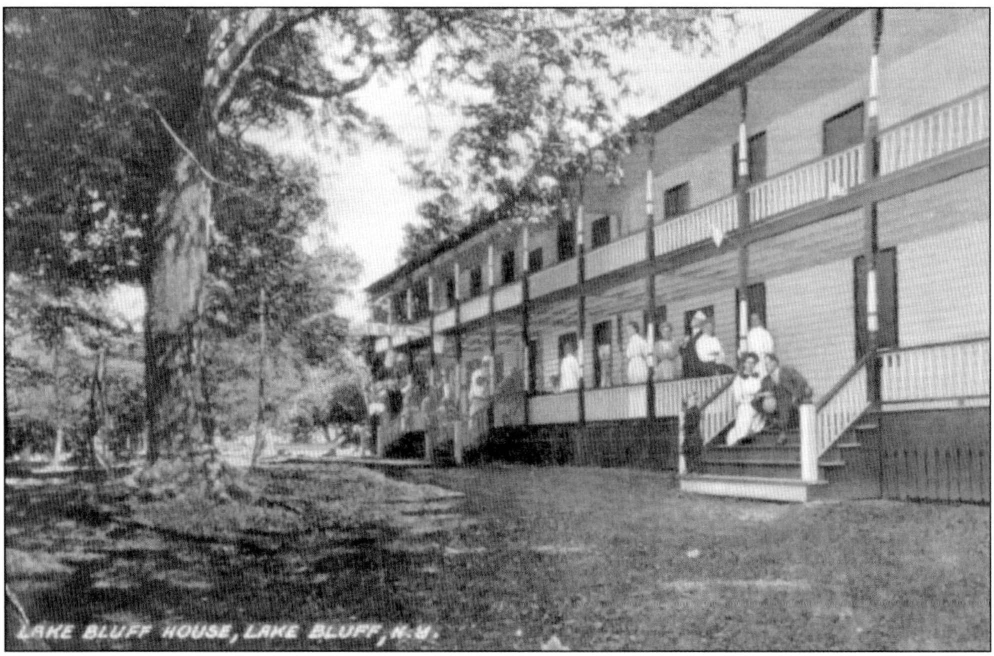

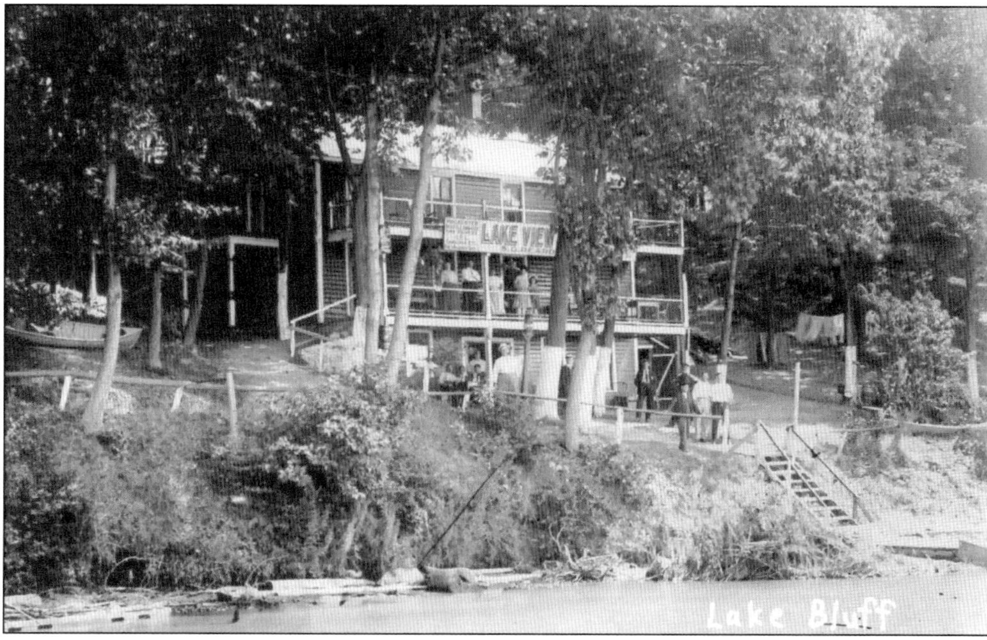


Lake Bluff had two hotels. The Lake View (Cottis) Hotel was near the steamboat landing on the bay front (above). Primarily fishermen and hunters frequented the Lake View. Erected in the 1880s, the Lake Bluff Hotel (below), at the top of the bluff, was owned and built by Erastus B. Fuller. It had about 20 rooms, a post office, a candy store, a dining room, and a grocery store. The hotel was home to the only telephone on the bluff. Food was grown in the fields in the valley to the east of the hotel. In 1927, the hotel was purchased by the Lake Bluff Hotel Corporation and continued serving guests until 1938. Declining business forced the Lake Bluff Hotel to cease operation, and it was torn down. (Above, TOH.)

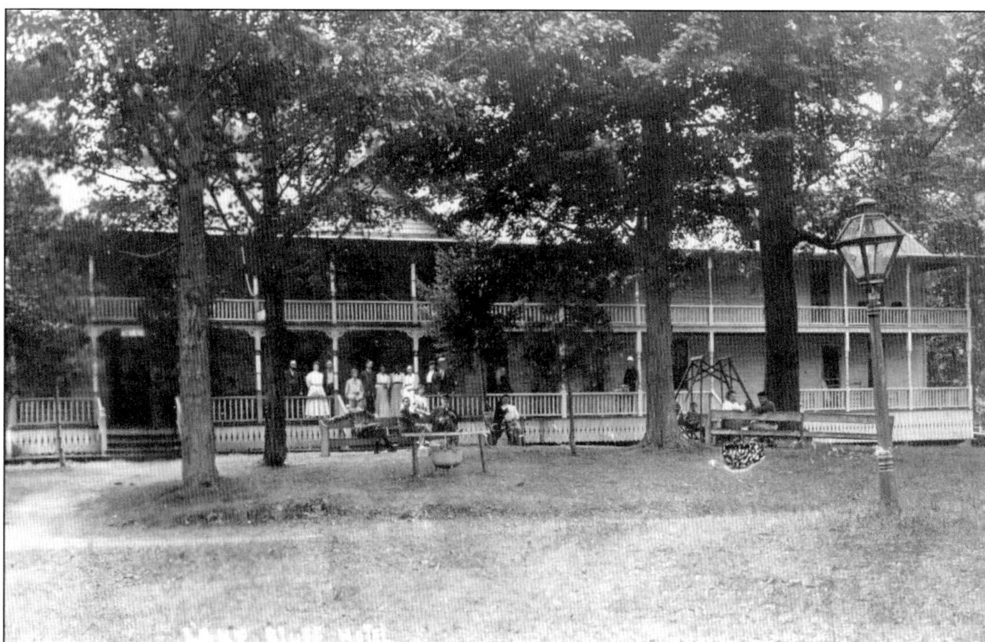

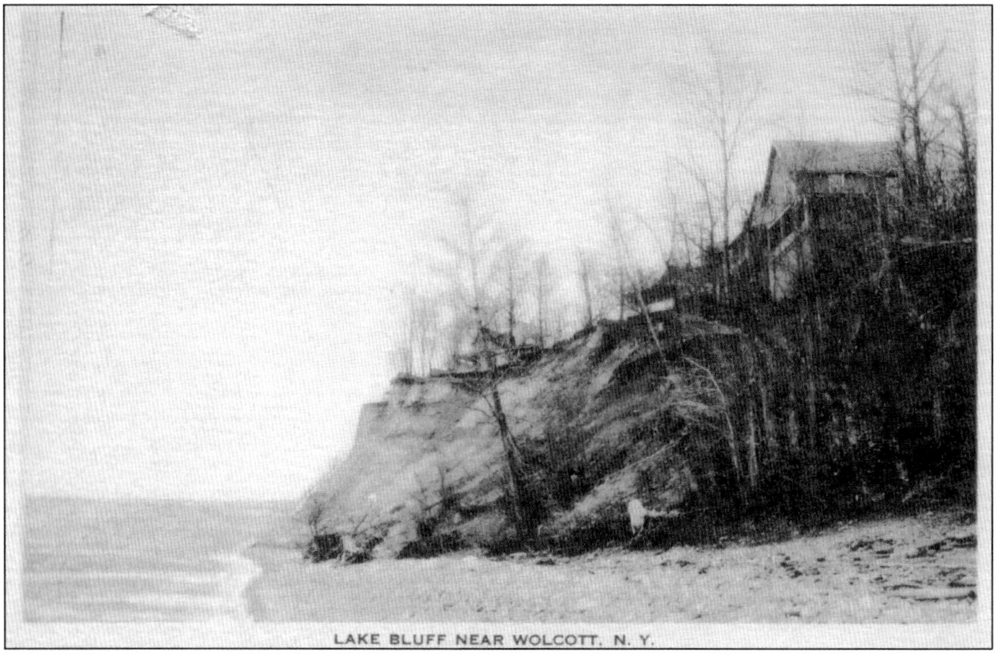


Lake Bluff cottages sit precariously at the edge of the bluff awaiting their owners' or Mother Nature's decision as to their destinies. For some of these cottages, their fates were to fall over the edge. Some were torn down, and still others had the good fortune to be moved a little farther back to "safe" ground. (TOH.)

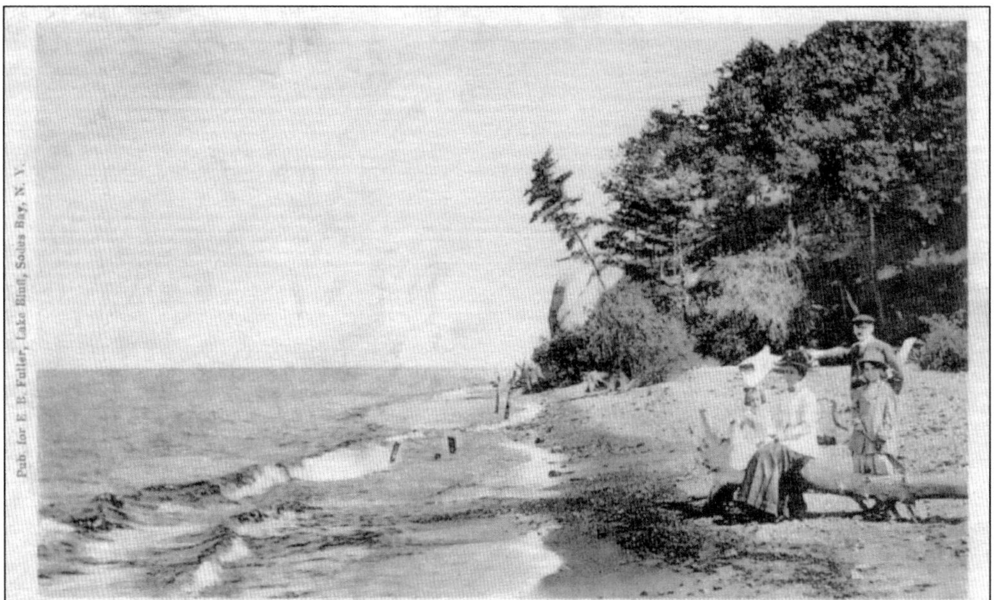


This postcard is one of the rare cards published for Erastus B. Fuller, owner of the Lake Bluff Resort. With Lake Bluff in the background, a family poses, appearing to seriously enjoy the view of Lake Ontario from the beach at the point where Lake Bluff and Crescent Beach merge. Perhaps a sailboat race or a flock of water birds captures their interest.

# *Six*

# Crescent Beach and Charles Point

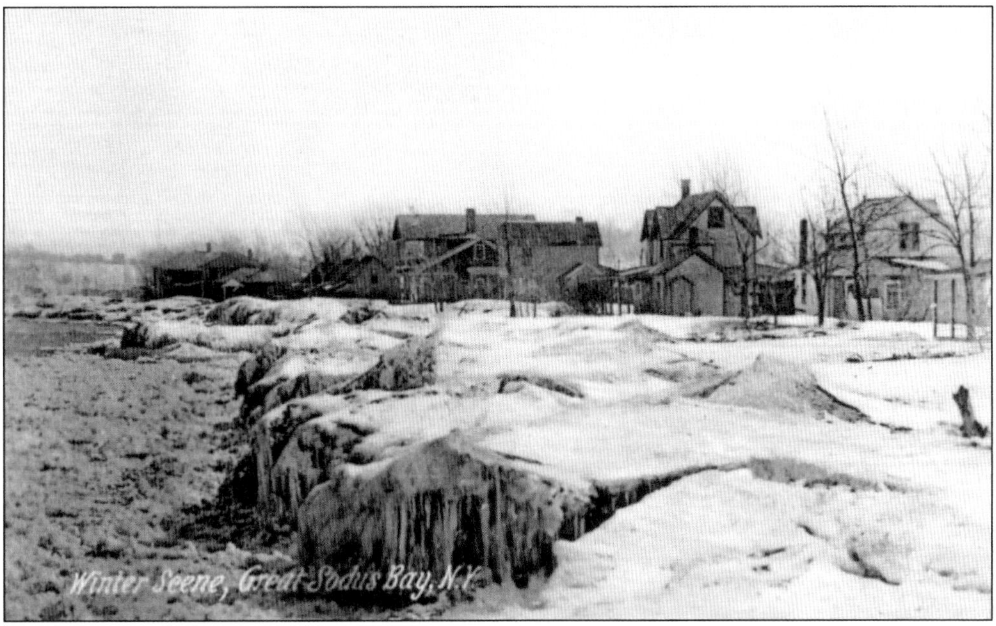


Winter postcard scenes of Sodus Bay are a rarity. This view was taken near Charles Point and looks west along the lakeside of Crescent Beach toward Lake Bluff. Lake waves beat against the shore, building up ice formations over the course of the winter. Some of these formations extend into the lake for hundreds of feet. Blowholes, ice volcanoes, and crevices are part of the icy contour, making for treacherous walking.

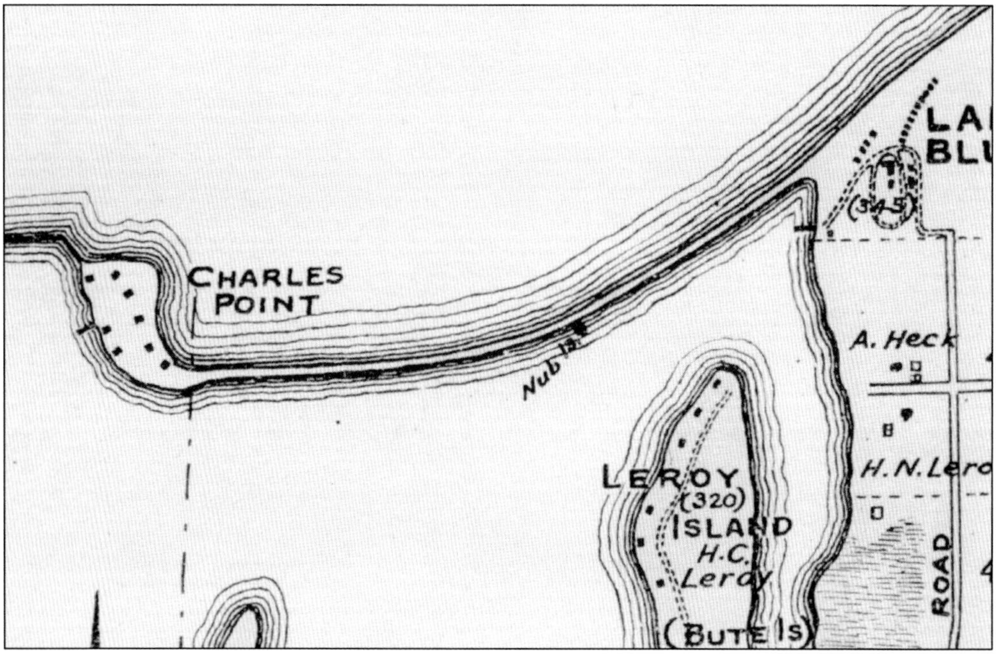


The map from the *1904 New Century Atlas* shows Crescent Beach, Nub (Knob) Island, and Charles Point. Crescent Beach has now merged with Nub Island. At the junction of Lake Bluff, the bar has moved back to nearly where the dock is shown. Near Charles Point, the bar lies more to the south with a dogleg to Charles Point. Today, the beach may be nearly 200 feet wide from lake to bay. Other spots may only be 50 feet wide. The postcard below shows a bird's-eye view of Crescent Beach from atop Lake Bluff looking west. Sodus Bay is on the left, and Lake Ontario is on the right. Newark Island juts out into the bay at the upper left. Nub Island is the little dot of land in the center left between Newark Island and Crescent Beach. (Above, TOH.)

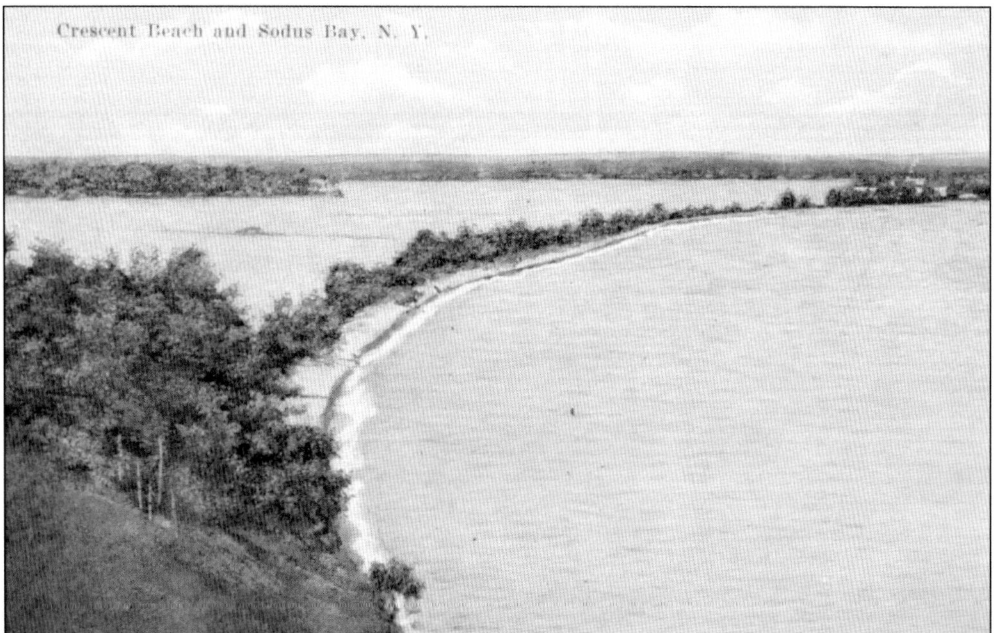

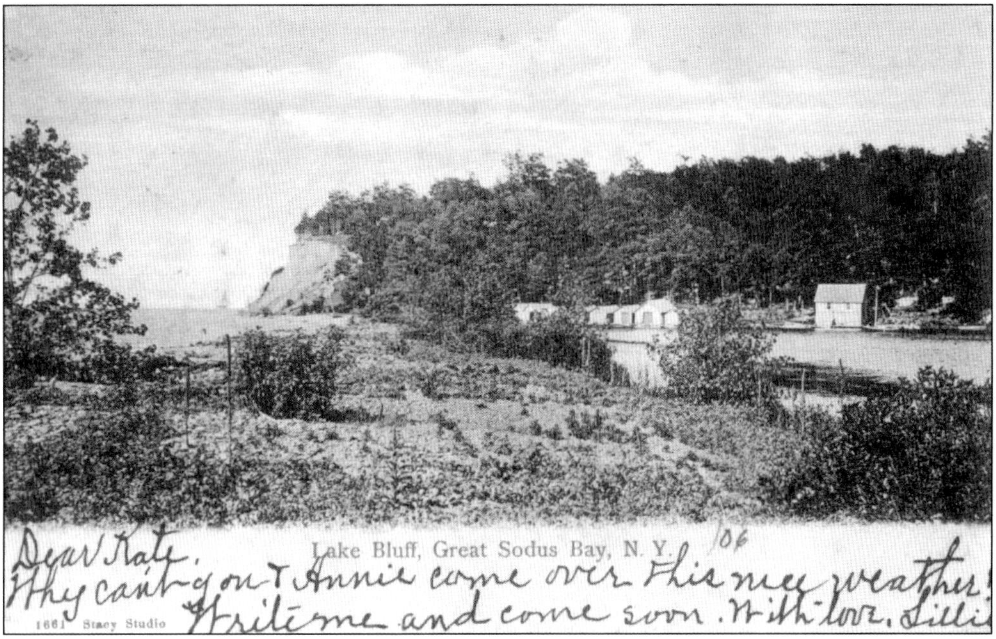


Crescent Beach is also known as the Sandbar, but is affectionately referred to by locals as simply "the Bar." The Bar has long been a favorite swimming place and promenade. The lake's sandy bottom makes for excellent family swimming, and the cobbled beach provides rock hounds many hours of study and collecting. The land on the bar is privately owned, and access is restricted to owners and their guests.

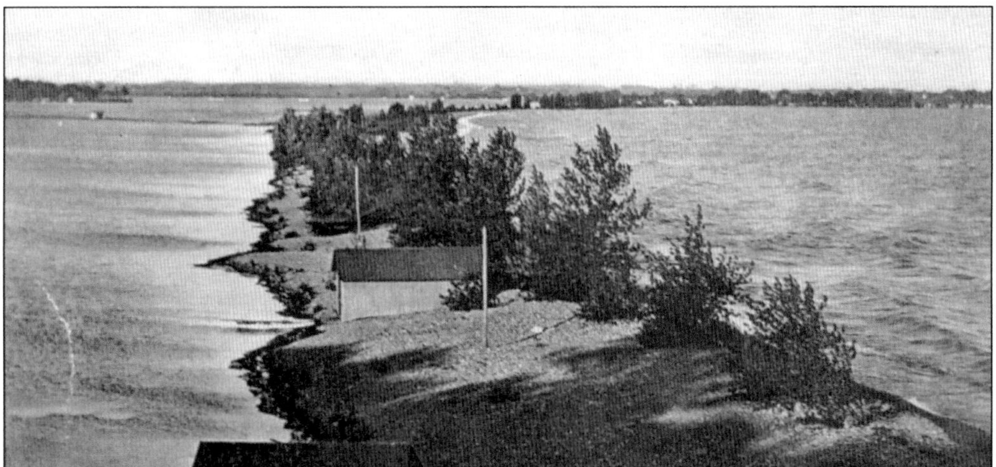


Postmarked at Lake Bluff in 1907, this view of Crescent Beach may have been taken from the Lake Bluff windmill. From here, the tiny Nub (Knob) Island can be seen in the upper left corner. In the upper right corner, at the far end of Crescent Beach, is Charles Point. Vegetation is sparse on the bar due to the battering weather conditions.

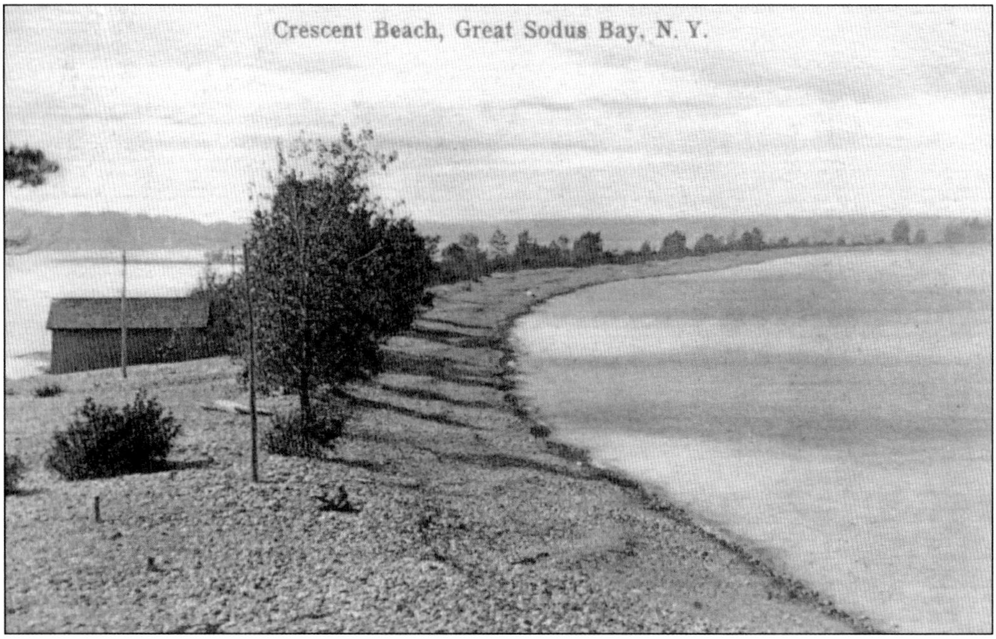


Crescent Beach experiences interesting transitions throughout a single year as a result of storms, and over the years due to coastal shifting. The beach could one day be covered with wonderful beach sand. Following a storm, the beach could be strewn with various sized lake stones. It is always changing, never the same—a land of many appearances.

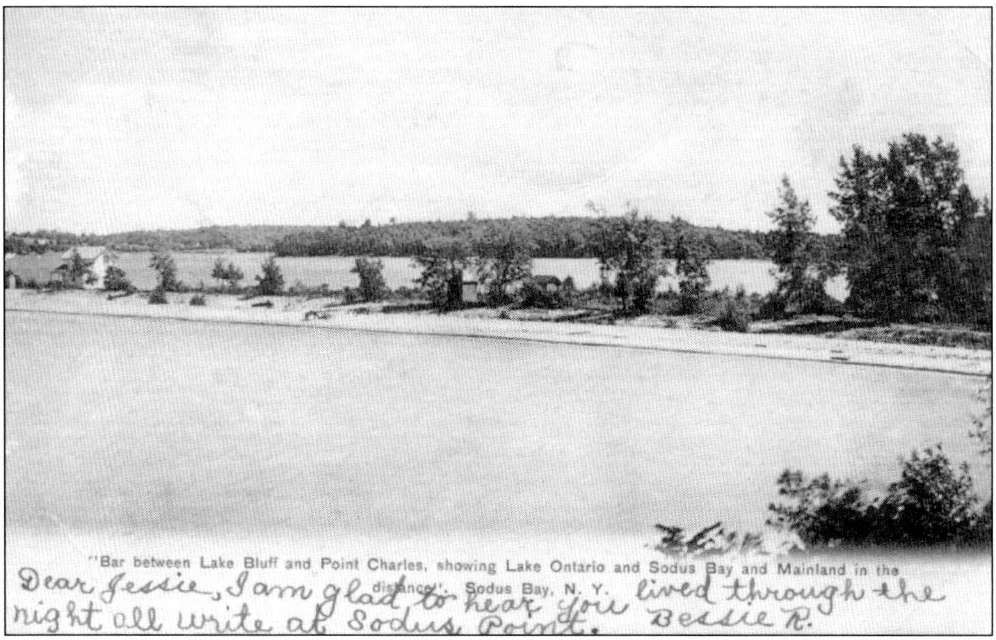


This image, postmarked in 1906, shows Crescent Beach in the foreground with Eagle Island in the center at the horizon. The mainland is to the left above the cottage. This photograph was probably taken from Charles Point. In the early 1900s, there were more cottages built up on the sandbar at this location than near the bluff. The vegetation appears to be denser along this stretch.

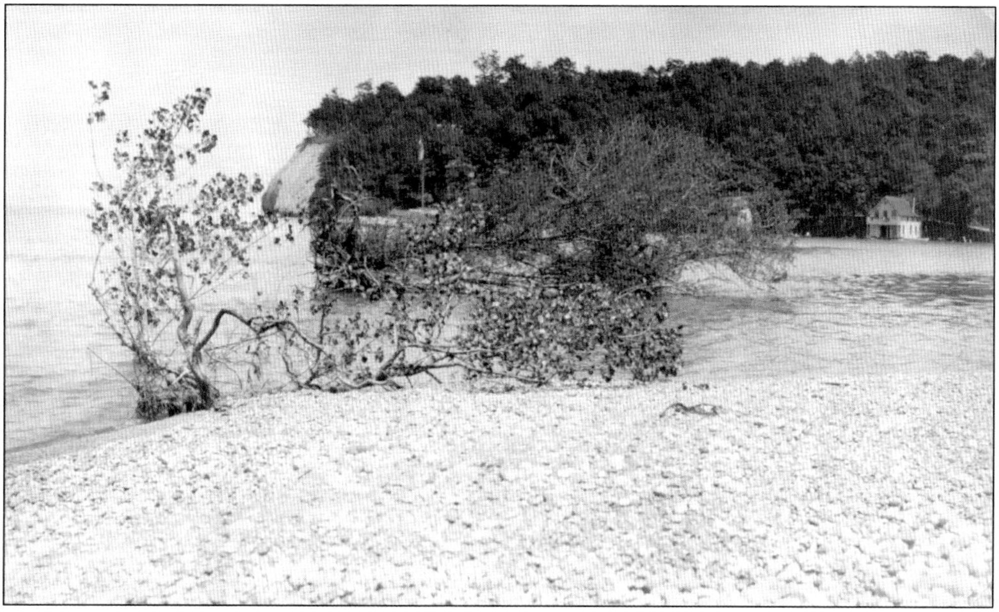

A "break" in Crescent Beach, as seen in this view looking toward Lake Bluff, reveals the severe impact the lake storms can have on the barrier bars in the Great Lakes. The breaks create a buildup of underwater sandbars in the bay that can cause a navigational problem for boats, especially sailboats with deeper keels. Careful study of the bluff shows erosion at the bluff toe from the storm that caused this damage.

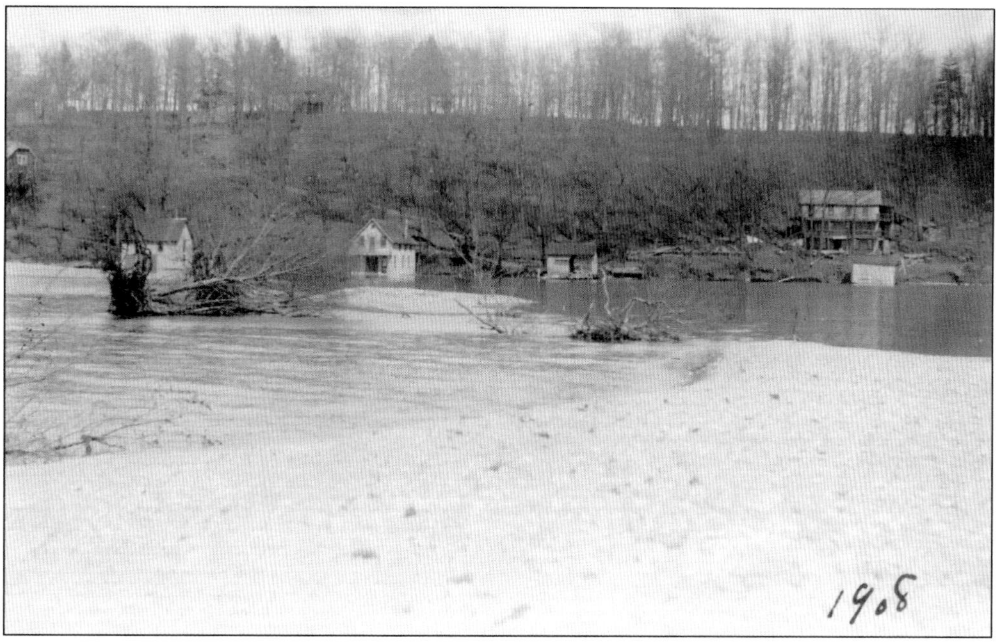


The break in this image appears to be from the same storm pictured previously. This photograph, taken in the spring or fall of 1908, reveals lasting storm damage. Today, there is a sizable underwater sandbar in the bay where this break occurred, and the barrier bar is now quite wide at this point. Strong winds and large waves from forceful storms can have a severe impact on the barrier bar.

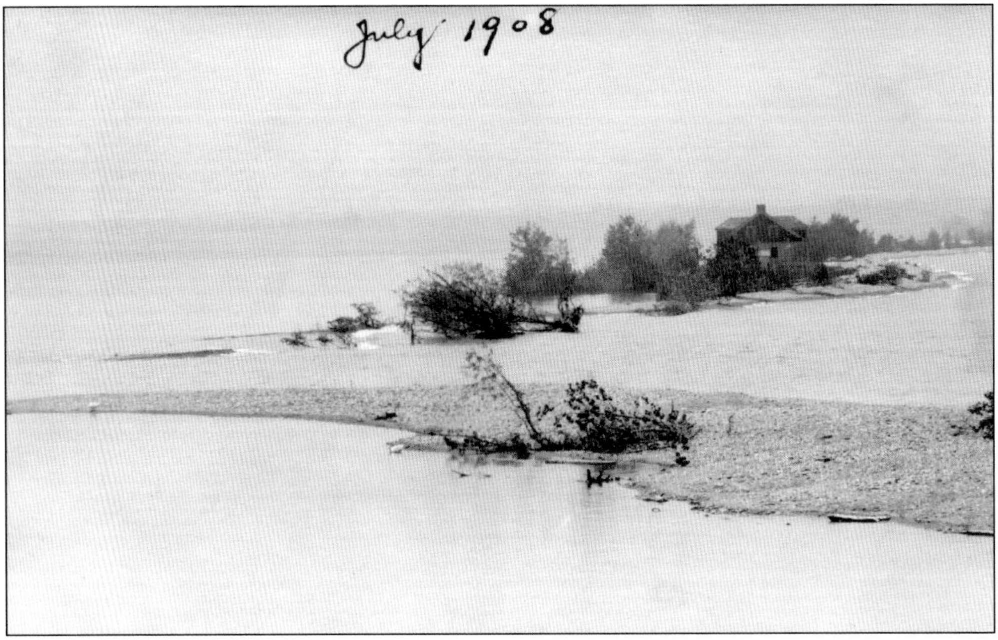


Looking west, this view of the same bar break as in the previous postcards reveals the expansiveness of the opening in the sandbar. The owners of the cottage in the background were very lucky the bar broke where it did. The cottage is no longer there, nor is the bar at this point in the lake any more. This cottage may have eventually been lost to waves or torn down. (TOH.)

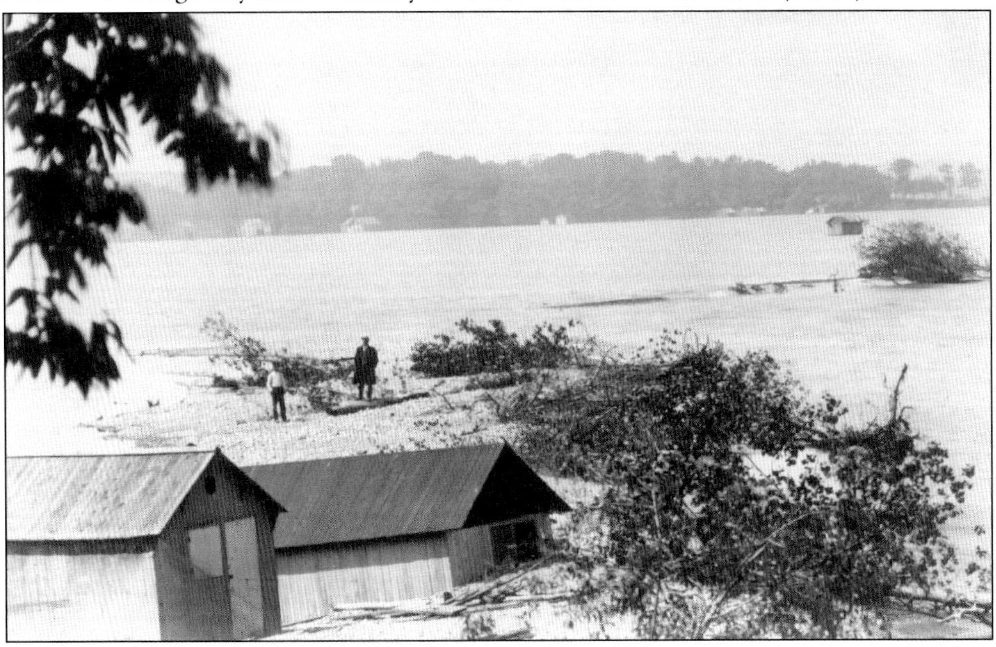

Two explorers survey the damage from the storm's onslaught. In the distance is Newark Island. The little shack on the water between Newark Island and the break in the bar is Knob Island, underwater except for the duck blind. Today, Crescent Beach has moved back into the bay to join with Knob Island. The two boathouses in the foreground were lucky then. Their footings can now be seen in the lake.

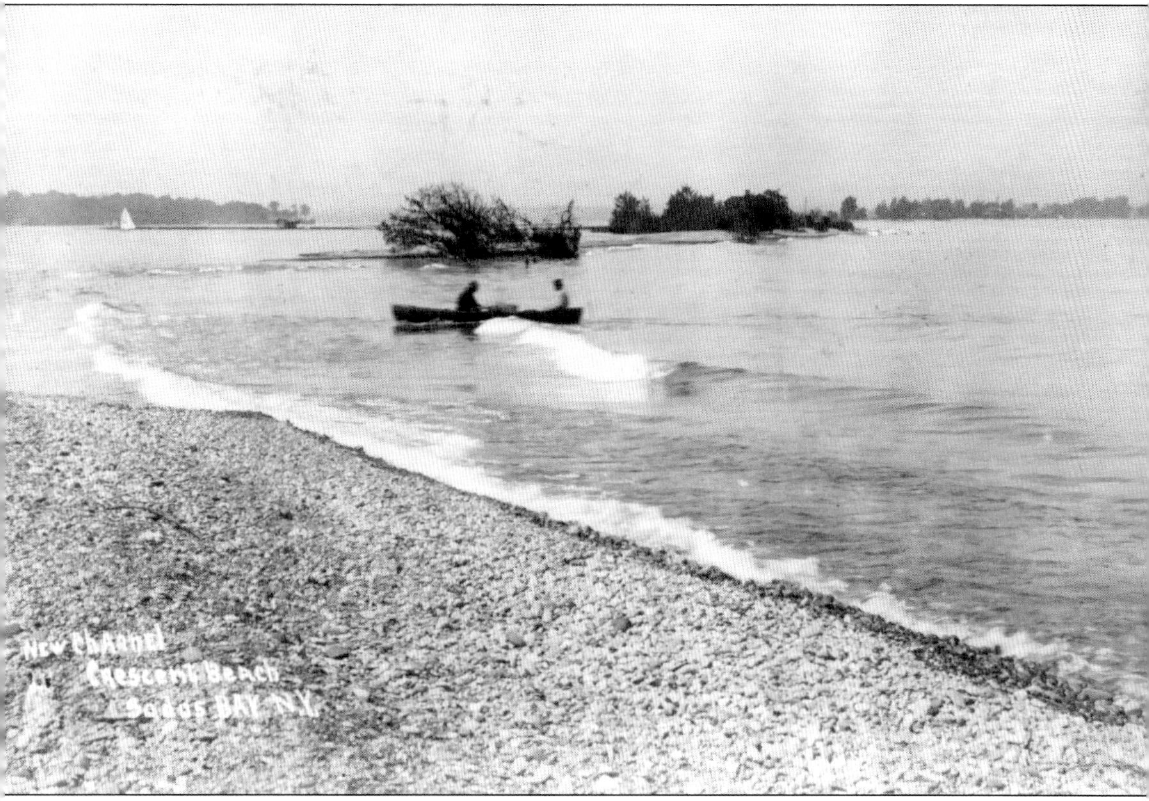


After the storm, life must carry on. Though destructive in many ways, the storm created fresh new opportunities for the residents of Sodus Bay. The bar break was looked upon as a new channel opening. This new channel allowed easy passage between the bay and lake for shallow-draft boats. This was great for east side residents who now did not need to go a full mile to reach the channel piers to head out into the lake to fish or enjoy a lake swim. Bar breaks in this location, close to Lake Bluff, have occurred over the years. Early maps, dating back to the early 1800s, show an opening in the bar at this section very close to Lake Bluff. As with all storms, there is recovery, and the bar has renewed itself over the years. The land seems to seal itself back up, closing the channel naturally. Time allows for a new storm to come along determining the future of the land along this fragile yet resilient coastline.

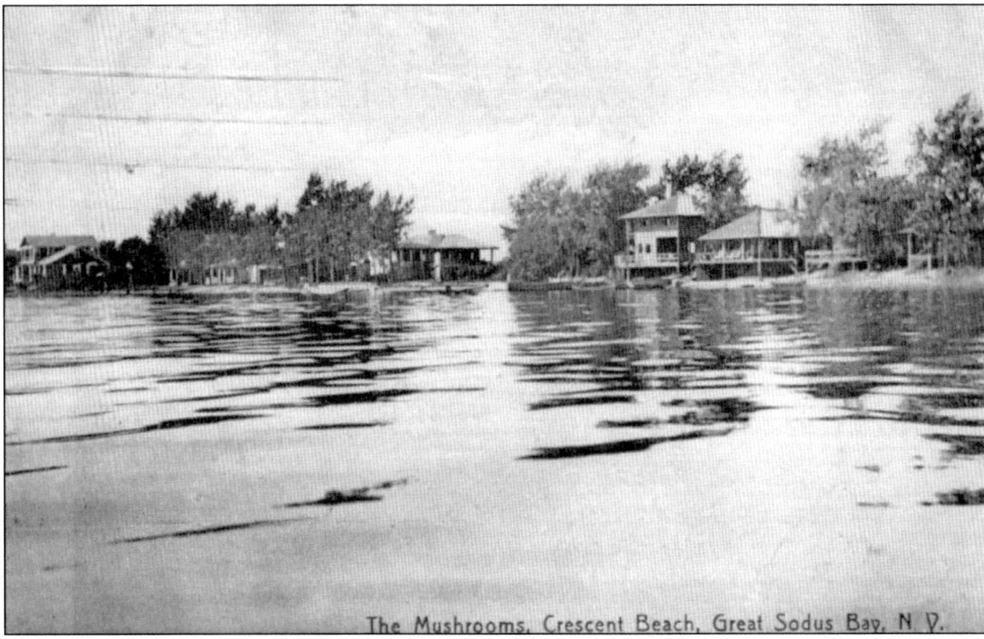


The "Mushroom" cottages on Crescent Beach were so named after the architectural style of the house, designed with a pyramidal roof shape, making the cottage look like a mushroom. These substantial cottages were ultimately washed out into the bay during a storm in the 1930s. One of the boathouses on the west side of LeRoy Island is one of these former Mushroom cottages. This card is postmarked in 1907.

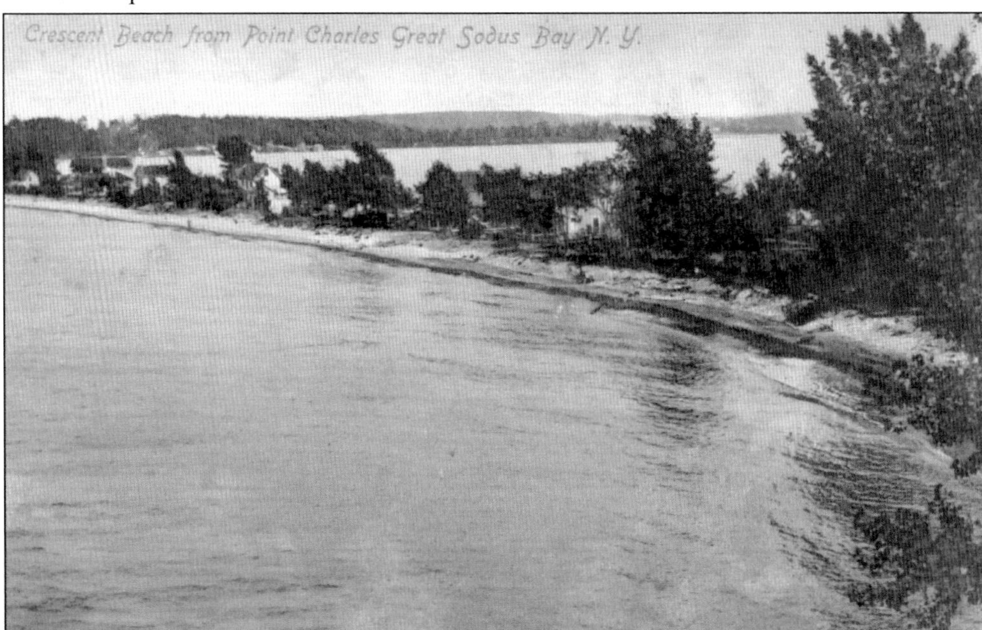


A final look back at Crescent Beach from Charles Point reveals more vegetation and a buildup of cottages. LeRoy Island and the mainland are in the distance. Somehow, despite the wear and tear on its shores from the wind and waves, Crescent Beach is always able to restore itself each season for the dedicated returning summer residents.

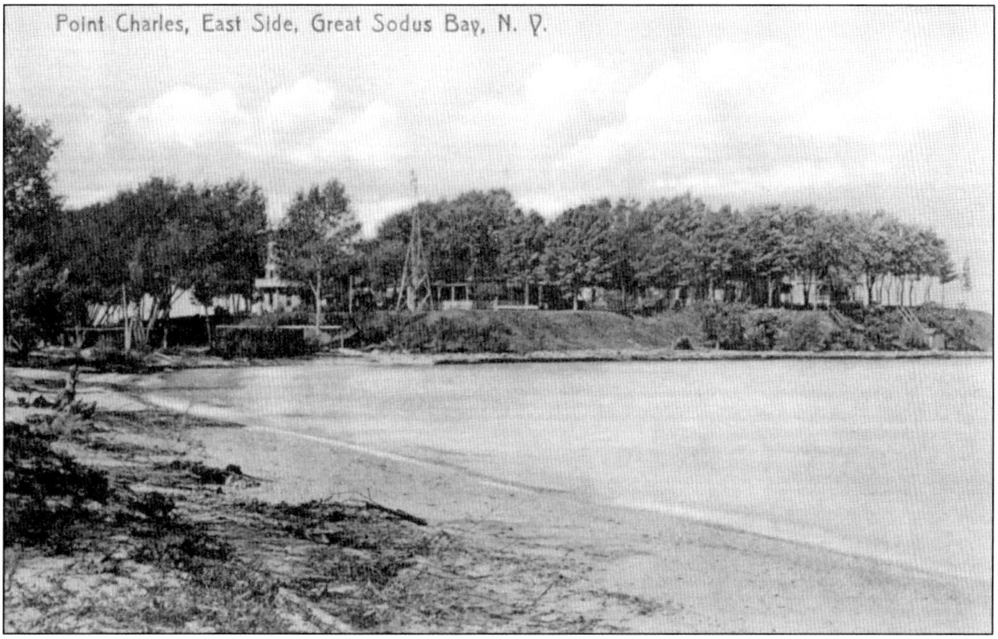


This view of Charles Point is from the lakeside of Crescent Beach, looking west. The windmill on Charles Point was used to provide power to draw water to the water tower for the residents. The windmill is now gone, but the water tower continued to be an important facet of the daily summer life of the residents of Charles Point until recently.

This popular Charles Point postcard, postmarked 1906, features a view from the bay where the channel and bay meet. Charles Point was purchased from Benjamin Rush Lummis in 1880 by a group of 12 families for a grand sum of $1,200. It did not take long for the summer residents of the then-named Point Charles to establish boathouses, docks, an icehouse, break walls, and cottages on this one-time farm.

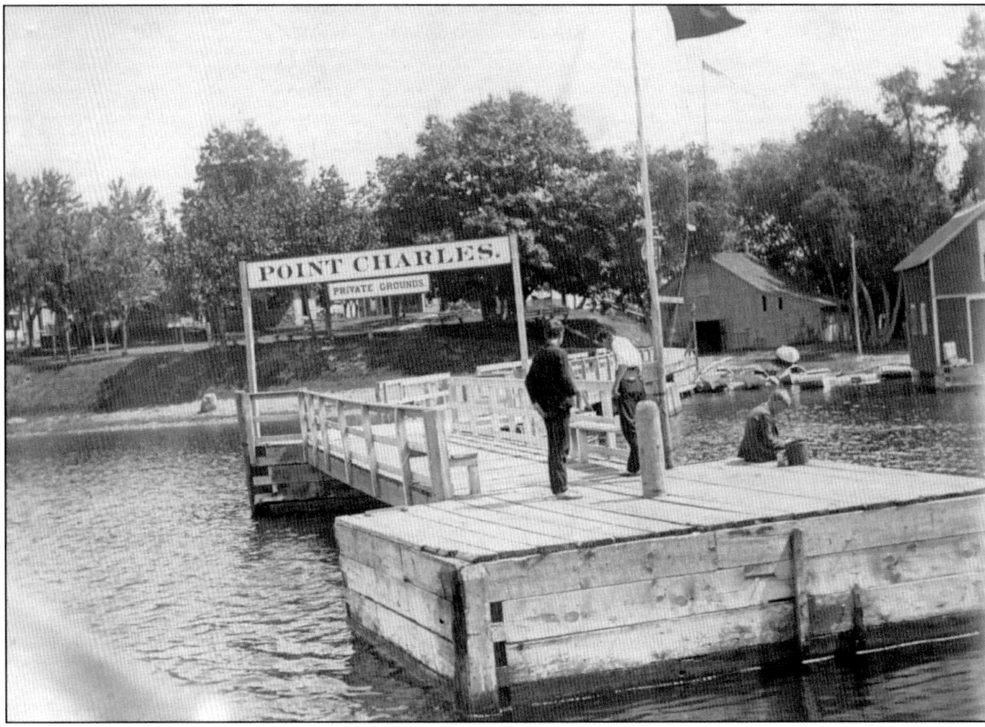


Sitting on the dock of the bay, one boy appears to be fishing, a can of worms by his side, while the other boy is having some sort of "dock lesson" from the gentleman leaning over the wharf bench. This photograph of the Point Charles steamer landing alerts visitors that this is private property. A collection of rowboats and canoes is onshore. (SBHS.)

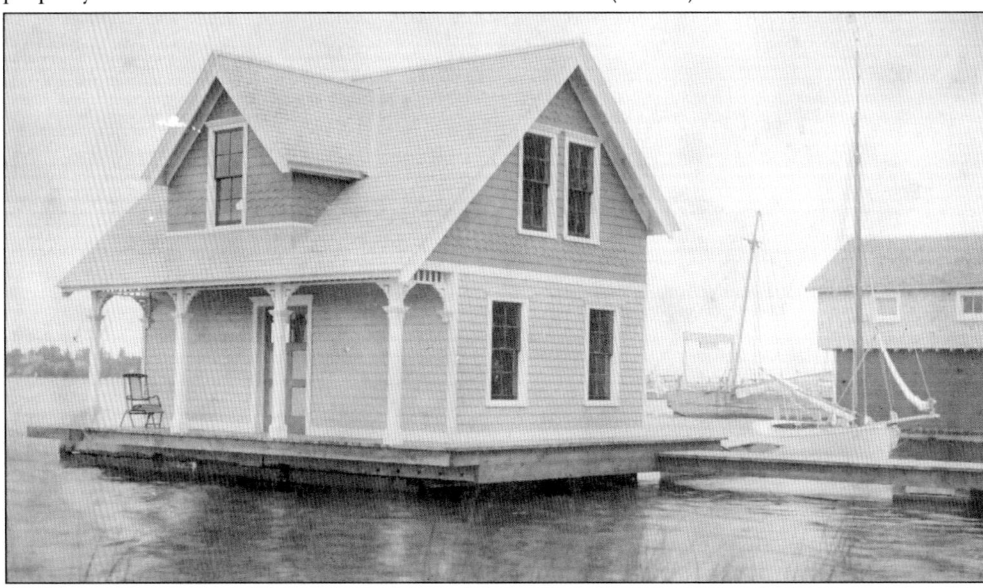

The Charles Point Steamer Landing can be seen between the two boathouses in this photograph dated 1899. The charming boathouse looks as if it may have been built as a cottage over the water. Notes written on the back of the photograph reveal that the upstairs was an apartment for the individual who served as the owner's handyman, chauffeur, and boatman. (SBHS.)

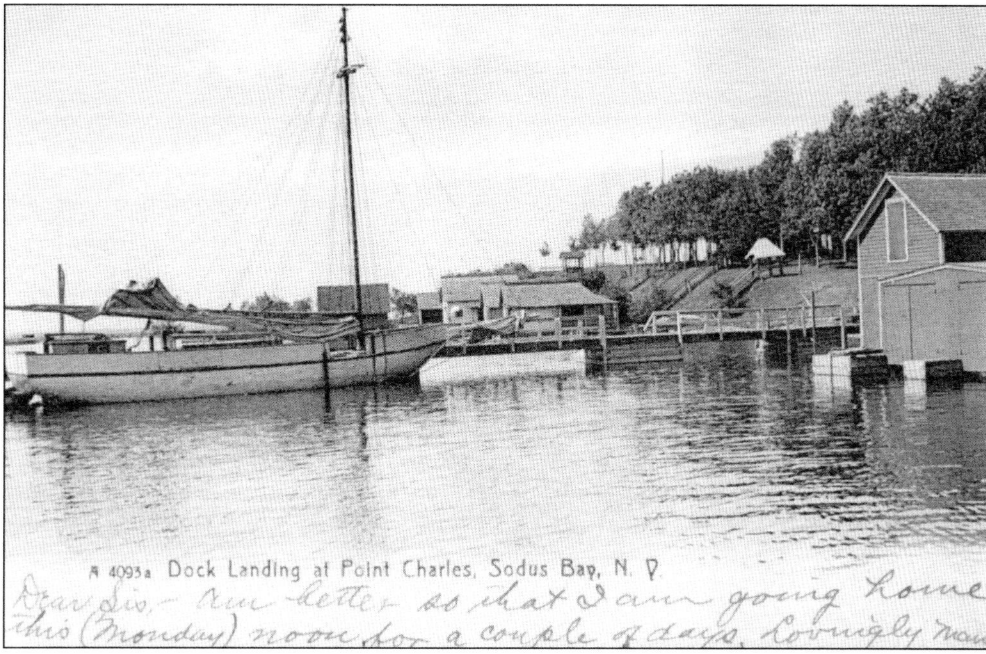


This gaff-rigged sloop sits at the Charles Point dock in calm water, awaiting some good sailing weather. Sailing was a popular activity for many of the residents at Charles Point. In *Point Charles Sketch*, Sheffield reports of one sailboat on Charles Point the children liked to play on—the *Polly Hopkins*. This vessel looks like it would have made a wonderful boat to explore.

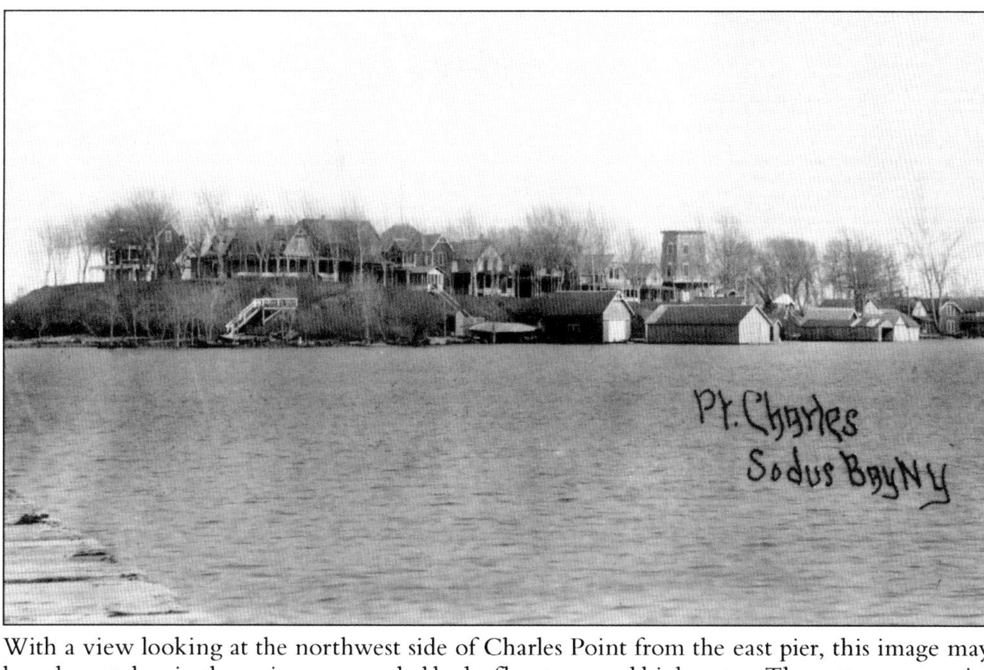


With a view looking at the northwest side of Charles Point from the east pier, this image may have been taken in the spring, as revealed by leafless trees and high water. The cottages are quite close together due to their location on original 40-foot tent sites. The tall building on the right side of the image is not a lighthouse; it is a cottage.

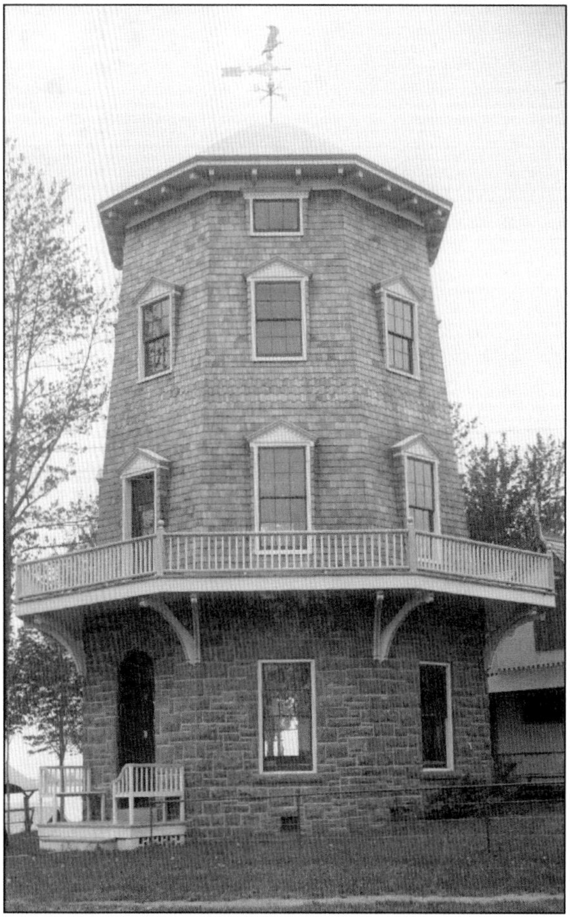

This octagonal four-story cottage on Charles Point was built in 1900. Called "The Tower" in the caption of this 1920 photograph, the building resembles a Dutch windmill or possibly a small lighthouse. The cottage served as a playhouse for the former owner. Some items noted on the back of the photograph are a Victrola for tin records on the first floor, a reading room on the second, and a pool table on the third. (SBHS.)

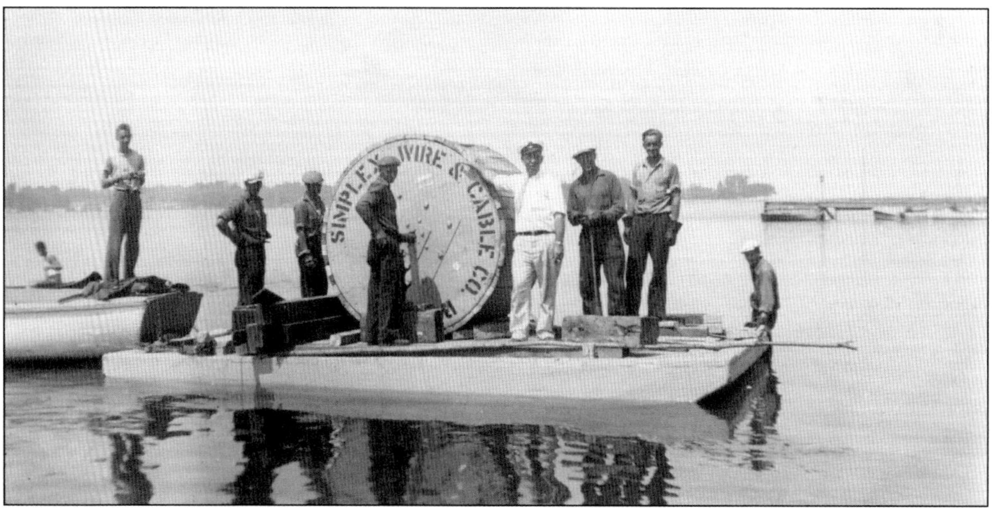


Electricity was brought across the bay from Sodus Point and installed in 1939. Until that time, kerosene lanterns gave nighttime illumination and ice for refrigeration was delivered from Sodus Point. A note on the back of this image tells that well-known Sodus Point resident George Helfer, dressed in white, is on the barge. (SBHS.)

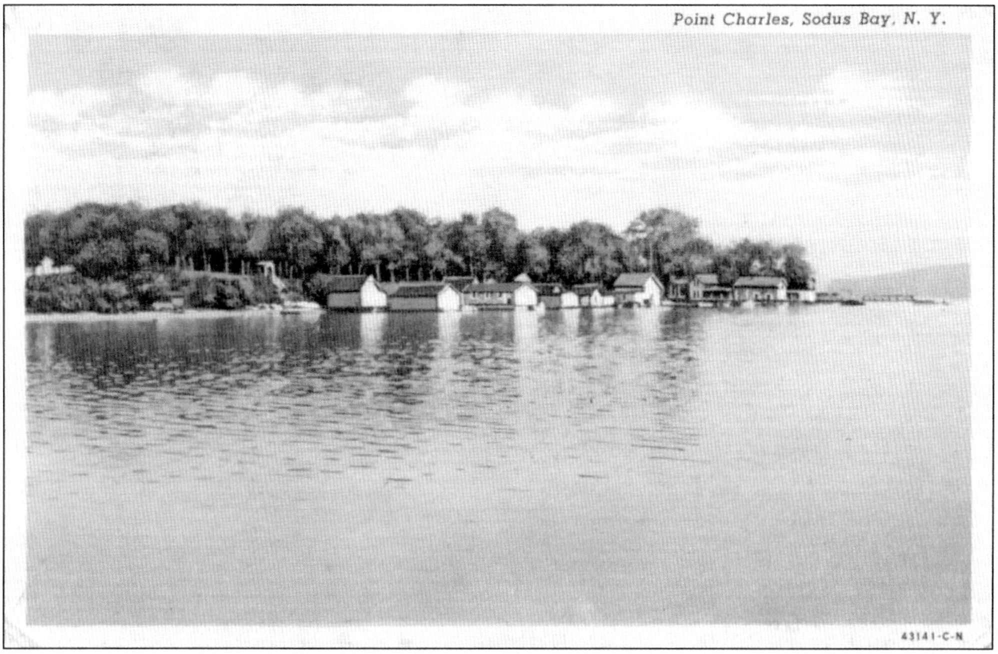


A popular Charles Point postcard, this image captures the resort colony with its row of boathouses reflecting in the calm Sodus Bay waters. It is told that, years before Charles Point became a cottage colony, the author James Fennimore Cooper spent time at Sodus Bay, possibly on Charles Point. Cooper's Leatherstocking Tales are based, in part, upon his impressions of Sodus Bay.

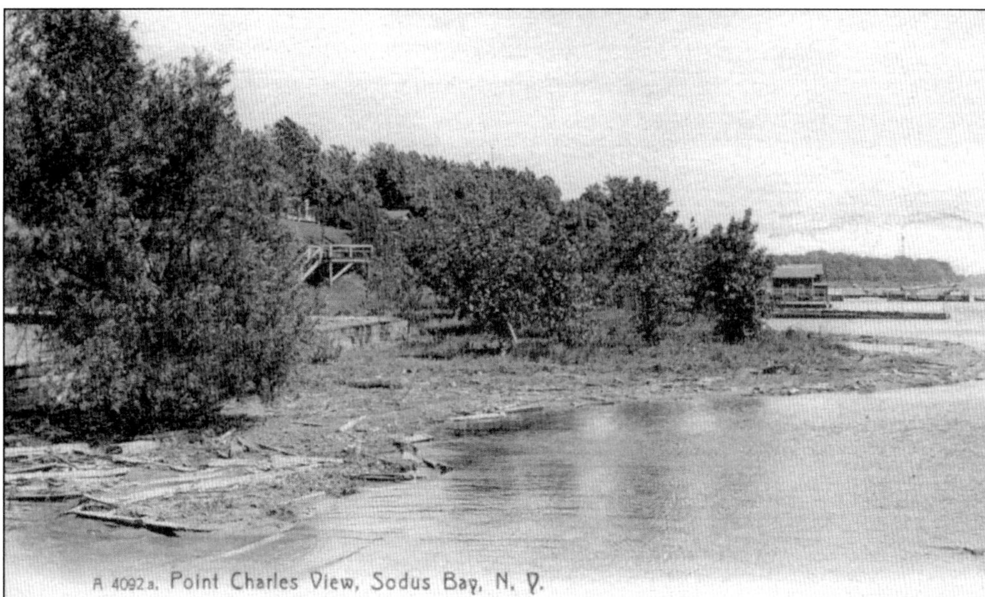


This little cove at the northwest corner of Charles Point is where the leg of break wall begins that joins with the east pier of the Sodus Bay channel. Standing near this cove at the end of Charles Point, the photographer looks back at the Charles Point boathouses and steamer landing in the bay. Behind the photographer is Lake Ontario.

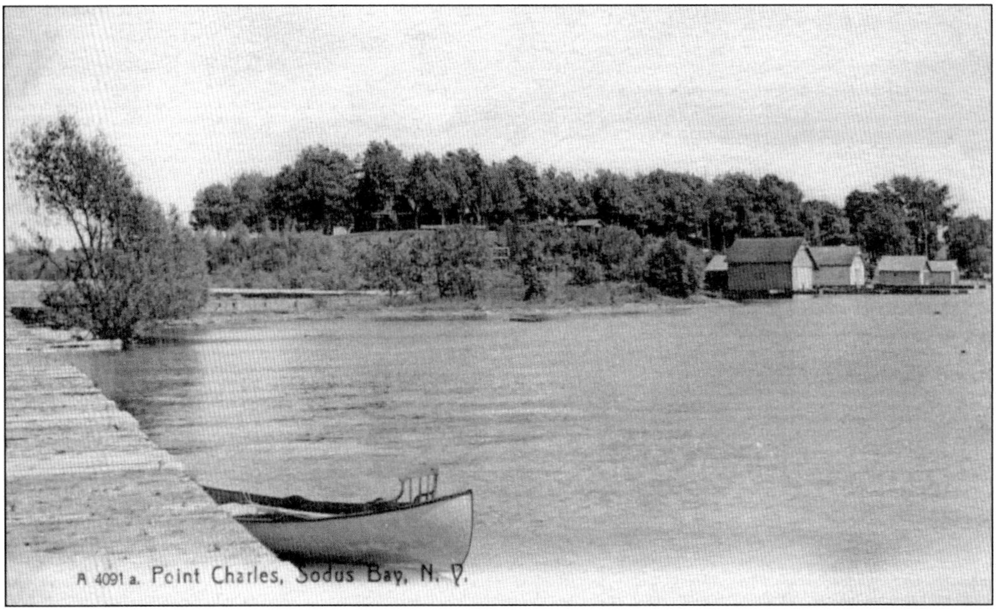


This view is from farther out on the connecting arm to the east pier. This stretch of pier and the east pier were a popular promenade for Charles Point residents and remain so today. While the waters on the bay side of Charles Point are calm, just a few feet away on the other side of the pier, the lake could be producing whitecaps and large crests of three to six feet or more.

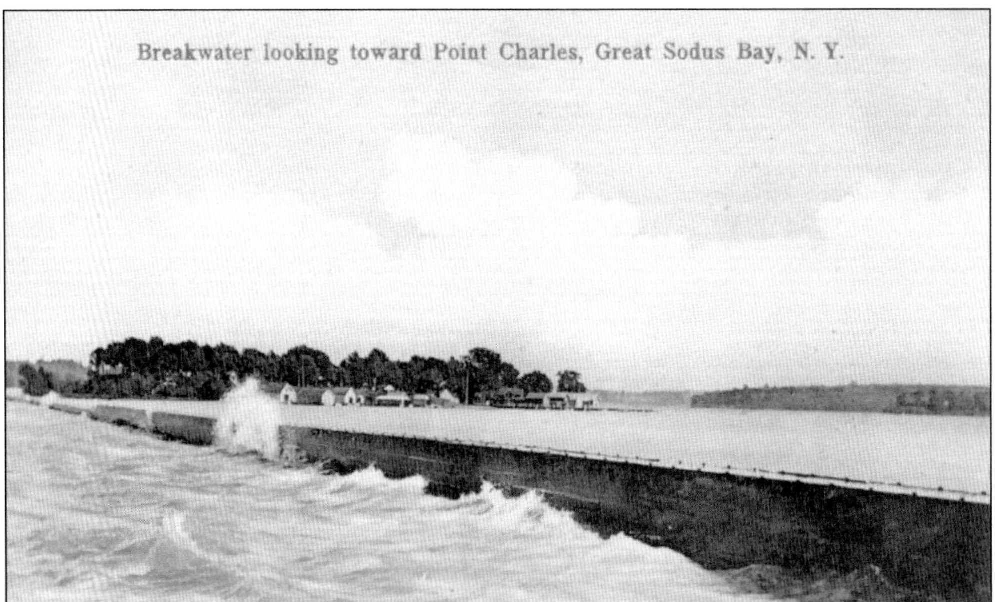


A view looking back toward Charles Point from the east pier is reminiscent of the first owners who bravely farmed this land, bringing their cattle here by water and ice, when it was still an island. It also pays homage to the early residents who built their summer tent colony in 1880, so loving the land that they built beautiful cottages on this small point situated between two engaging bodies of water.

# *Seven*

# Sodus Point

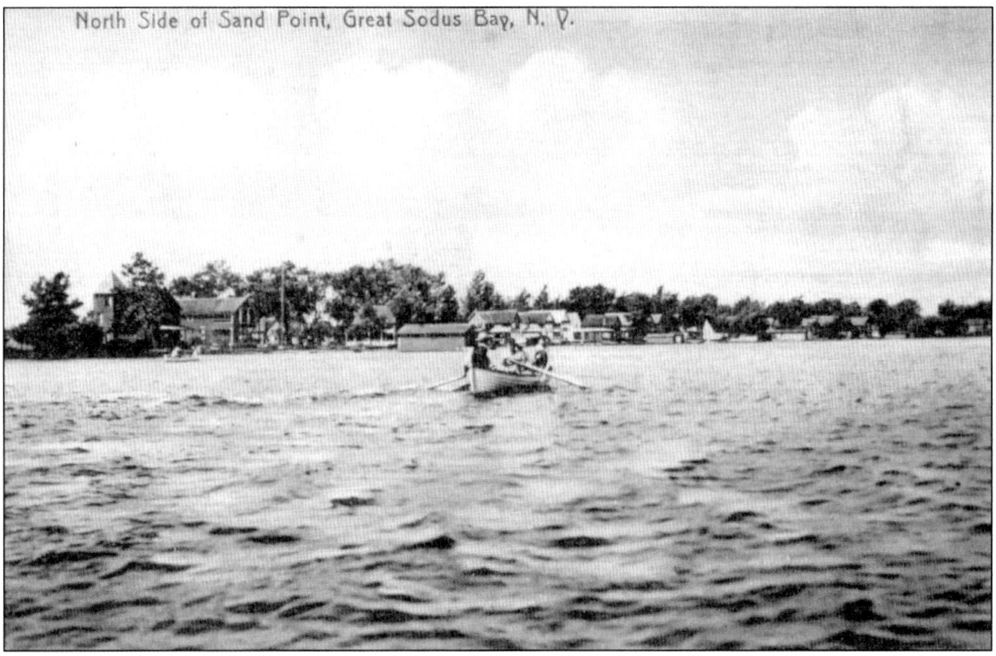


On the northwest side of Sodus Bay is Sand Point, a peninsula extending into the bay toward the east from the village of Sodus Point. The north side of Sand Point was originally lakeshore. When the channel piers and break walls were constructed in 1830, sand filled in between the piers and lighthouse bluff, creating new land on the lakeshore and thus placing Sand Point fully within the bay.

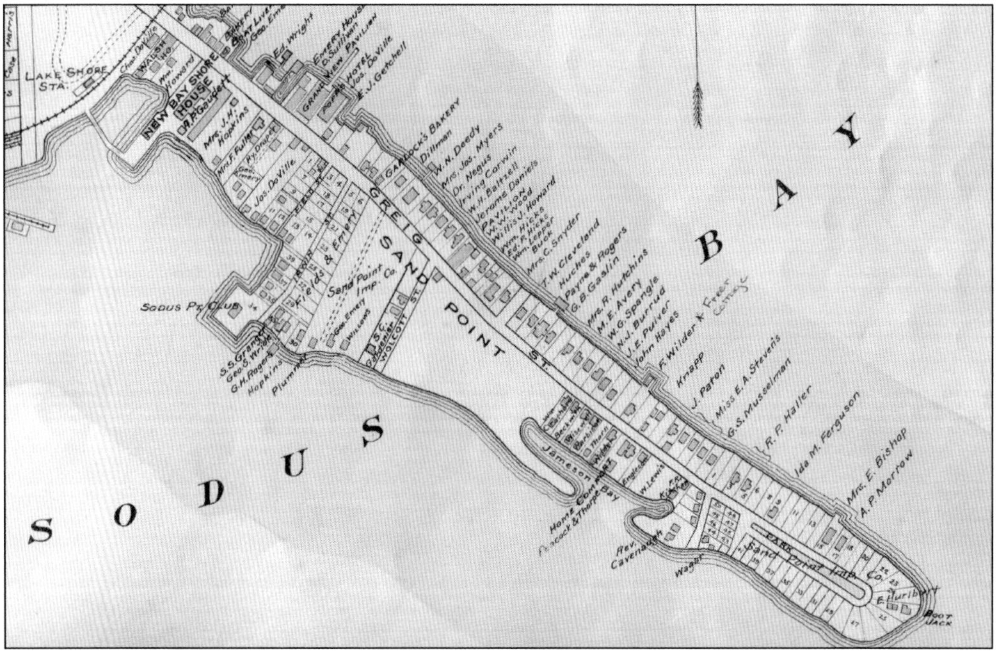


The village of Sodus Point map in the *1904 New Century Atlas of Wayne County* provides the map sections on this and the facing page. This map shows considerable development of Sand Point and notable points like the Grandview Pavilion, DoVille properties, Boot Jack's, Peacock and Thorpe's, the Sodus Point Club (Sodus Bay Yacht Club), and the Bay Shore House. (TOH.)

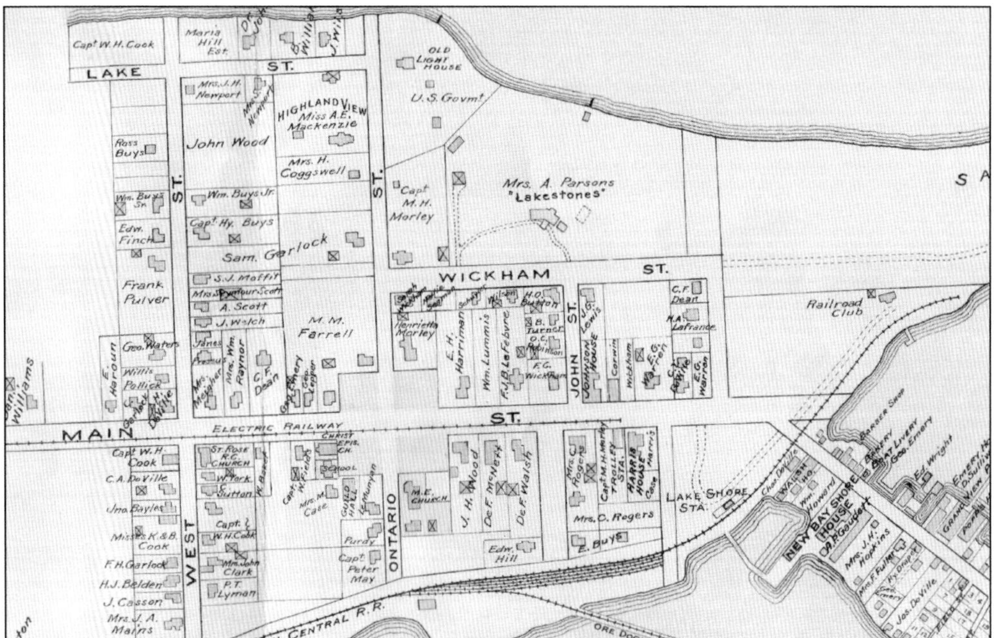


Prominent locations like Col. Enos Blossom Parson's Lakestones estate next to the Old Light House, the Lake Shore Station, the Ore Dock, the Guild Hall, St. Rose Roman Catholic Church (formerly known as Lummis Hall), and the school next to Christ Episcopal Church are just a few of the historic buildings shown on this section of the 1904 village of Sodus Point map. (TOH.)

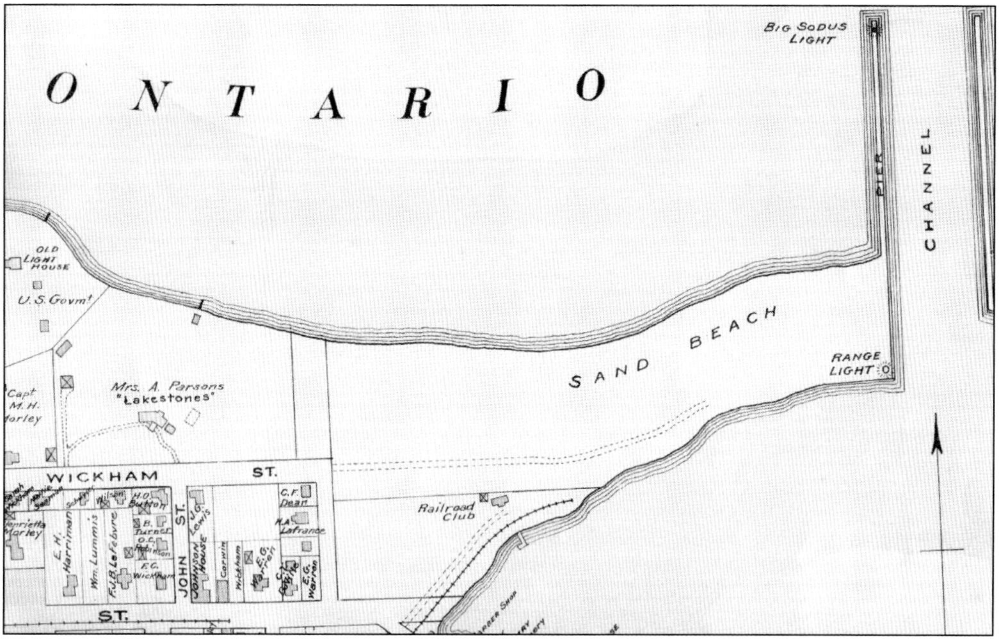


This map reveals the "new" land created since the 1830 construction of the piers for the outer lighthouse and channel. All the area from the bottom center of this map where the railroad tracks enter the image straight up to the lakeshore was the original lakeshore. The addition of the piers allowed sand to accrete, forming the sand beach, eventually becoming the continuation of Wickham Boulevard and the numbered streets. (TOH.)

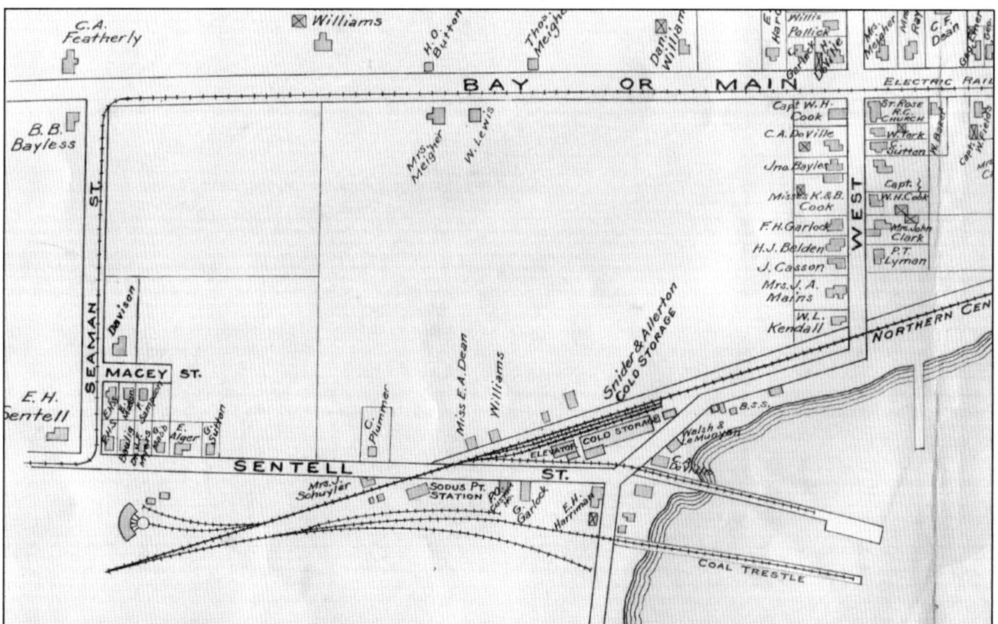


Along the bay-front southwest of Sodus Point is the area once known as Macyville, named after Sylvanus J. Macy, who built a bank here around 1881. The building became the US Customs Office and a post office for a time. Macyville was the industrial center of Sodus Point, home to the coal trestle, grain elevator, malt house, and roundhouse for the railcars. (TOH.)

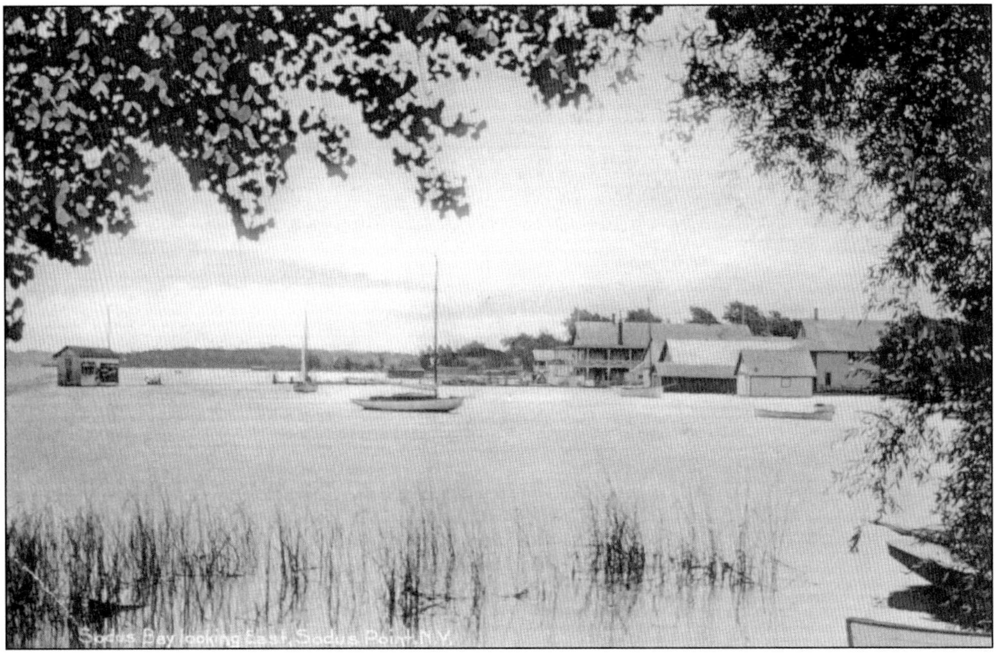


Located west of the "new" land known as the Sodus Point Sandbar, created by the addition of the piers in 1830, is the north side of Sand Point. In the distance is Newark Island. Sand Point has been the location of many summer cottages and several hotels. In the center of this image is the two-story balconied Grand View Pavilion and Hotel, with its long dock stretching out into the bay.

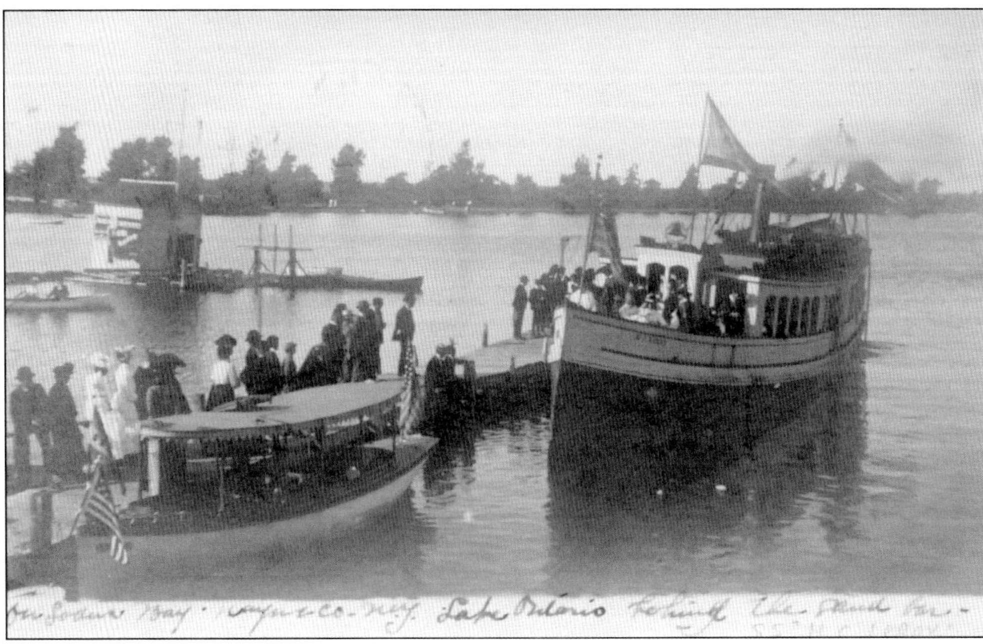

Established around 1899, the Grand View Pavilion and Hotel, owned by Frederick A. Welch, was a huge draw for people visiting Sodus Point around 1900. Dances, picnics, a bowling alley (added to the hotel in 1902) and the dock (built around 1905) were all attractions.

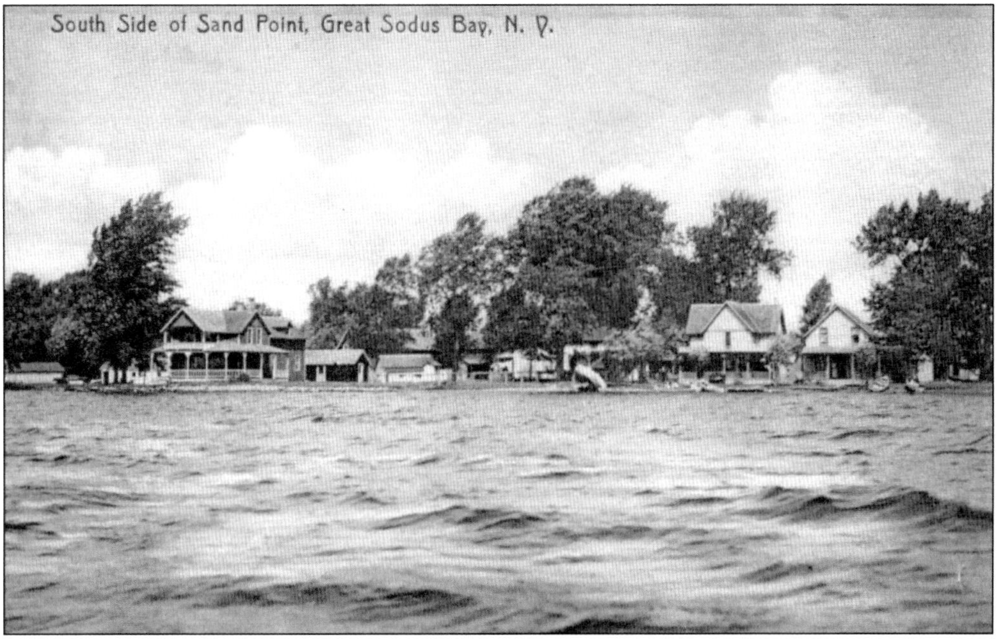


Rounding Sand Point, the south shore of this peninsula lies protected and makes a good home for moored sailboats and other yachts. This shore has been the home of the Sodus Bay Yacht Club since 1897. This part of Sand Point has also served as a refuge for summer visitors at several seasonal hotels and cottage facilities during the early days of resort activity at the point.

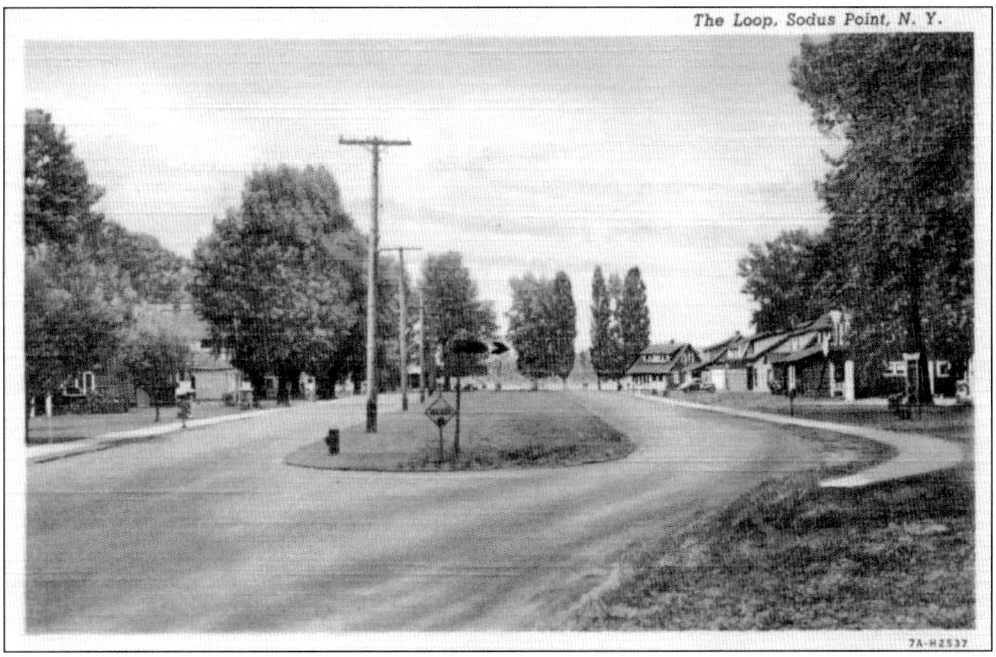


A March 31, 1917, *Newark-Union Gazette* newspaper article titled "Park to Replace Swamp on Sand Point," reports that the Sodus Town Board voted to appropriate $1,000 to improve the road around the end of Sand Point. R.J. Hailer, owner of the cottage at the end of Sand Point called Boot Jack, spent $1,500 for a curb around the loop to add to the parklike appearance.

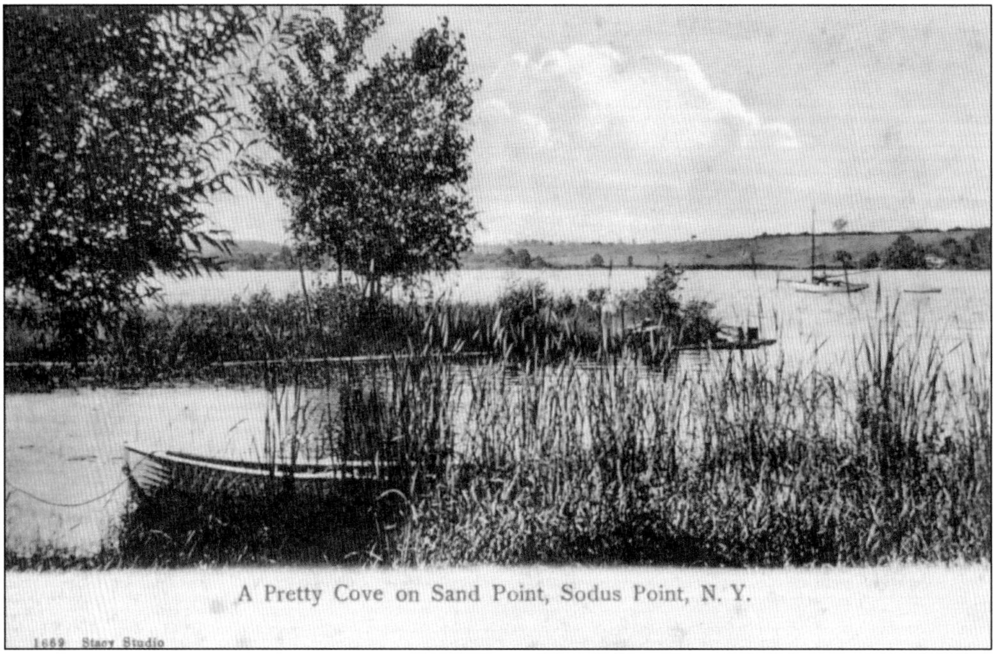


As cottages and tourist accommodations continued to be built along the Sand Point peninsula, locations of untouched nature and serenity became rarer. Jameson Bay, a small, quiet cove on the south side of Sand Point, was somehow able to retain that peace and natural beauty that drew visitors to Sodus Bay. A glance back at the first map in this chapter shows cottages built on the inner part of the Jameson Bay cove, but at the time of the 1904 map, the outer peninsula remained free of buildings.

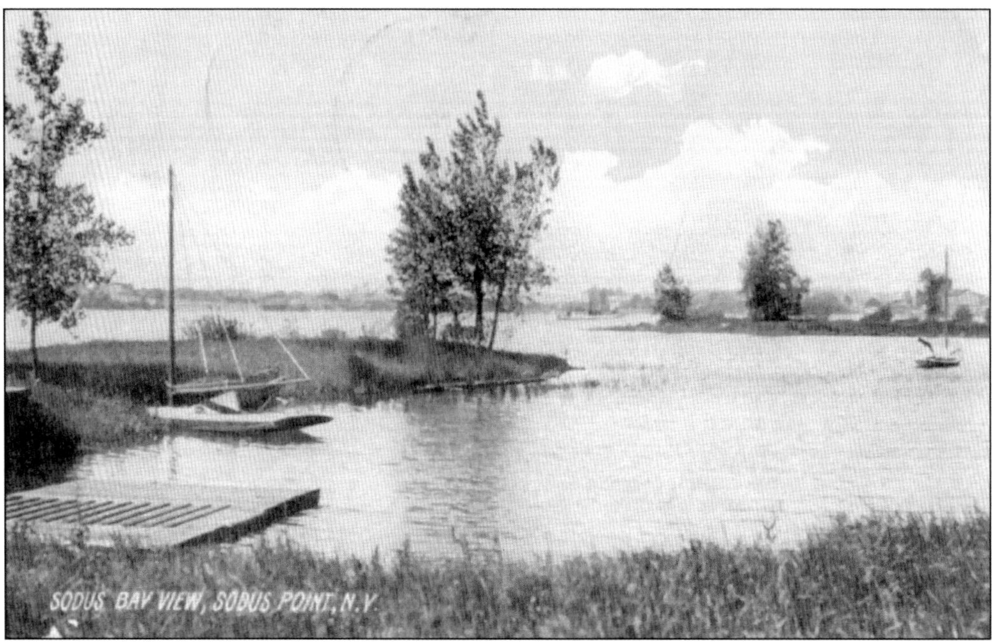

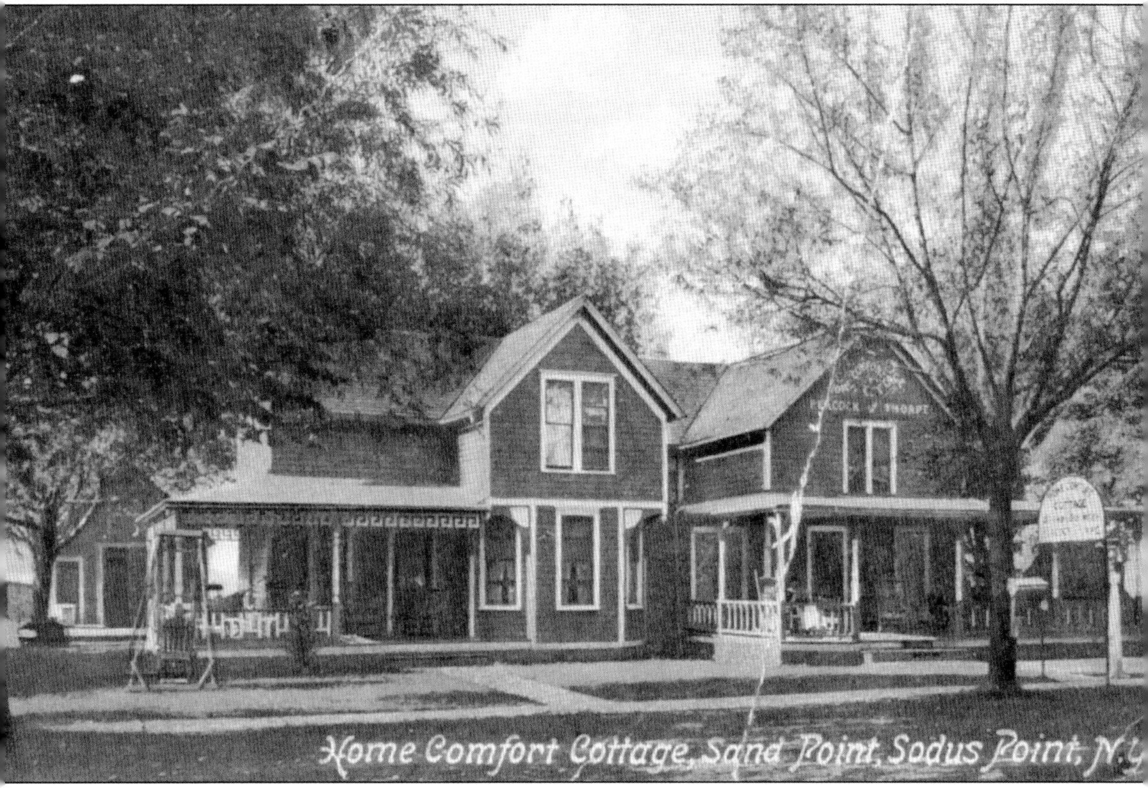


Hattie Peacock and Belle Thorpe were proprietors of the Peacock and Thorpe Home Comfort Cottage located on Jameson Bay. Quite the cooks, the two women also ran, for a period of time, the Home Bakery and Grocery in Newark, New York. Newspaper reports of guests visiting the Peacock and Thorpe cottage are common during the early 1900s. A front page report in an August 1916 *Newark-Union Gazette* relates the news about an outing to Sodus Point for employees of Chaffee's department store of Newark and provides a colorful document as to the diversity of Peacock and Thorpe's cooking. The article recounts that dinner was served at 8:00 p.m. The menu is given as follows: "Mildred Broth, Bull Heads A La Garick, Sweet Corn – Etta Style, Wayne Green Peas – Jewett Picked, New Potatoes in Nellie Jackets, Frogs Legs A La Waldo, Broilers – Beader Raised, McCarty Lemon ice, cake, and coffee." Further reading of the article reveals that the creative menu item names were drawn from the names of the Chaffee department store employees attending the outing.

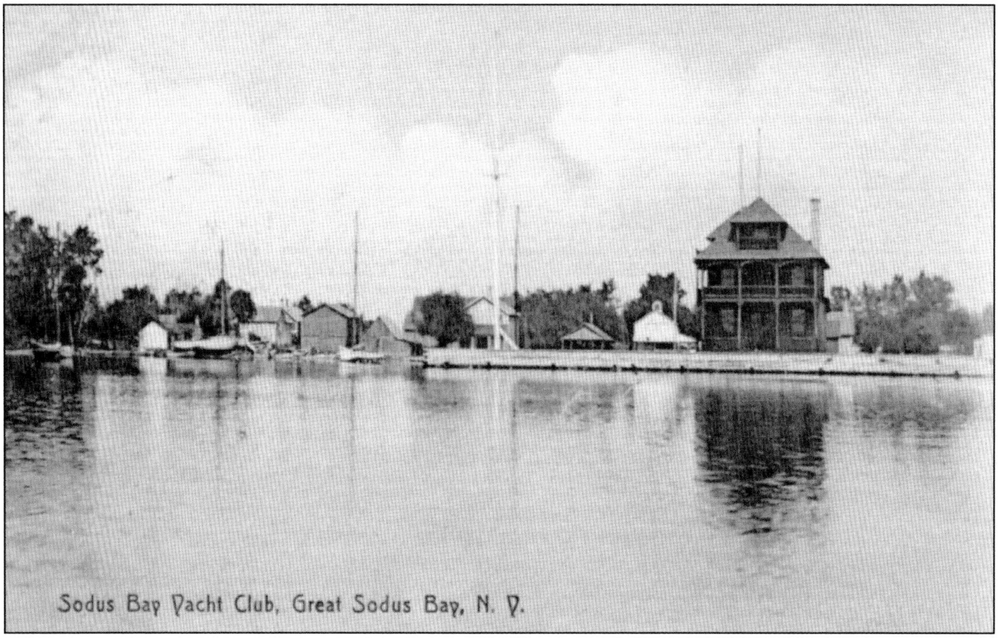


A little farther west along the south shore of Sand Point is the home of the Sodus Bay Yacht Club. Built in 1897, the Sodus Bay Yacht Club has been the hub of sailing and motorboat activity on the bay. Boaters find the south side of the Sand Point peninsula, protected from northerly winds, makes a good home for moored sailboats and other yachts.

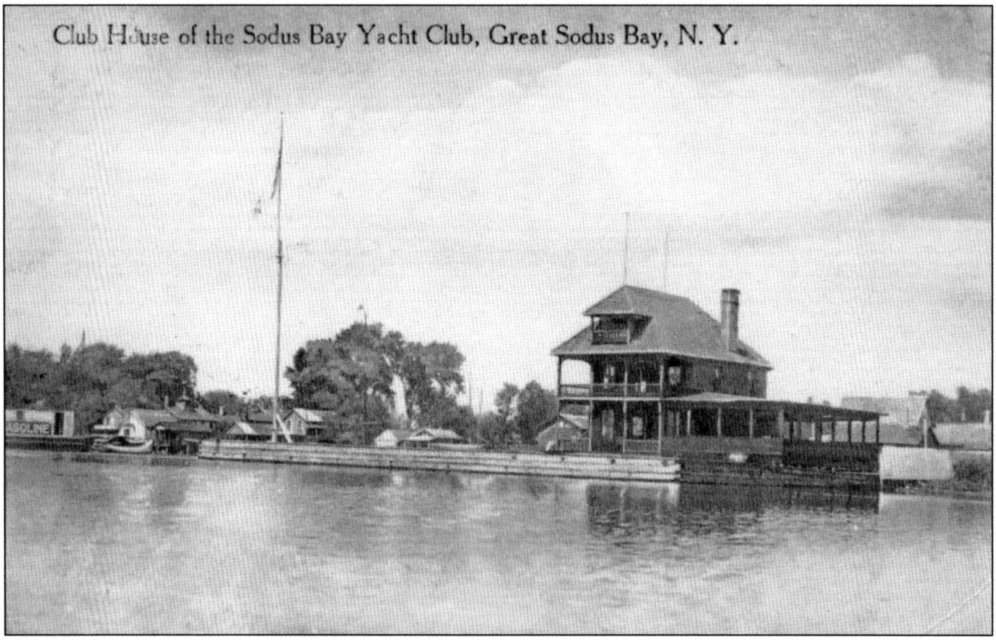


Over the years, the Sodus Bay Yacht Club facilities grew to include the dance pavilion on the east side (around 1913), as seen in this postcard. The message on the back of the postcard, written at Sodus Point on August 26, 1913, reads, "We twelve old maids are having a fine time camping here. Wish you might be here to have a good time with us."

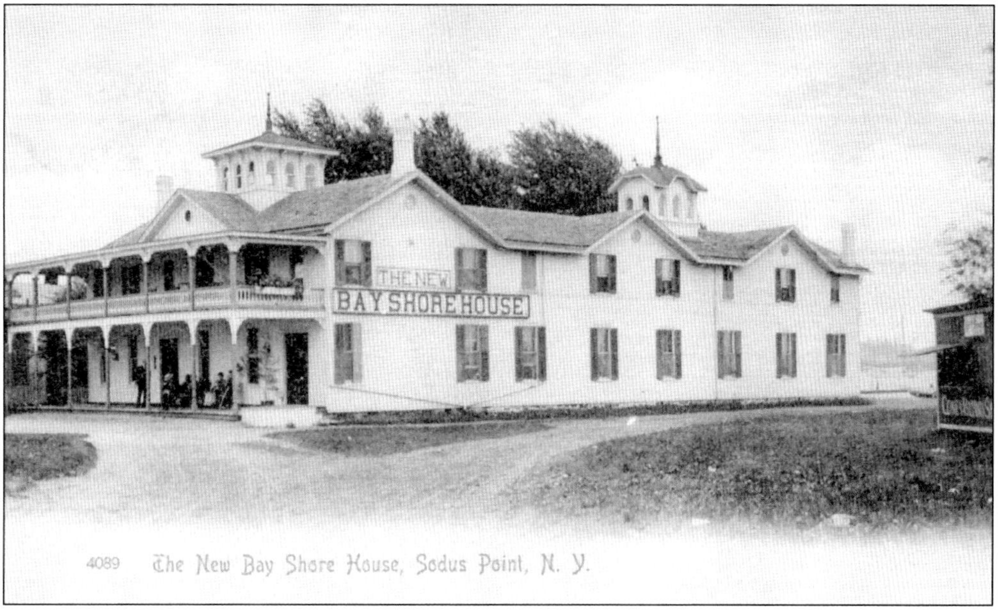


West of the Yacht Club, on what is now Krenzer's boat storage, was the location of a mid-1800s shipyard. From around 1880 to 1912, this was home to the New Bay Shore House, a commodious and popular hotel visited by people from as far away as New York City and Philadelphia. On July 12, 1884, the *Newark-Union* reported a skating rink was in operation in a room attached to the Bay Shore House. The Sodus Bay Yacht Club held a meeting here in which the club's constitution was adopted and the first officers elected. A prominent and wealthy individual who owned several other Sand Point properties, John Henry Hobart "Hobe" Hopkins was builder and primary owner of the Bay Shore. Hopkins ran the hotel until his death in 1903. The property was sold and divided at auction in 1912.

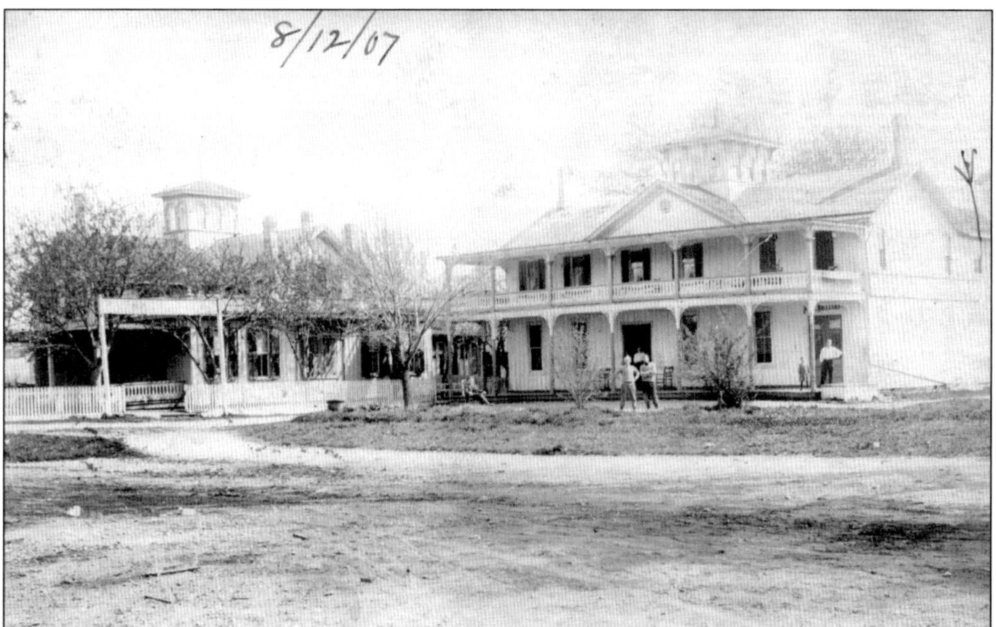

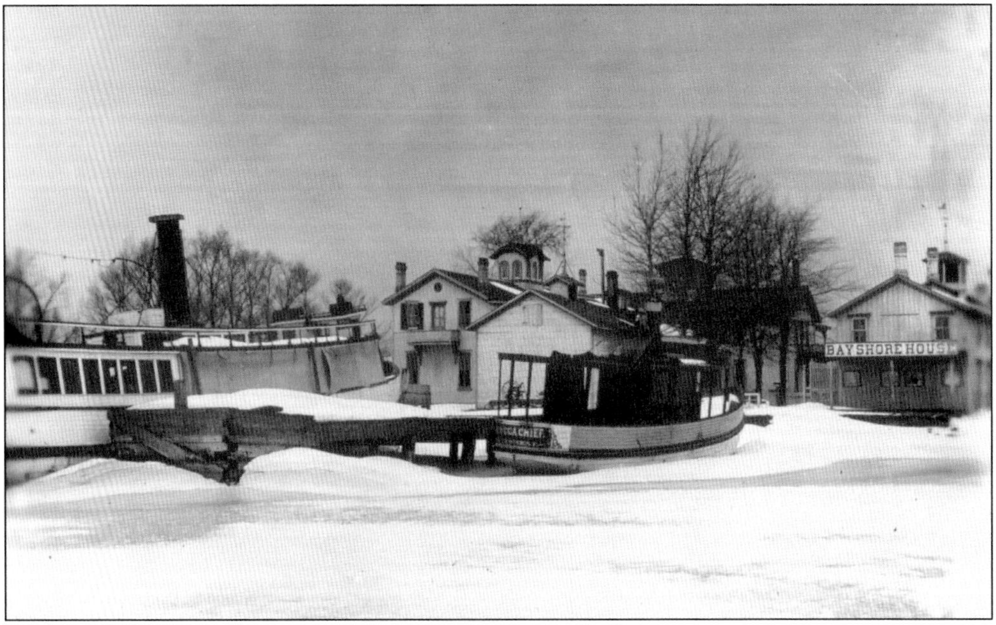


With a view just west of the Bay Shore's boathouse and dock, the image above shows the *Seneca Chief* and what appears to be the *Sunbeam* frozen in ice, reflecting a time when hauling large boats out of the water may not have been a common practice. The *1904 New Century Atlas of Wayne County* places the Walsh House and Boat Livery, seen below, on the south side of Sand Point, two lots west of the New Bay Shore House. A *Newark-Union* newspaper article from August 1887 reports that Capt. Frank Walsh, a Sodus Point pioneer, was a ship's captain and ran a shipyard where the Bay Shore Hotel stood. In 1887, he operated a boat rental and tackle shop. In 1901, a merry-go-round was built on the lot between the Bay Shore House and the Walsh House. (Both, SBHS.)

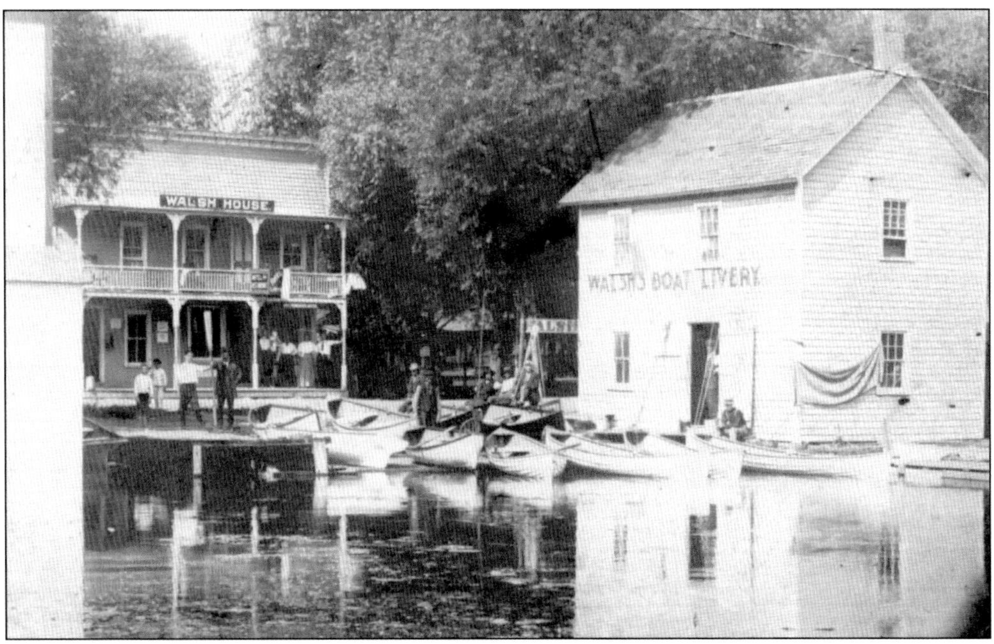

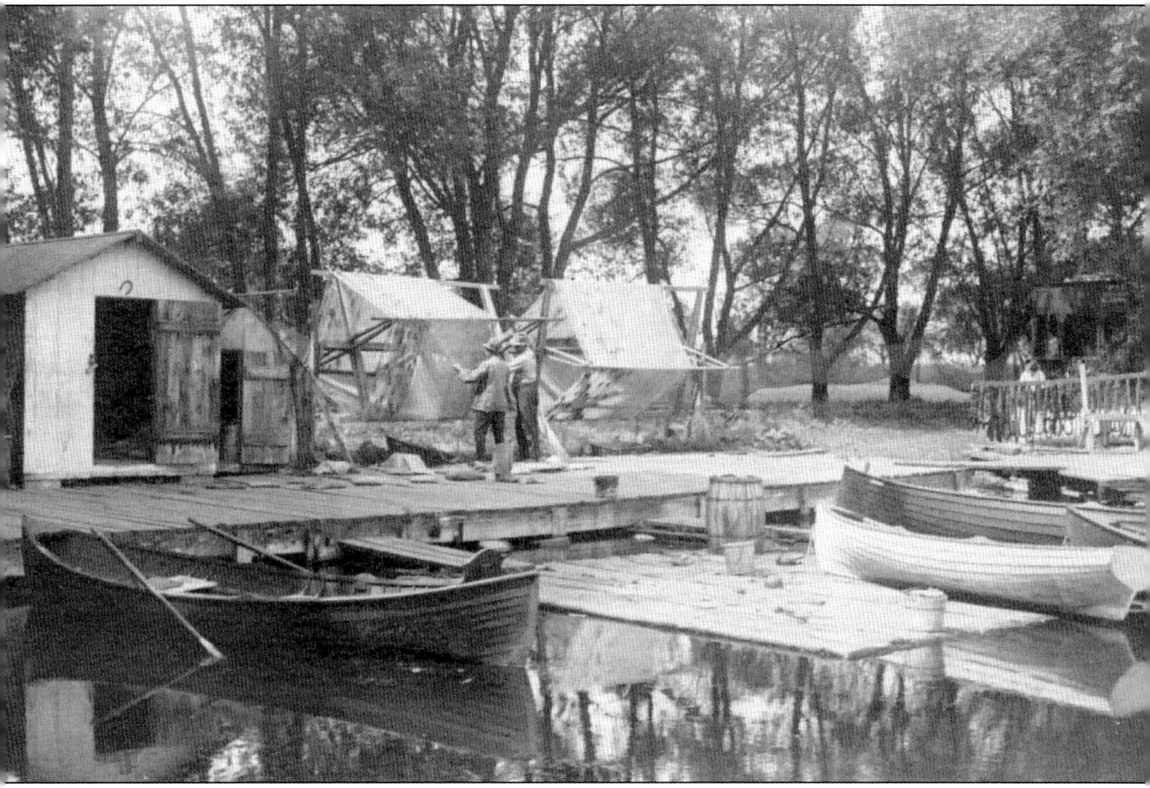

The DoVille name in Sodus Bay is synonymous with boats and ice-cream cones. Henry DoVille Sr. came with his parents from Sorel, Quebec, to Sodus Point in the early 1800s. DoVille, a boatbuilder and captain, had 12 children with his wife, Mary. Three children died before reaching the age of 8. Five sons became sailors. Charles T. DoVille was a boatbuilder, ice harvester, and fishing guide. Henry DoVille Jr. was captain of the *H.C. LeRoy* and other Sodus Bay boats. Henry Jr. was also an old-time fiddler. The DoVille Boat and Tackle (pictured) was located on Sand Point next to Walsh's Boat Livery. The DoVilles had many other properties on Sodus Point where they operated maritime and hotel businesses. Charles ran a refreshment stand in conjunction with his boat livery. Charles's daughter-in-law, May, worked with him and eventually took over the refreshment stand operation, which she ran from the 1920s to 1950s. May's special waffle cones were popular across the region. The refreshment stand was located at what is now Hot's Point on Sand Point. (SBHS.)

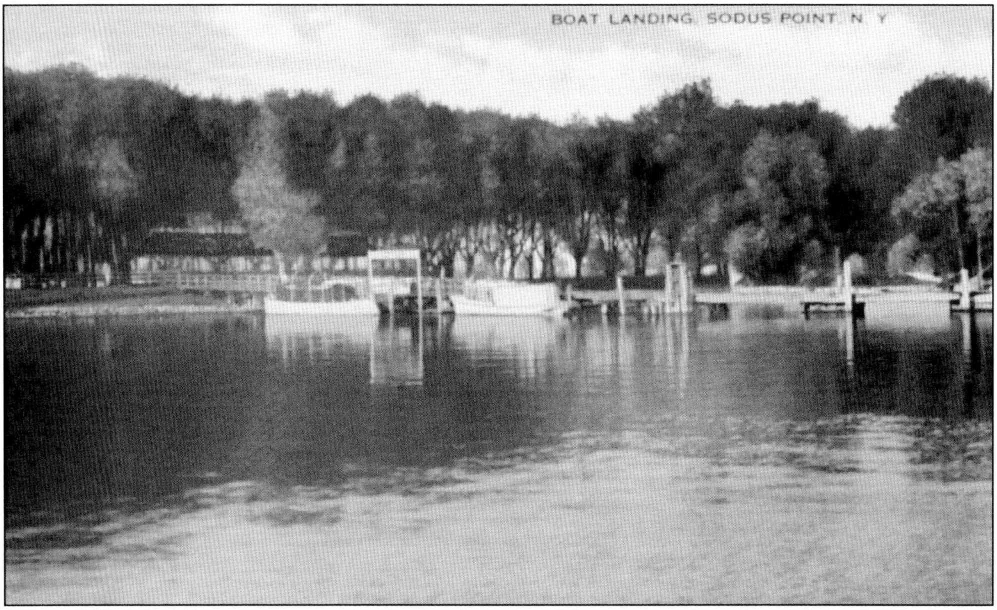


Located to the southwest, across the cove from the Bay Shore Hotel, were the Sodus Point Steamer Landing, the Northern Central Lake Shore Train Station, and Willow Park. The steamer landing and train station are long gone, along with the thousands of passengers who visited Sodus Point by rail from around 1880 to 1935. Willow Park remains a picturesque setting for family gatherings and a gentle reminder of days gone by.

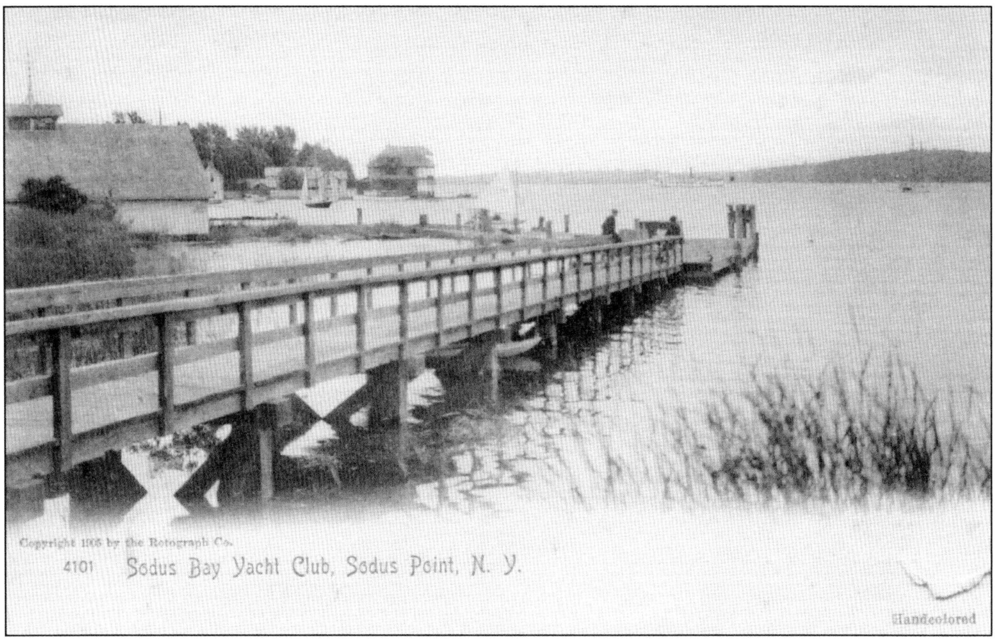


Visitors who arrived by rail at the Sodus Point Lake Shore Train Station while traveling to final destinations like Charles Point, Lake Bluff, Bonnicastle, Resort, or one of the islands, would venture out this dock to board a bay steamer. The steamer captain would transport the travelers and their baggage, heavy with food and other supplies, across the bay to their chosen vacation spots. This postcard is dated 1907.

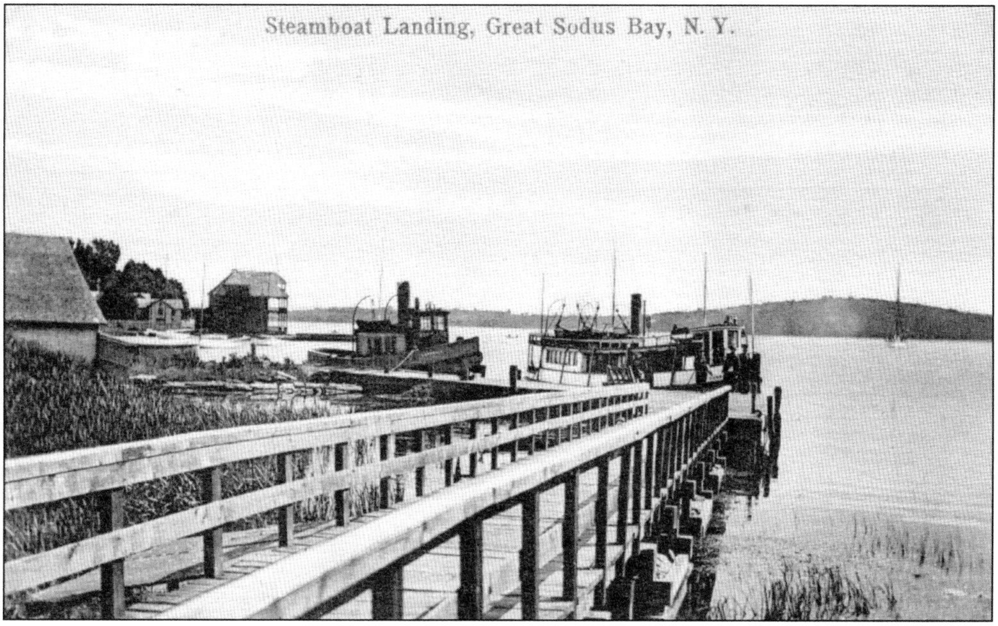


Awaiting business, the steamer *Sunbeam* and tugboat *Cornelia* sit in the calm waters at the boat landing. The Sodus Bay Yacht Club is the two-story building in the distance. Notice the cribbing for the pier leading to the dock on this postcard in comparison to the piles for the pier in the previous postcard. Postmarked 1909, this postcard features an image probably taken 10 years after the previous card's photograph.

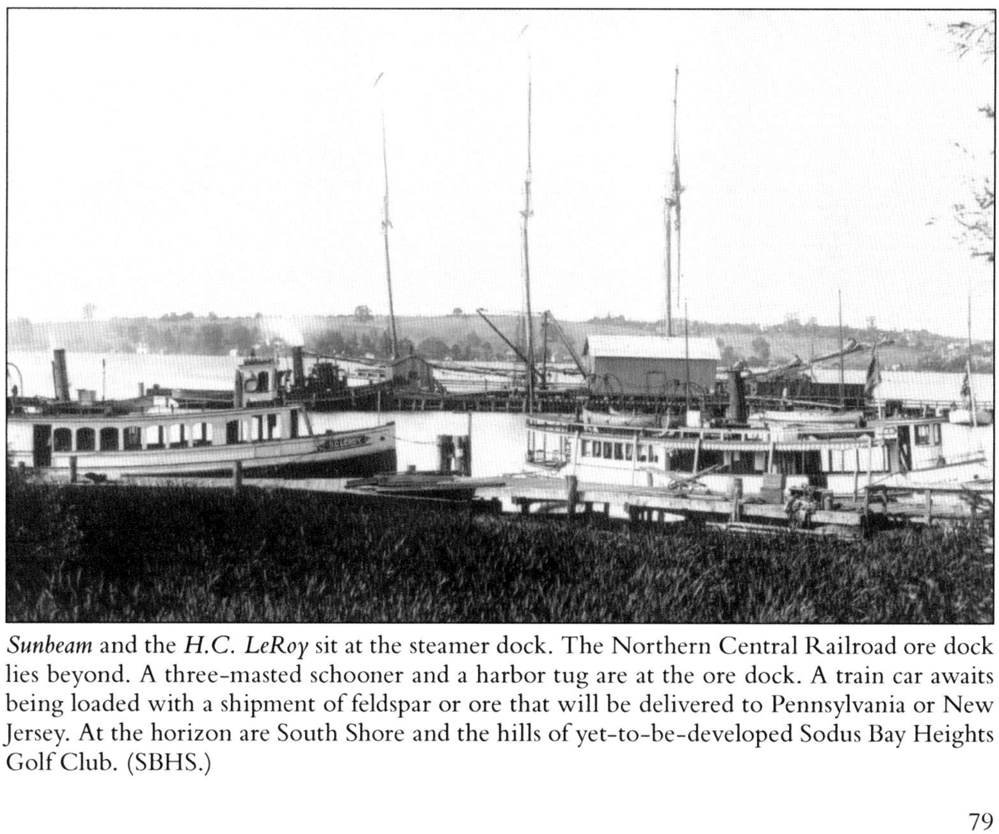

*Sunbeam* and the *H.C. LeRoy* sit at the steamer dock. The Northern Central Railroad ore dock lies beyond. A three-masted schooner and a harbor tug are at the ore dock. A train car awaits being loaded with a shipment of feldspar or ore that will be delivered to Pennsylvania or New Jersey. At the horizon are South Shore and the hills of yet-to-be-developed Sodus Bay Heights Golf Club. (SBHS.)

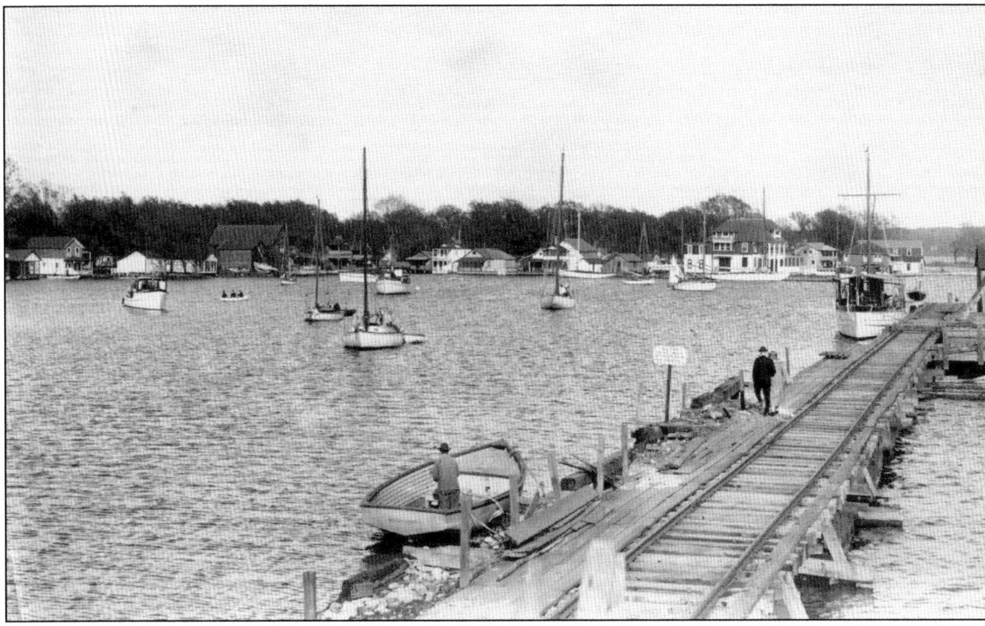

Shipping records reveal that feldspar was shipped to Sodus Point from Kingston, Ontario, in the early 1900s. Feldspar was used in the manufacture of pottery, wall and floor tile, and scouring soaps. Schooners *Two Brothers* and *Queen of the Lake* and steam barges *Robert McDonald* and *Owen* were some of the vessels that brought the feldspar to Sodus. The yacht club is in the cove east of the ore dock. (SBHS.)

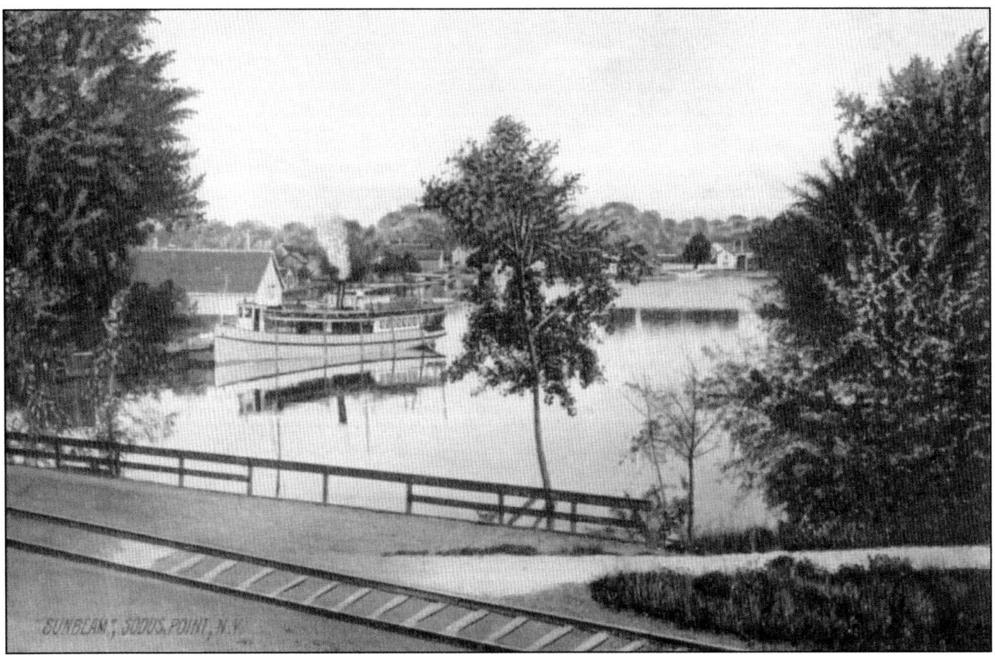


This quiet view of the steamer landing was taken from the Northern Central Railroad Lake Shore Station at Willow Park. The message on the back of this postcard reads, "We are having a dandy time. Caught one large fish this morning. Don't believe we will ever come back." Such was the sentiment of many who visited Sodus Point and Sodus Bay during this era.

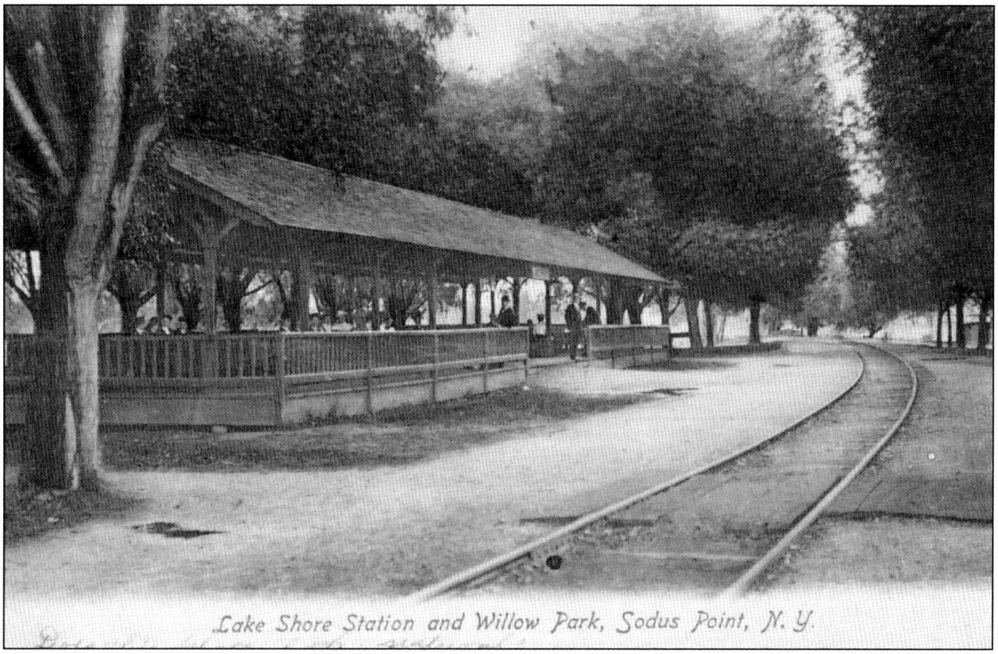


The view in the postcard above looks east at the Lake Shore Station, as people await the arrival of a Northern Central passenger train bringing guests to Sodus Bay, or to take those waiting south to Wallington, Sodus Center, Newark, and points beyond. Below, a Northern Central Railroad passenger train arrives at the Lake Shore Station. Left of the train, the Northern Central ore dock can be seen through the trees. The passenger line for the Northern Central began running around 1881 and ceased operation in 1935. Edward H. Harriman purchased and improved the poorly managed Lake Ontario and Southern Railroad in 1881. The Northern Central, a division of the Pennsylvania Railroad, purchased the Sodus Bay and Southern line from Harriman in 1884. The Northern Central Rail provided passenger service as well as freight service that included the transport of coal from Pennsylvania.

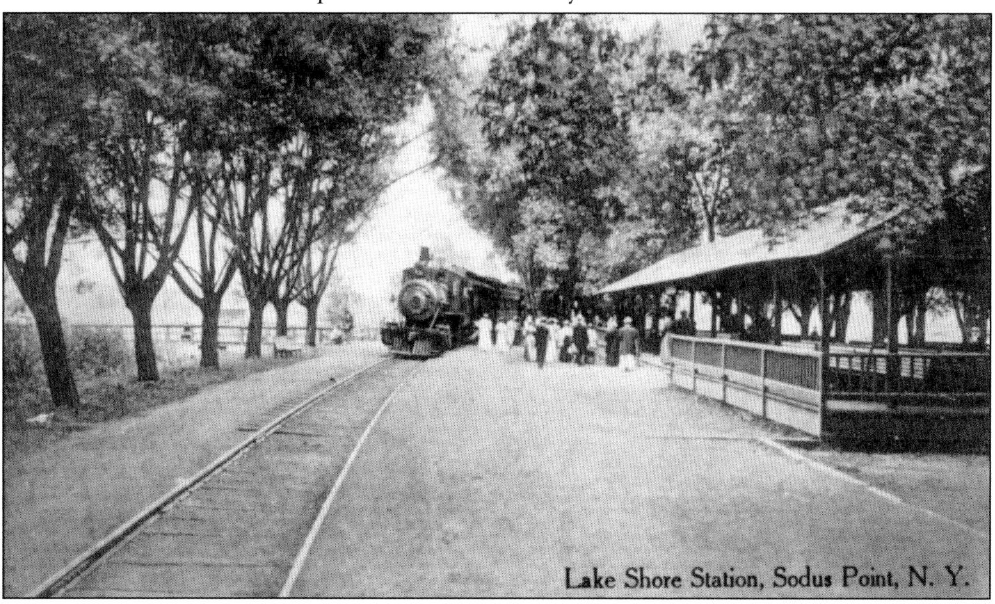

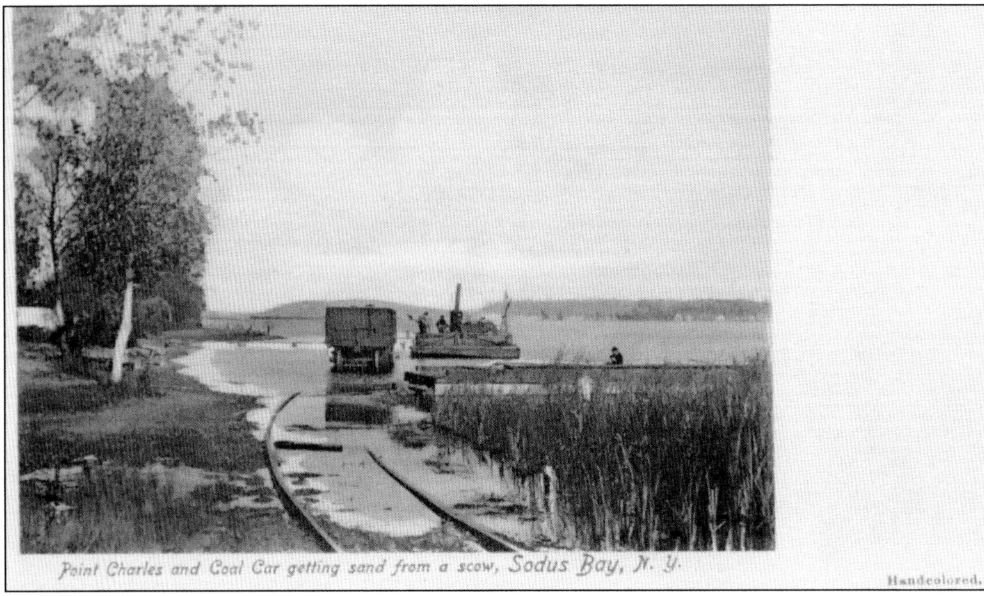


Buildup of sand in the channel, caused by the prevailing northwesterly winds off Lake Ontario, presented a problem for navigation through the channel from the time shipping began in the early 1800s. Dredging reports go back to the original construction of the piers beginning in 1829. Around 1884, the Northern Central extended its rail bed to the west pier, where railcars collected sand for use on the rails to provide traction. (SBHS.)

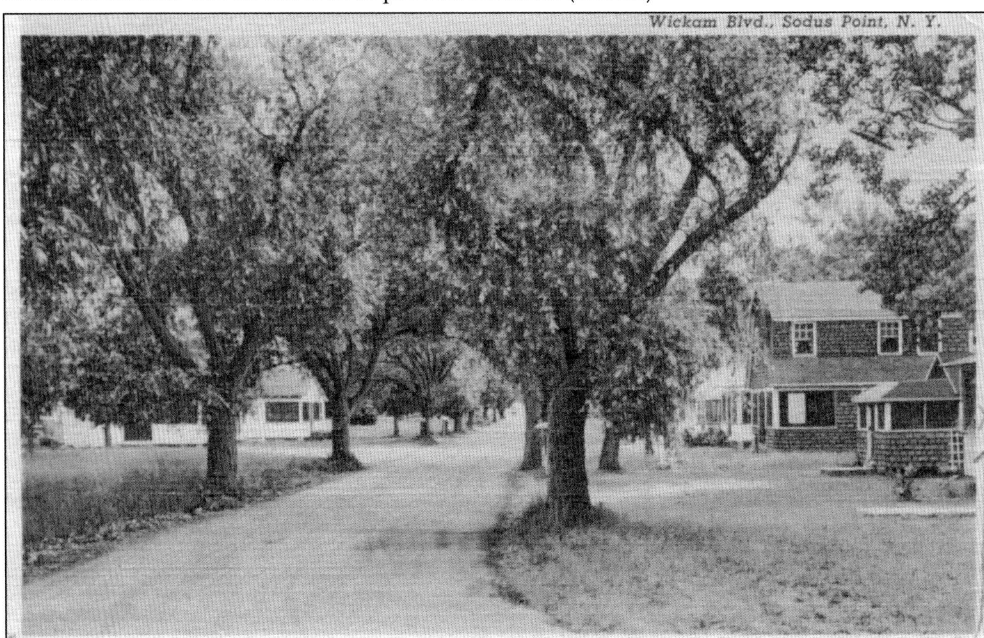


Capt. William Wickham served in the US Navy during the British war with the French (1792). An early settler, Wickham was important to the development of Sodus Point. He built the first general store, served as postmaster from 1814 to 1856, was harbormaster, and was a founding member of the Sodus Point Episcopal Church. The family cemetery is located on Wickham Boulevard, which is named in Wickham's honor.

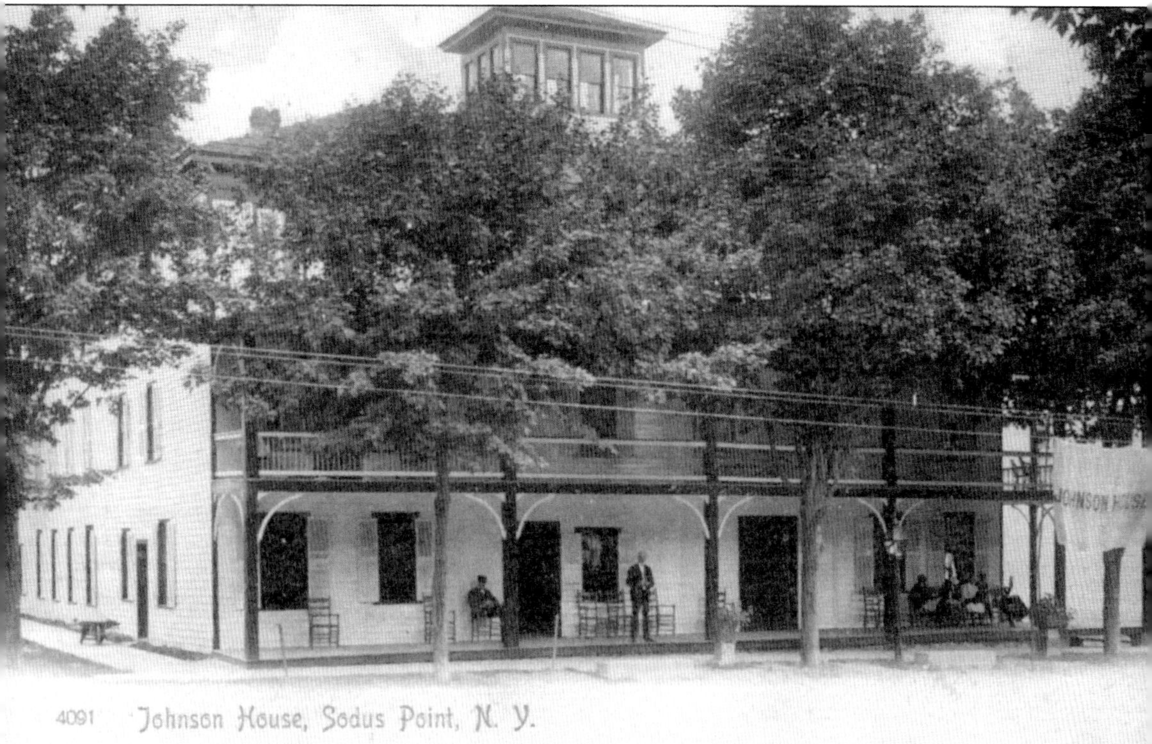


Built prior to 1860, the Johnson House is listed in the *1863 Wayne County Business Directory*. An advertisement in Mrs. D.F. McNett's 1912 pamphlet *Sodus Bay* describes the Johnson House as the oldest hotel in Sodus Point. The cupola was added to the building in 1889. Around 1871, George H. Case became proprietor of the Johnson House. His father-in-law, S.P. Johnson, was the founder of the Johnson House. Case was renowned for being a very gracious host who paid attention to his guests' comfort. The hotel was always busy, with group event activities and visitors from out of town. Case and his wife, Julia, ran the hotel until around 1905, at which time their son Harrison took over as proprietor. Sold in 1912 to three businessmen, including Harry H. Williams, a Sodus banker and Charles Point cottager, the Johnson House found itself under several managers through 1937. The hotel kept a steady pace with customers for several years, but gradually, the newer and attentively managed Harris House, across the road, took over in popularity.

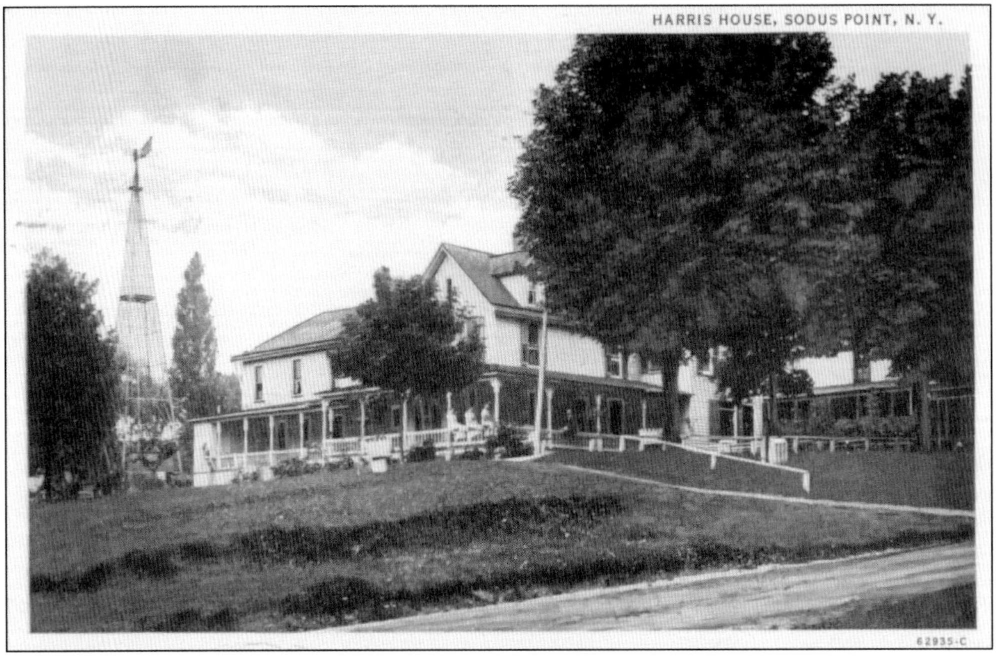


The Harris House sits atop the high crest of Sodus Point. James Harris and wife, Mary, ran the Harris House from around 1900 through the 1920s. Advertised as being open year-round with rooms from $3 a day, Harris House became Sodus Point's most popular hotel. Mary fell gravely ill in 1924, and the hotel's business dwindled after her death at 59 years of age in January 1925. James died in 1936.

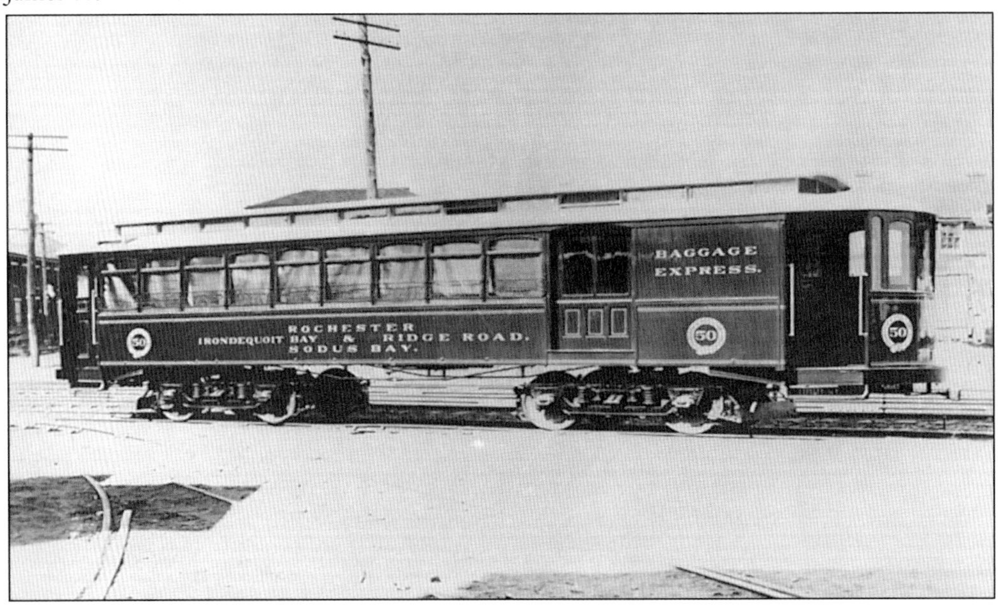


It cost a nickel to ride the Rochester & Sodus Bay Railway trolley, which ran from 1900 to 1929, until the automobile became more popular. The Sodus Point tracks originally ran to the base of Greig Street hill. The pitch of the hill made it difficult to get enough speed going to get back up the hill, so the tracks ended at the Johnson House. (New York Museum of Transportation Collection.)

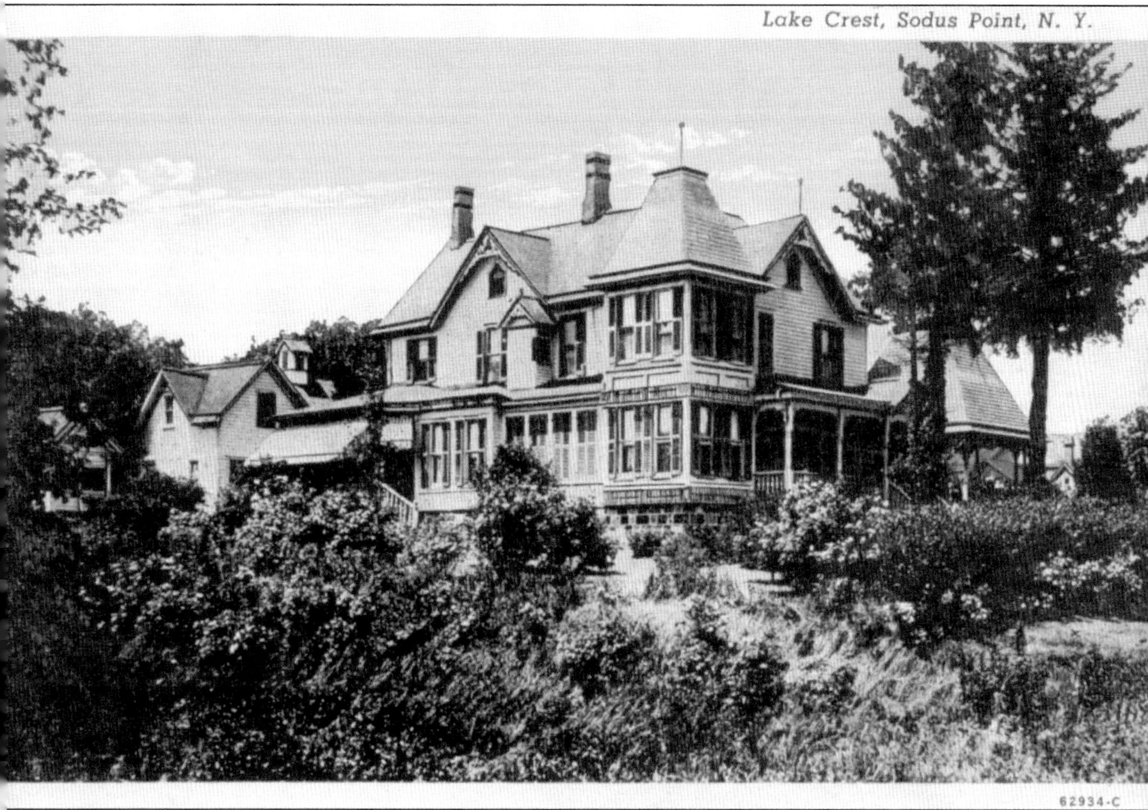


Lake Crest was the estate of Anne Elizabeth MacKenzie (1822–1904). Anne's brother John T. MacKenzie donated to the Presbyterian mission. She was heir to his great fortune. Following her brother's example, Anne bequeathed her home to the Presbyterian Church Foreign Mission as an education center for returning foreign missionaries. With all close relatives deceased, Anne's cousins contested her will, challenging that she was not of her right mind. Her brief obituary in the *Arcadian Weekly Gazette* on November 20, 1904, conveys that "she was a very eccentric character, possessed of considerable means." One of Anne's peculiarities was that she owned a parrot that said naughty words. After nearly six years of appellate court proceedings, the final verdict in 1910 ruled in favor of the Presbyterian Church. Around 1934, Lake Crest became a popular dinner and picnic site for large groups and a guesthouse for private individuals; it was managed by the DoVille family.

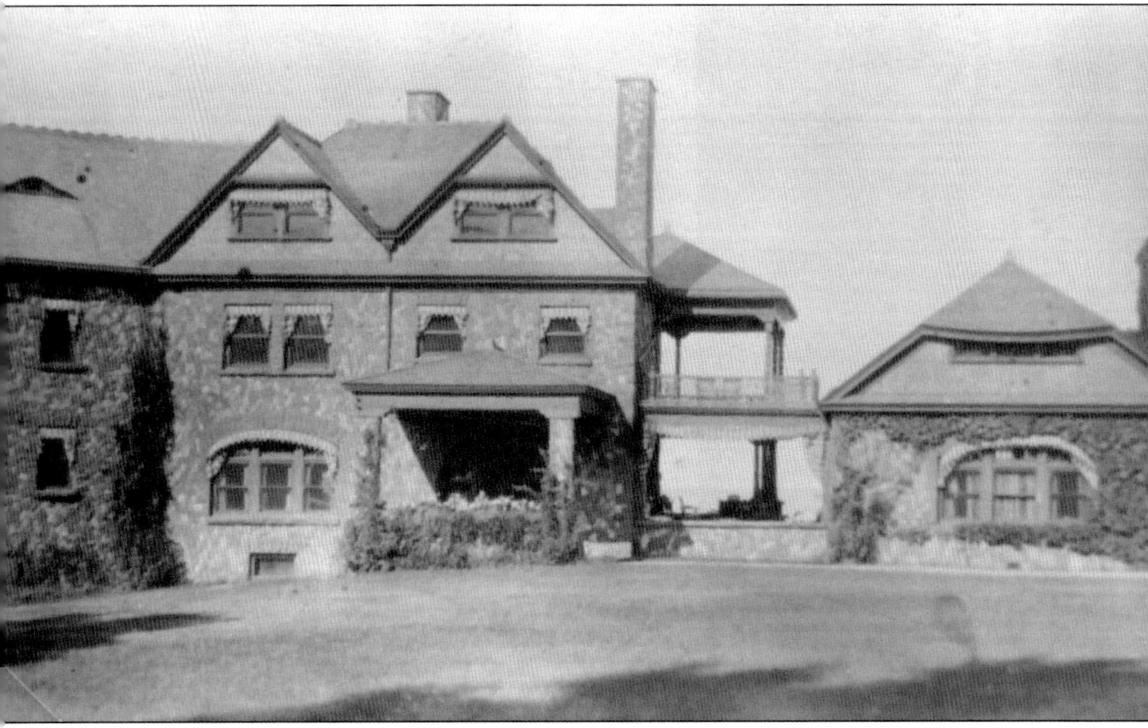

Lakestones was the home of Civil War veteran Col. Enos Blossom Parsons (1840–1897) and his wife, Augusta. Built around 1880, the castle-like residence was constructed of stones collected from the shores of Lake Ontario. The scenic view from the estate overlooks the lake as far as the eye can see. Parsons served with distinction as a cavalry officer for the Union army. Following the war, he built a malting enterprise in Rochester, but sold that to move to Sodus Point. Parsons was the builder and owner of the Sodus Point Malt House. He was also director of the Northern Central Railroad at the time of his death. In addition to the Lakestones estate and malt house, Parsons owned other properties, including Eagle Island on Sodus Bay and Preston's Mill and Maxwell property west of Sodus Point. He intended to use the Preston/Maxwell property as pasture for fancy cattle and horses. (SBHS.)

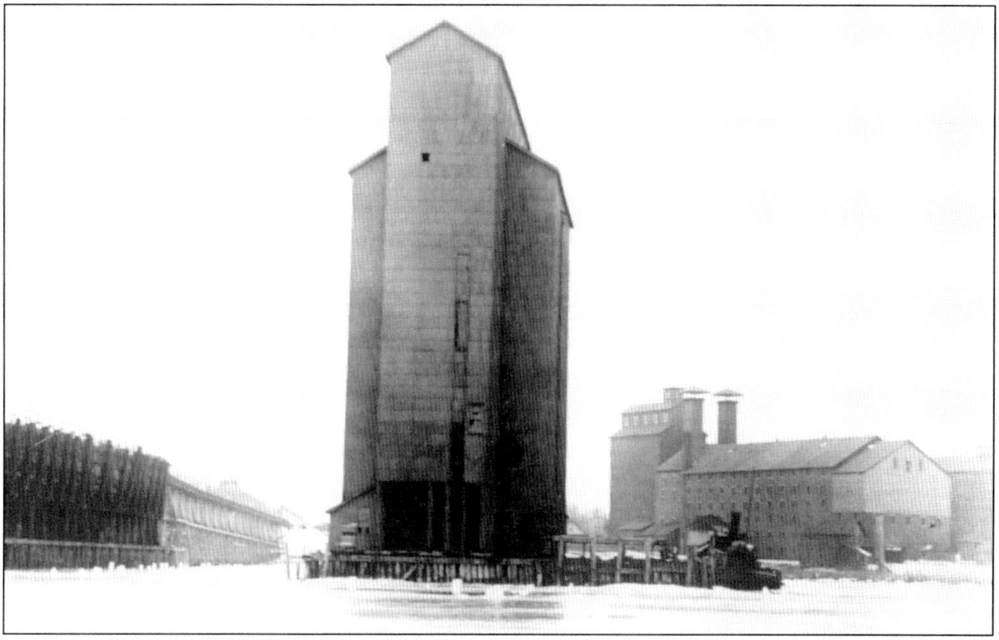

E.B. Parson's malt house, on the right, was constructed in 1880 using limestone from a local quarry. E.H. Harriman bought the malt house around 1900, converting the facility to a cold storage. Louis Wehle of Rochester purchased the malt house in 1936. After two years of renovation, Wehle returned the building to its intended operation. It was used as a malt house for the Genesee Brewing Company until 1986. (SBHS.)

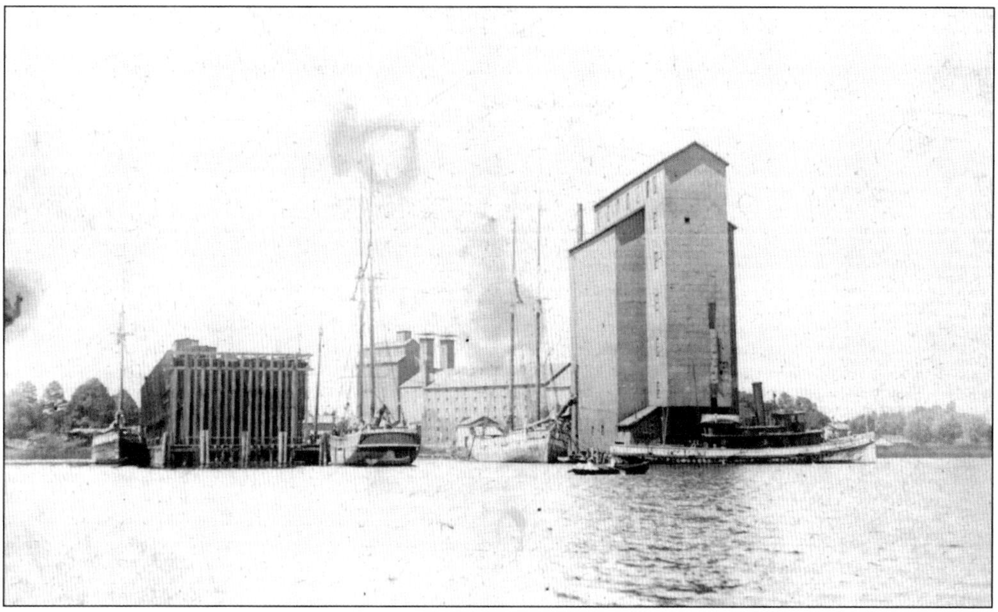

The grain elevator (at right in this image and in the center in the image at the top of the page) was erected to receive shipments of barley from Canadian fields. The grain would be delivered to the six-story malt house by horse teams. The towers were removed in the 1950s, and three floors of the malt house were taken down prior to that. The first coal trestle is on the left in both images. (SBHS.)

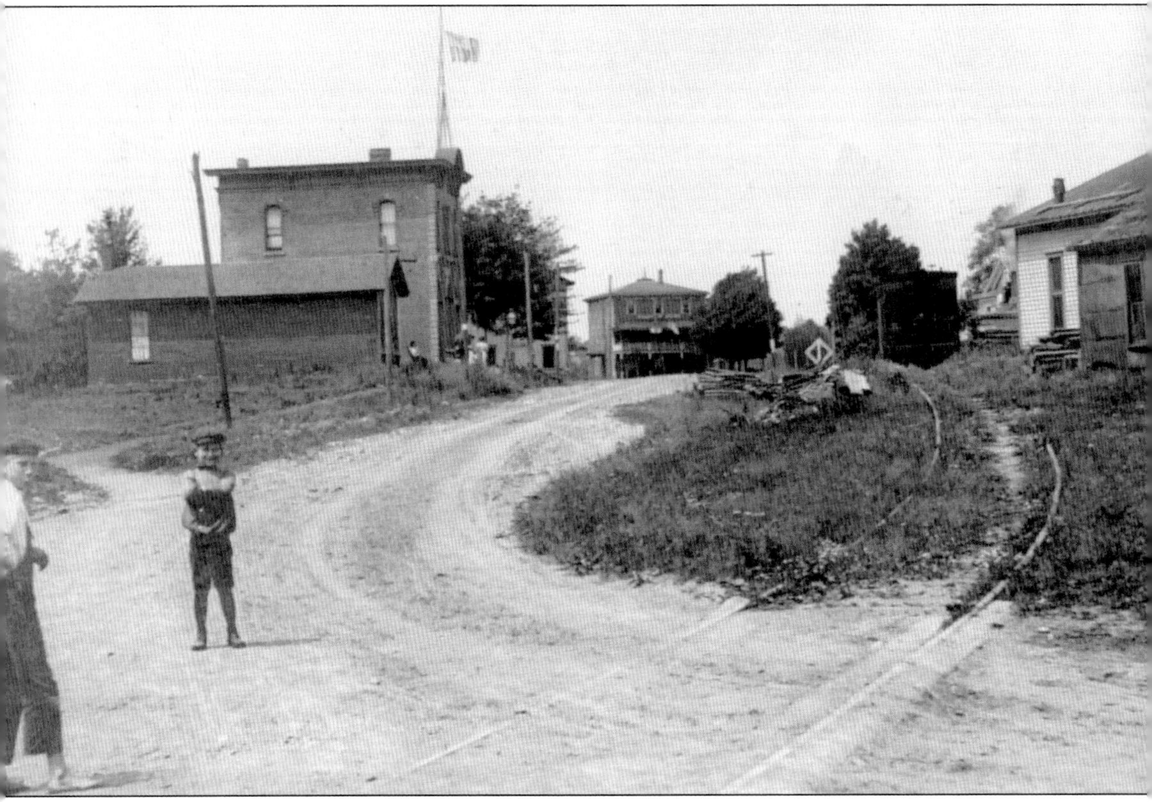

In this view looking west along Sentell Street, the building on the left was erected by S.J. Macy in 1874. Macy used the building as a bank during his short tenure at Sodus Point. The Pennsylvania Railroad purchased the structure in 1885 and leased it to the federal government for use as a customhouse and post office. Use by the government ceased in 1968. The Macy building was listed in the National Register of Historic Places in 1980 but was sadly demolished in 2001. In the center of the view, at the horizon, sits the Franklin House, a popular restaurant and tavern for locals, railroad workers, and coal boat crews. Between the two buildings is the Sodus Point Railroad Station, also known as the Bunk House and Railroad "Y" restaurant. This building, so popular in its day, was torn down in 1992. (SBHS.)

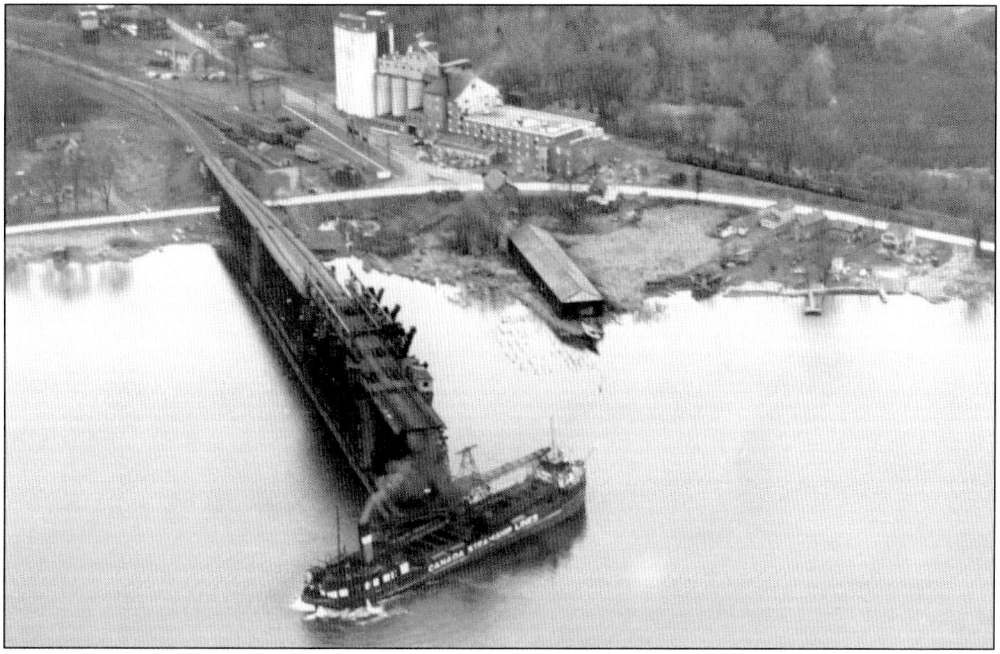

This aerial view of Macyville provides a view of the malt house, the remaining piers of the grain elevator, coal trestle, customhouse, railroad bunkhouse, and, at the top of the image, the Franklin House. Cutting through the collection of Macyville buildings are the tracks for the Northern Central Railroad. As the towers and the upper floors of the malt house have been removed, this image dates from around 1950. (SBHS.)

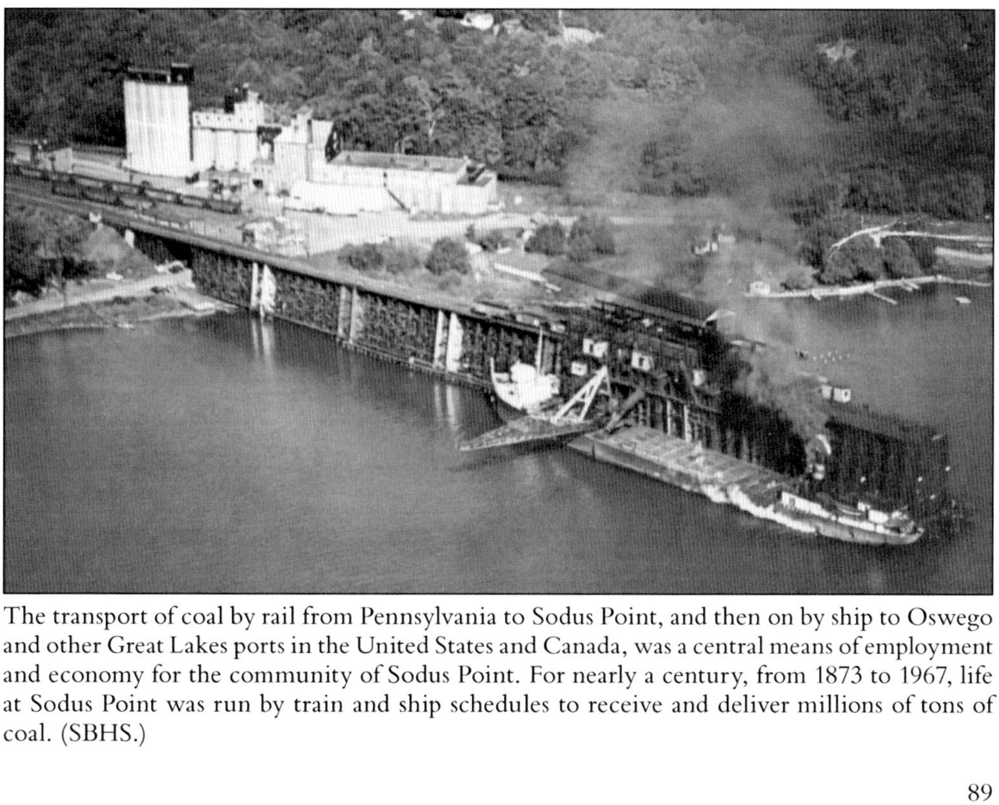

The transport of coal by rail from Pennsylvania to Sodus Point, and then on by ship to Oswego and other Great Lakes ports in the United States and Canada, was a central means of employment and economy for the community of Sodus Point. For nearly a century, from 1873 to 1967, life at Sodus Point was run by train and ship schedules to receive and deliver millions of tons of coal. (SBHS.)

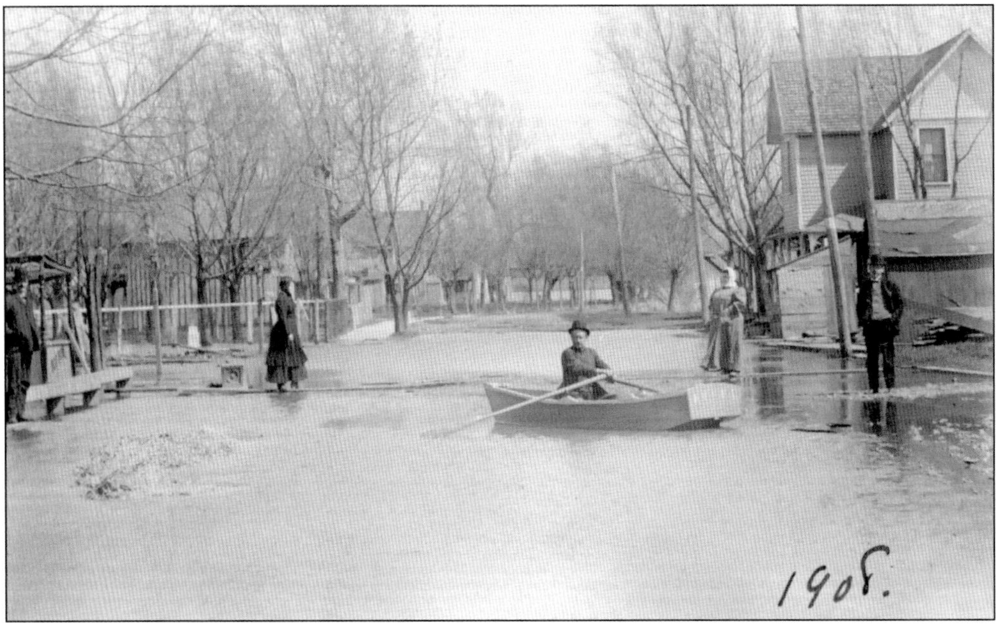


The *Union Gazette* of Newark, New York, dated April 18, 1908, reports in a lead line: "Wreck and Wrack at Sodus Bay: Damage by Wind and Water Worst in History of Bay." Fifty-two-mile-per-hour winds "blew great guns" on Saturday, April 11, 1908. The opening of the article continues: "Sand Point afloat, Piers and Breakwaters covered, Crescent Beach partly submerged, boats and boathouses wrecked in all directions, and the water is still rising." The photographs for the postcards on this page were taken at Sand Point a day or two following the big storm. (Above, SBHS.)

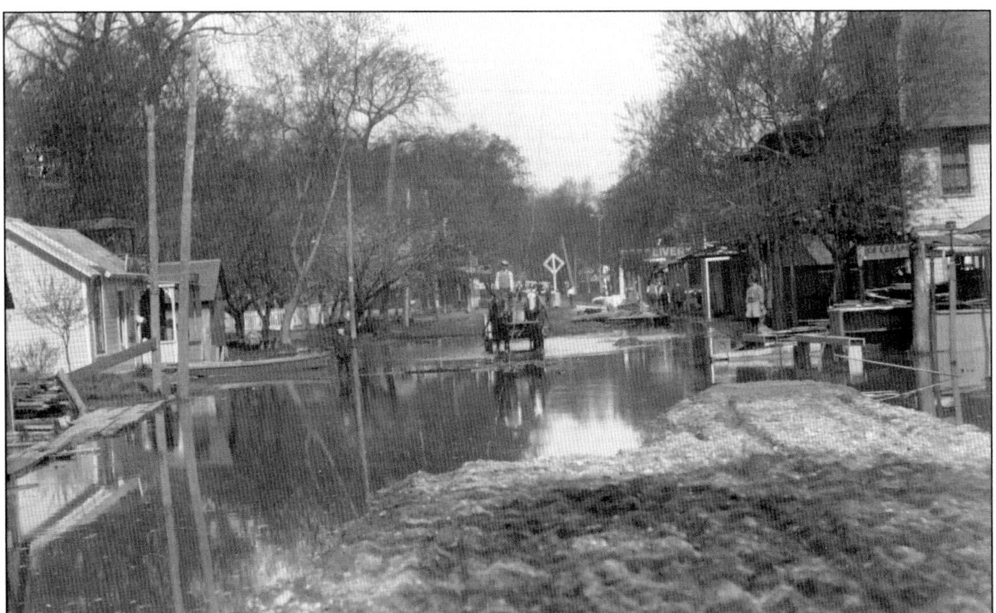

# *Eight*

# Lighthouses

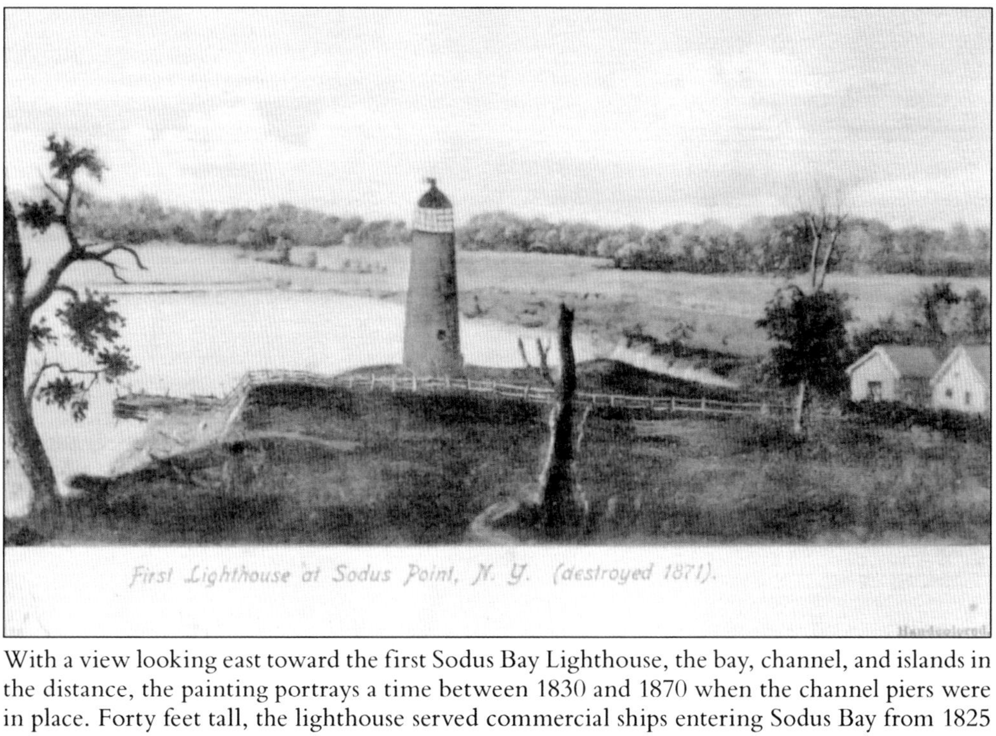


With a view looking east toward the first Sodus Bay Lighthouse, the bay, channel, and islands in the distance, the painting portrays a time between 1830 and 1870 when the channel piers were in place. Forty feet tall, the lighthouse served commercial ships entering Sodus Bay from 1825 through 1870. War of 1812 veteran Ishmael D. Hill petitioned the secretary of the treasury and was appointed the first Sodus Bay Lighthouse keeper in November 1826.

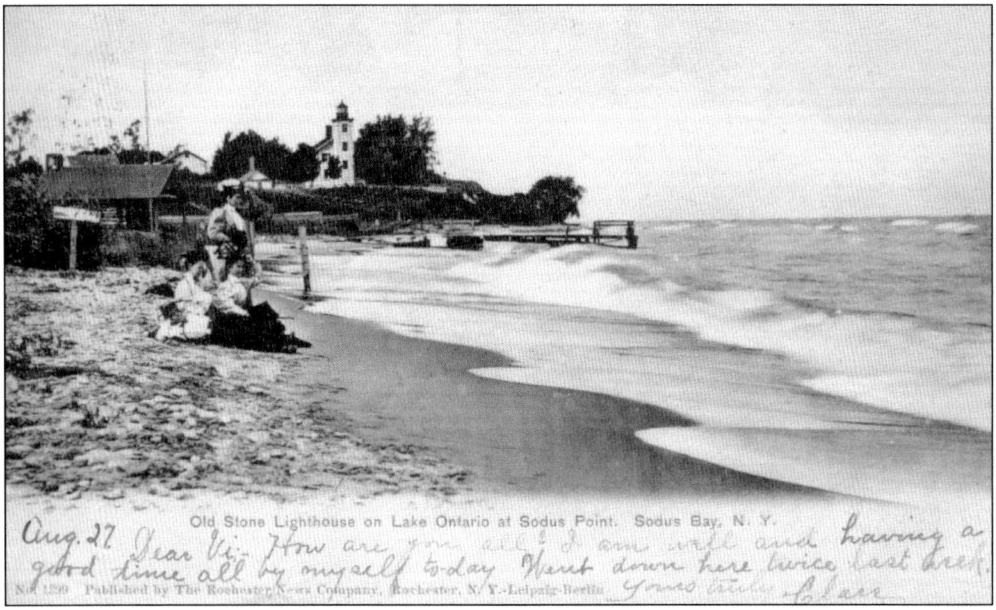


The caption on this postcard reads "Old Stone Lighthouse." Actually, the Old Stone Lighthouse was only 35 years old when this postcard was mailed in 1905. The lighthouse was built in 1870 to replace the deteriorating lighthouse tower on the bluff, which had served ships on Lake Ontario for 44 years. This second lighthouse was the Sodus Bay beacon for 30 years before being discontinued in 1901.

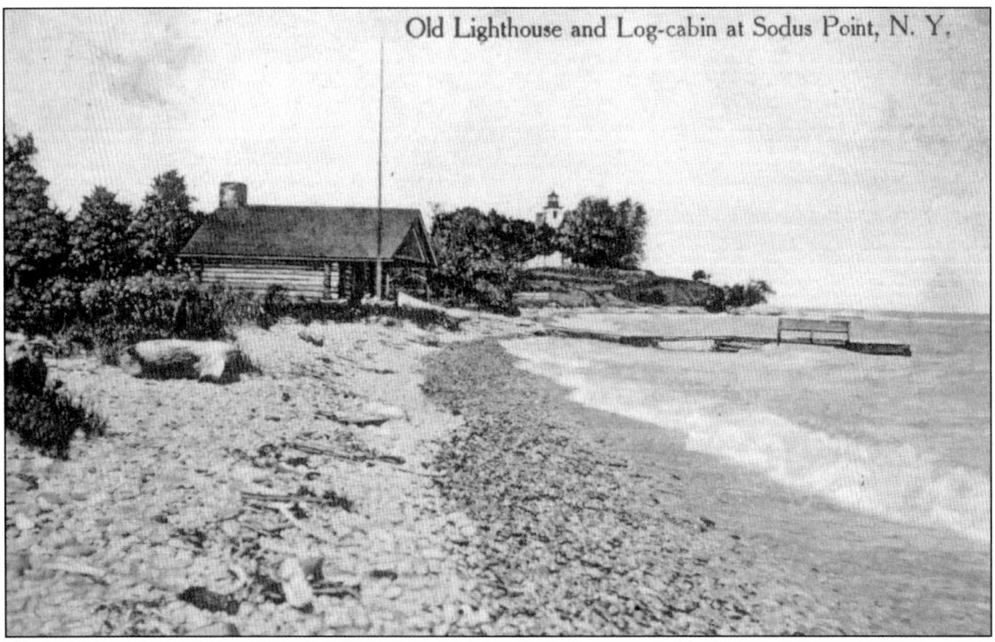


The log cabin pictured in front of the Old Stone Lighthouse belonged to adjacent property owner Col. E.B. Parsons, who was builder and owner of the Sodus Point Malt House. Parsons's estate was called Lakestones, as the castle-like building was constructed of stones taken from Lake Ontario. In contrast to Lakestones, the lighthouse was built using limestone shipped across the lake from Kingston, Ontario.

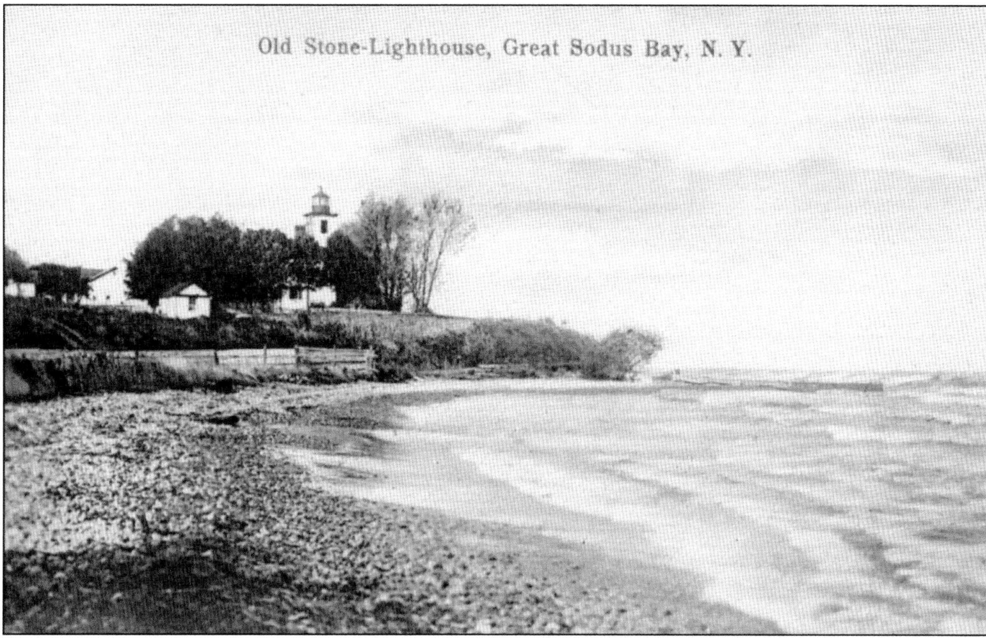


Crops, barns, and other outbuildings reveal that the early lighthouse keepers and their families farmed the "Old Stone Lighthouse" bluff where they resided all year long. Life on this bluff was a rugged one. Winds that could exceed 50 or 60 miles per hour were particularly brutal in the winter months when the lighthouse still needed to be tended. The unrelenting demands of the job, combined with the isolation of the location, resulted in the need for individuals of strong will and spirit. The jetty, constructed of stones from the first lighthouse and lighthouse keeper's dwelling, can be seen to the right of the bluff in each postcard. This jetty was built in hopes of reducing the erosion of the lighthouse bluff. The message on the back of the bottom postcard, which has a 1911 cancellation mark, reads, "This is one of the pretty sights from our back door."

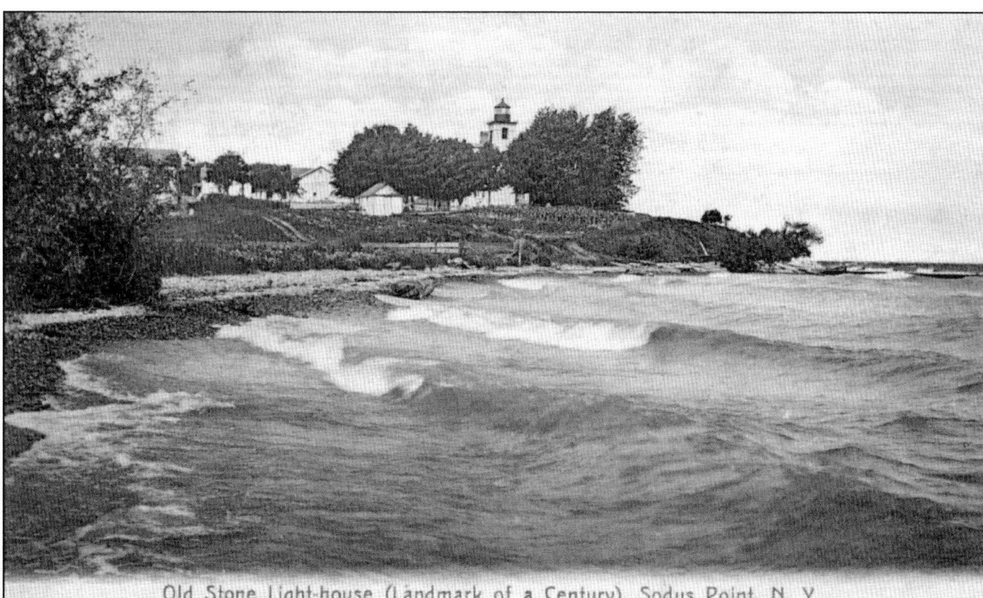

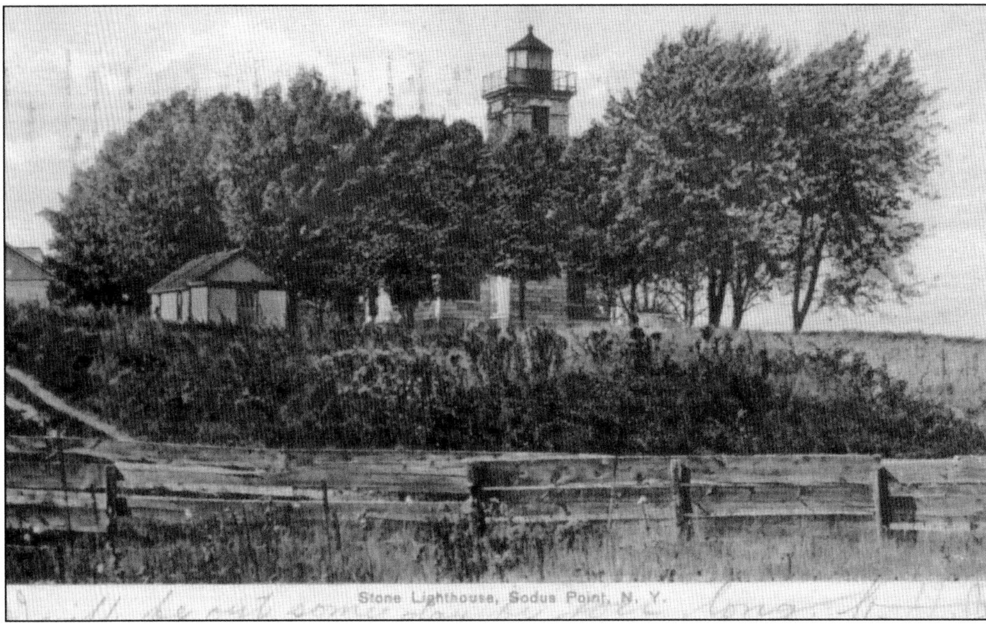


The postcard above shows the east side of the lighthouse as seen from the lakeshore. Below is a roadside view, looking northeast, of the Old Stone Lighthouse around 1890. Lighthouse keeper Charles Degan served from 1866 to 1881. In 1871, Degan oversaw the closing and demolition of the old tower and the opening of the Old Stone Lighthouse. Daniel Phillips became keeper of the lighthouse in 1882. The Old Stone Lighthouse was taken out of service in 1901 and the outer pier lighthouse, built in 1872, assumed official duty. Phillips and his family continued to live in the lighthouse keeper's residence that was part of the Old Stone Lighthouse as he tended the outer pier lighthouse. Phillips served until 1917, holding the post for the longest run of any lighthouse keeper—35 years. (Below, SBHS.)

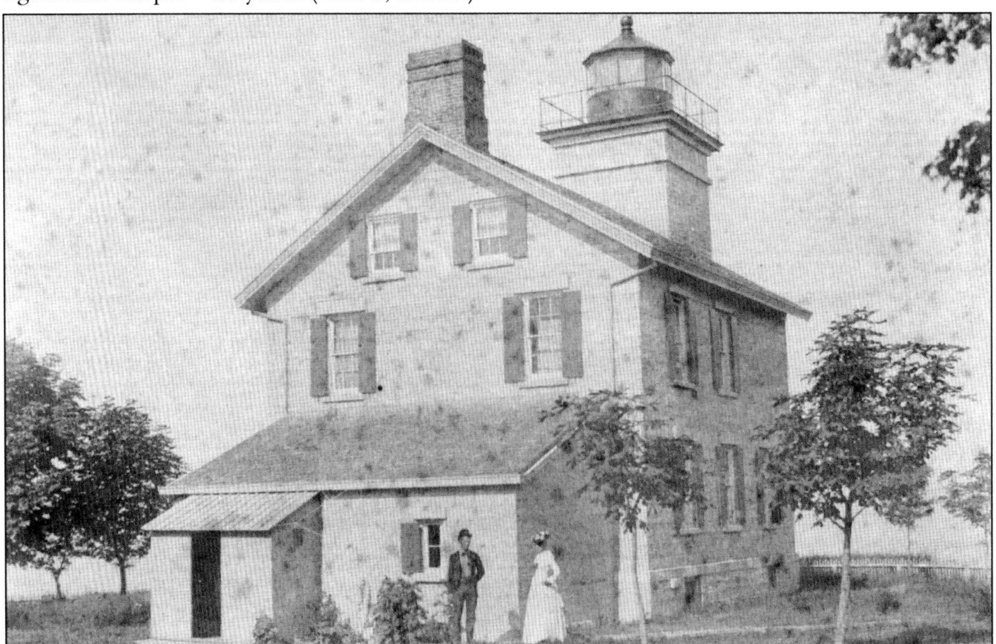

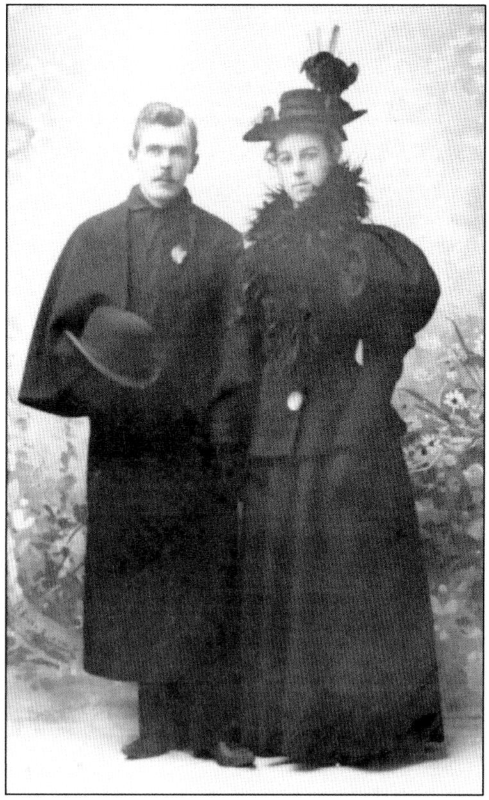

Lighthouse keeper Wilford Lewis and his wife, Bertha Phillips Lewis, pose in the July 1885 photograph at right. Bertha was the former lighthouse keeper Daniel Phillips's daughter. Lewis was lighthouse keeper for 22 years, from 1917 to 1939, second in duration at the light to his father-in-law. Lewis also served under his father-in-law as first assistant keeper of the Sodus Pier Head Lighthouse from 1905 to 1917, making his run as Sodus Bay lighthouse keeper 34 years long. Bertha had grown up, married, and raised her own children living at the Old Stone Lighthouse at Sodus Point for 57 of her 66 years. Shown in the c. 1905 photograph below is the Lewis family with son Elmer and daughter Marion. (Both, SBHS.)

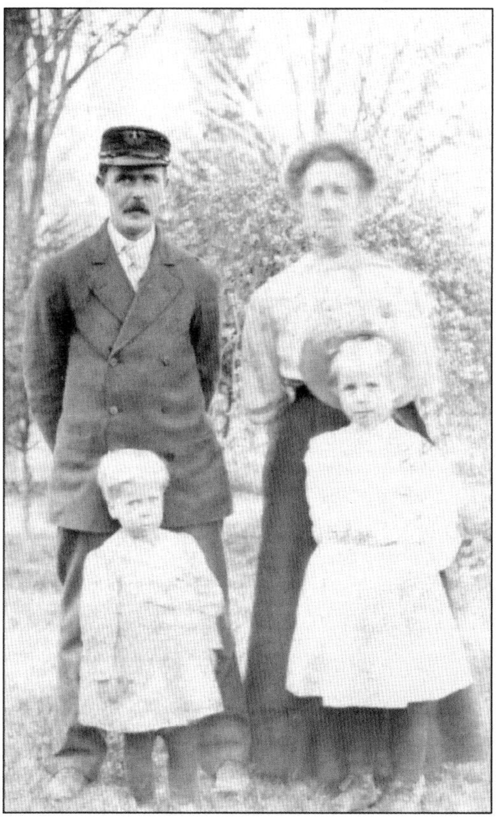

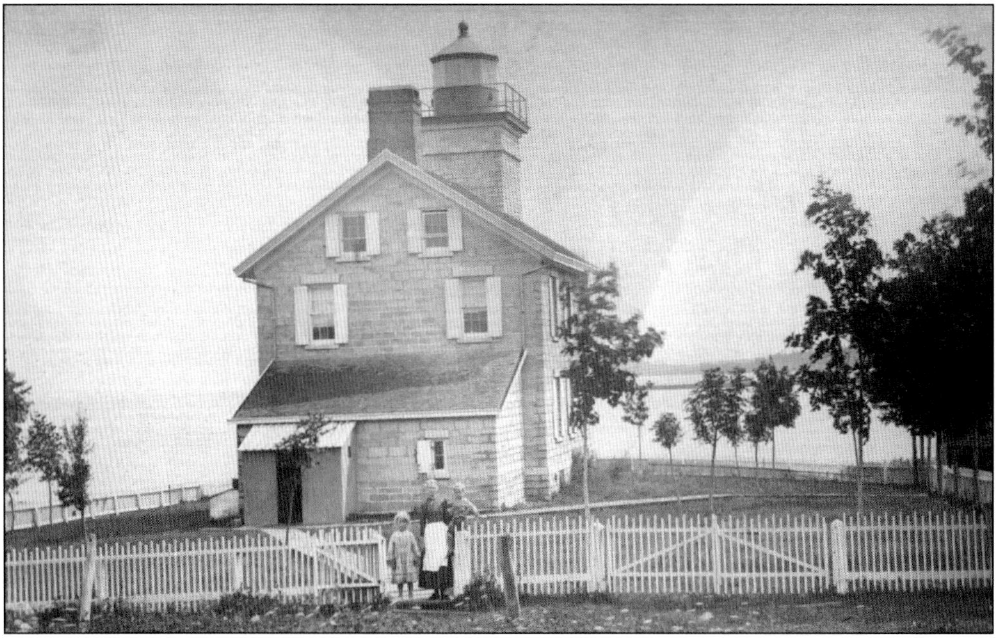

Bertha Phillips Lewis and her children, Elmer and Marion, pose on the street side of the Old Stone Lighthouse in the photograph above. Marion looks as if she may have been playing in the wind. The location of the lighthouse on the bluff provides exposure to ample wind from nearly all directions. The picket fence pictured here was an improvement added to the lighthouse grounds around 1902. The rare postcard below shows the bluff-side garden in the early 1900s. (Both, SBHS.)

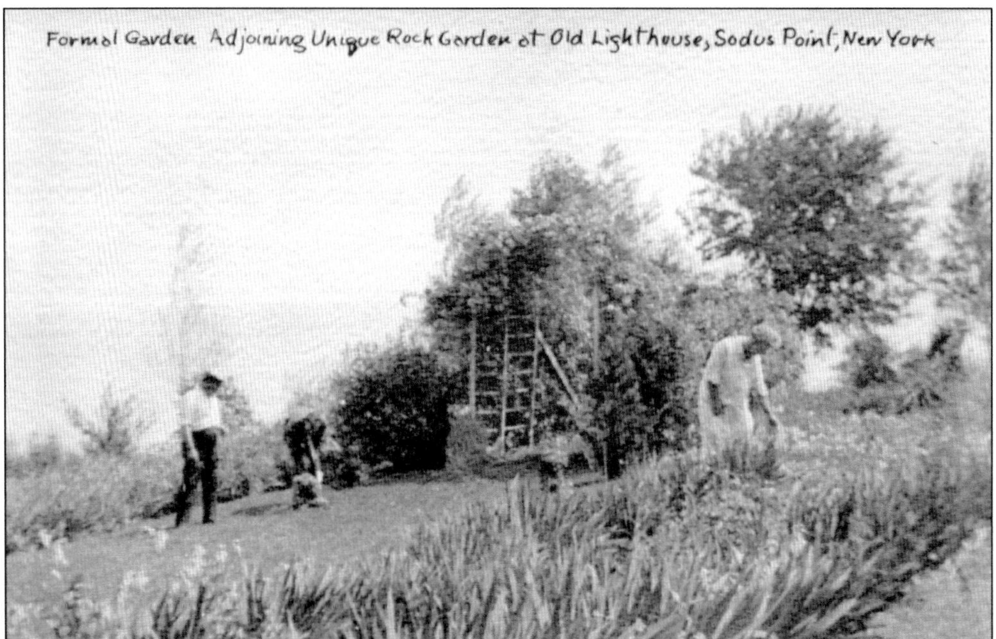

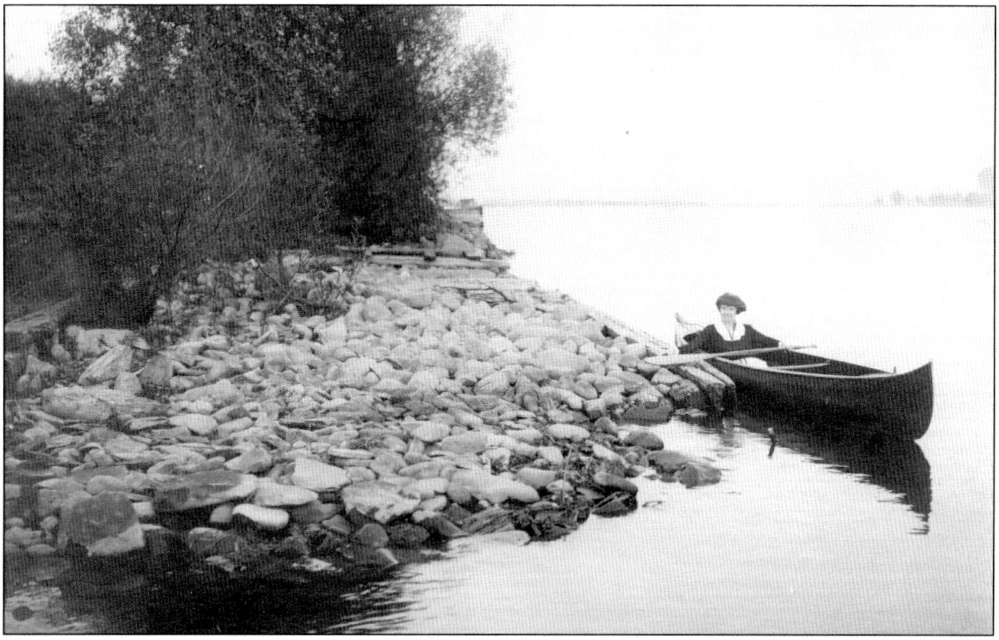

This photograph of a girl in her canoe, resting in the quiet waters along the ruins of the wooden cribbing of the old break wall, is visual poetry. Constructed between 1829 and 1834, this section of break wall spanned between the mainland at Sodus Point and the west channel pier, separating Lake Ontario from Sodus Bay, and is, in part, responsible for the creation of the "new" land of Sodus Point. (SBHS.)

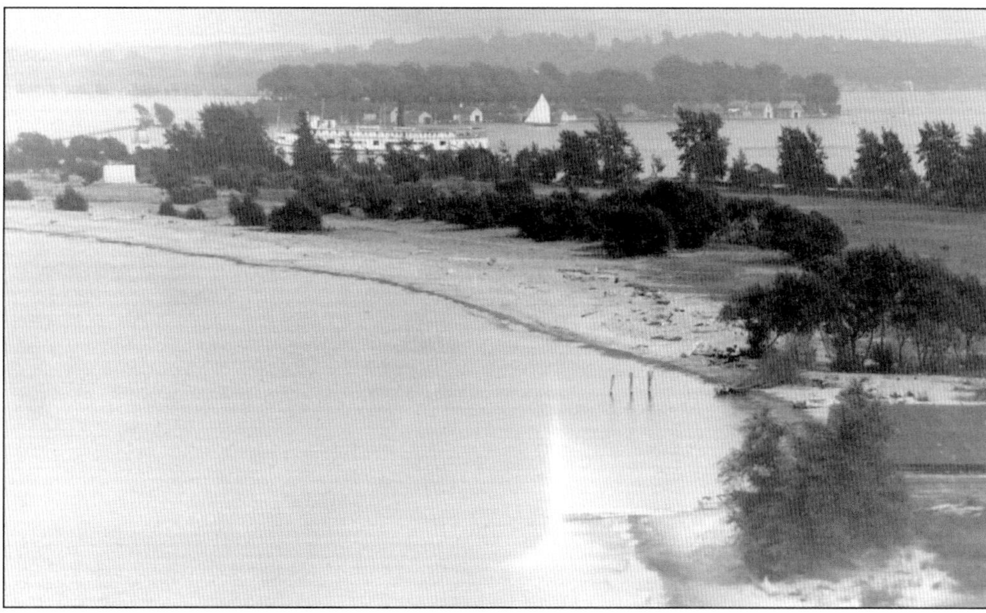

The Old Stone Lighthouse tower provides a profound panoramic view of Lake Ontario and Sodus Bay from 45 feet above the bluff. In the view looking east, Charles Point with its row of boathouses sets a background for the passenger steamer *Arundell* exiting the bay through the channel to Lake Ontario. Spanning the foreground is the vacant beach area that built up over time since the completion of the pier construction in 1834.

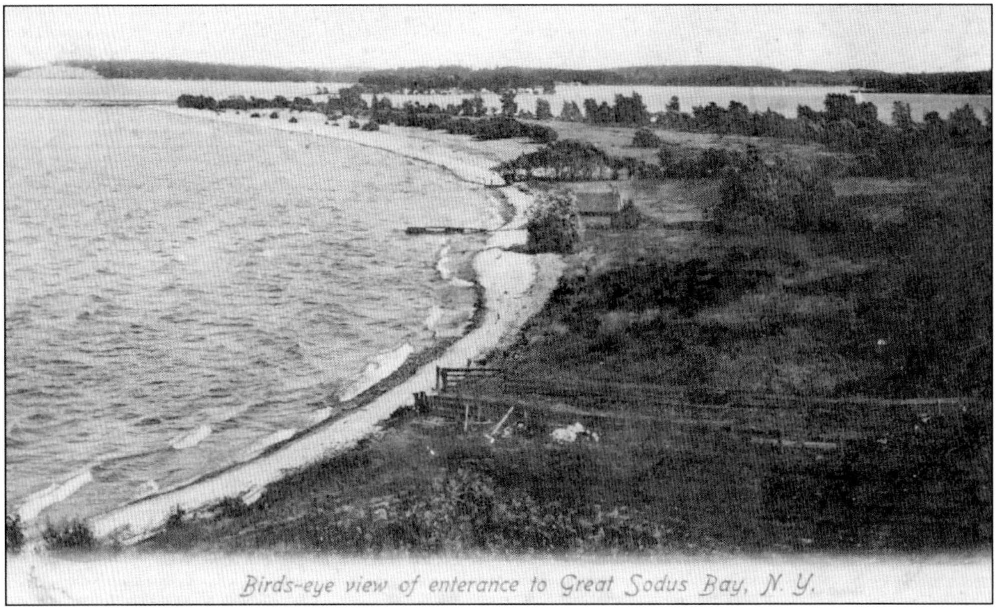


The photographer for this postcard image must have had a wide-angle lens, as Lake Bluff can be seen in the upper left with the channel piers slightly below. The tip of Newark Island can be seen in the upper right. The span of Charles Point and its boathouses are in the top center. The cottages along Wickham Boulevard and the numbered streets are still decades away from being developed.

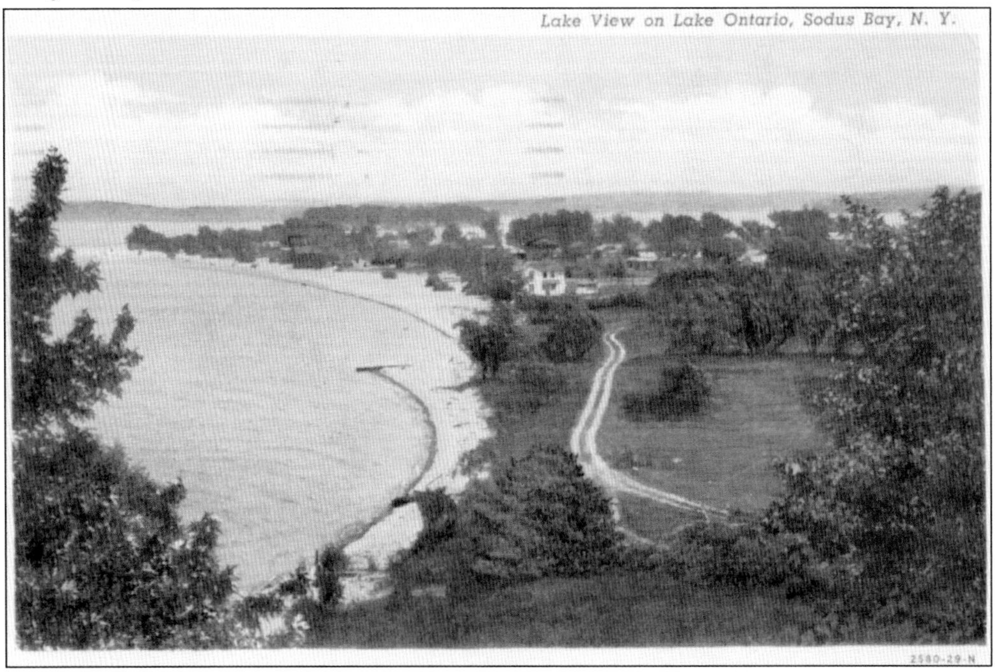


Postmarked in 1942, this postcard shows some development of cottages along Wickham Boulevard, as well as some lakeshore homes along the beach that have been built over the last 40 years. Comparing this image to the postcard at the top of this page, the dock in the center of both postcards reveals the buildup of sand over the years as a result of the piers and northwesterly winds.

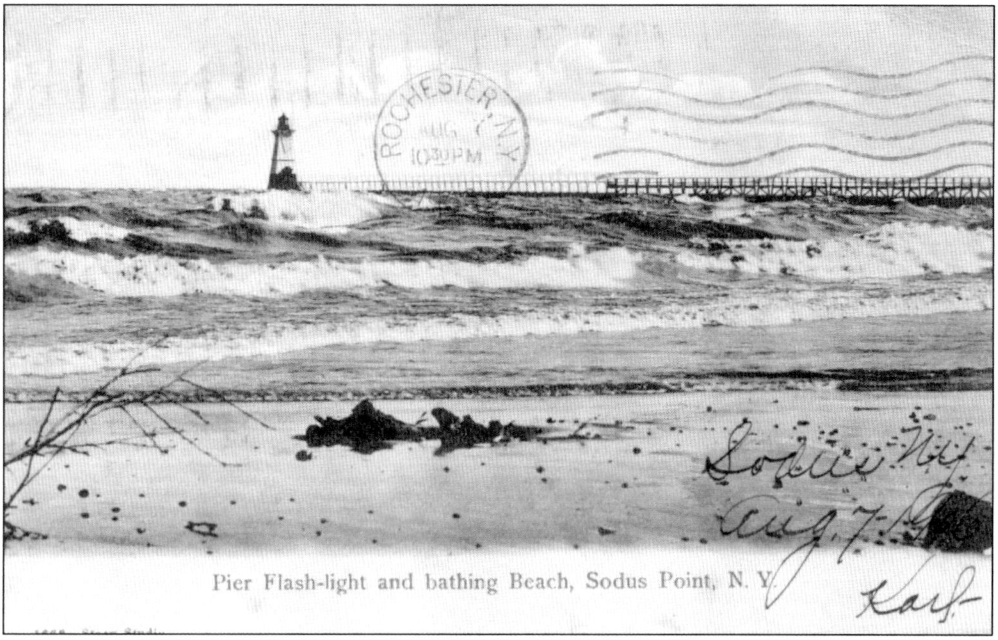


The first outer pier light was a 30-foot stone tower constructed in 1837. It was destroyed by a storm in 1857. Over the years, the pier light was replaced several times, until a 27-foot wooden lighthouse was built in 1884. In 1901, that lighthouse was raised 15 feet and became the active lighthouse for Sodus Bay. The first piers, built of stone and timber cribbing, date from 1834.

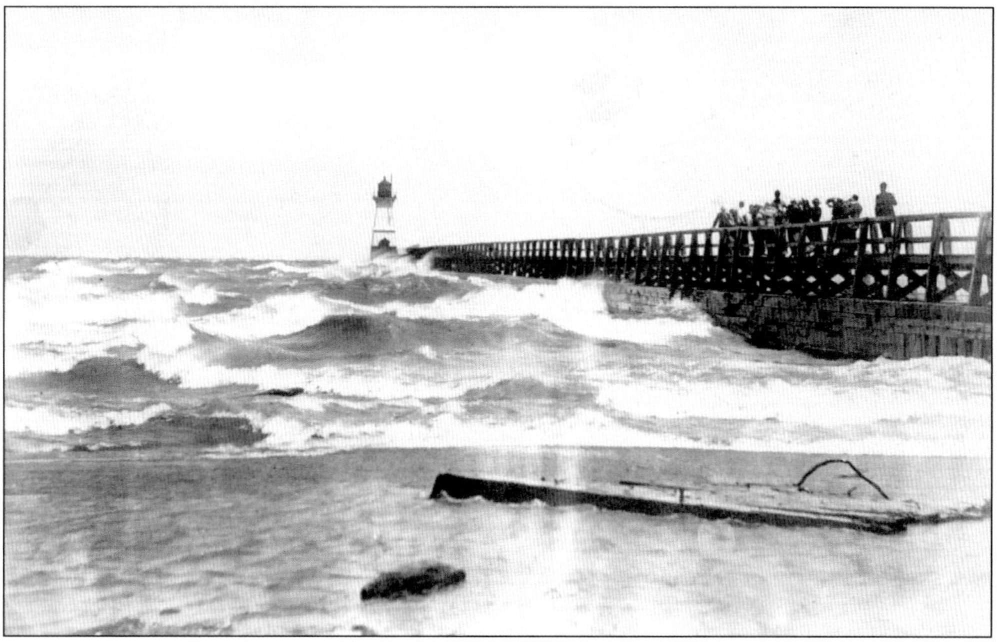

The west pier has been a popular public walkway, especially during the summer months when the breeze off Lake Ontario can be quite cooling. The elevated wooden catwalk was added in 1872, easing the journey for the lighthouse keeper over the pier in foul weather. The catwalk also provided a nice platform for the public to enjoy a stroll in times when waves would splash over the pier.

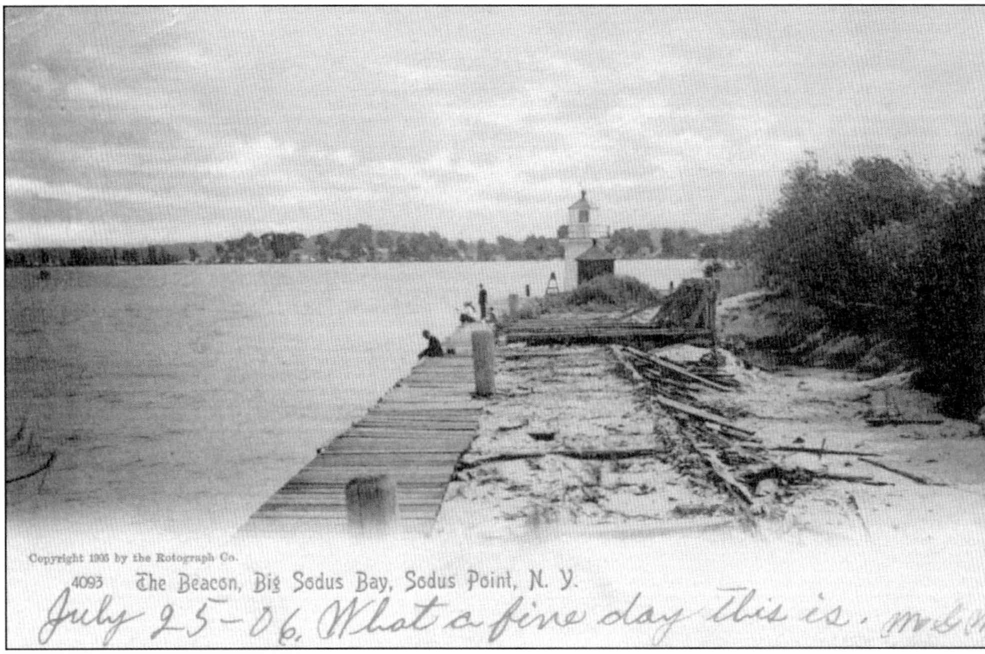


An inner light beacon, round in shape, was built on the west pier after the storm of 1857. It was only 18 feet tall and served as a guide for vessels leaving the harbor. Rebuilt in 1895, the inner light, pictured here, included a balcony, was painted white, and was square in shape. A skeletal tower replaced this light in 1938. In 1948, a marker radio beacon replaced the skeletal tower.

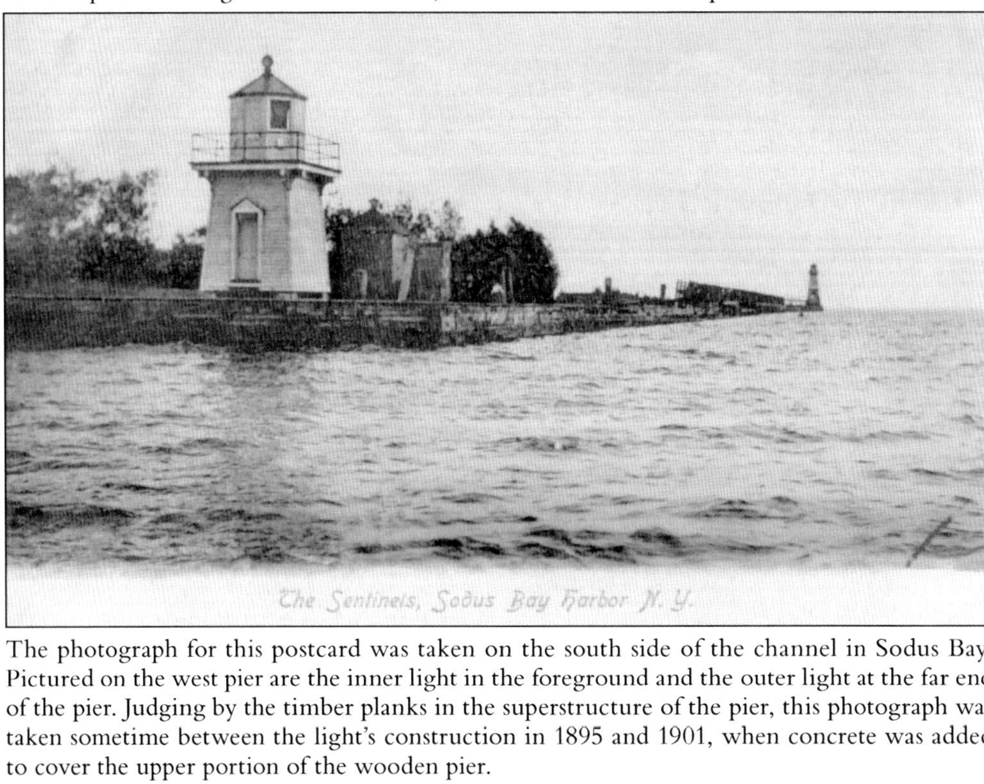


The photograph for this postcard was taken on the south side of the channel in Sodus Bay. Pictured on the west pier are the inner light in the foreground and the outer light at the far end of the pier. Judging by the timber planks in the superstructure of the pier, this photograph was taken sometime between the light's construction in 1895 and 1901, when concrete was added to cover the upper portion of the wooden pier.

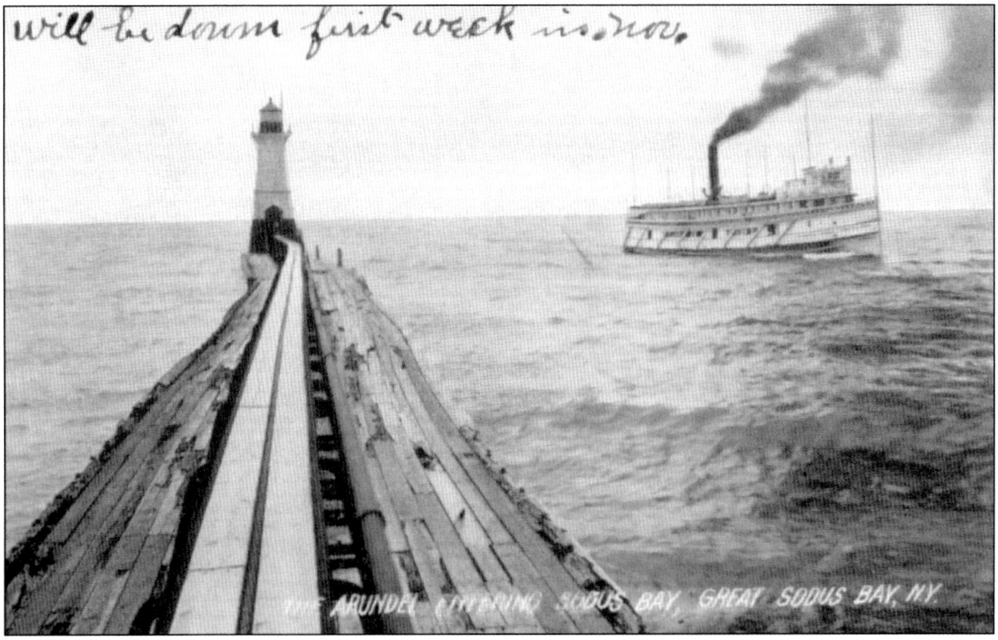


With passengers on board, the most revered steamer at the turn of the 20th century to travel Lake Ontario's south shore, *Arundell*, enters the Sodus channel (above) and departs (below) for its return to the Port of Rochester at Charlotte, New York. *Arundell* represents the many vessels of various sizes and purposes that have made their way with the aid of the Sodus Bay lighthouses. The condition of the pier in these two postcards, dated 1907, shows the wear the timber planking had taken from the beating of the waves, wind, and sand. These two photographs were taken prior to 1901, when concrete was applied over the superstructure of the piers, making for a smoother walking surface and protecting the piers from the elements. The postcard below shows a barge on the left side of the pier that may have been the concrete work area.

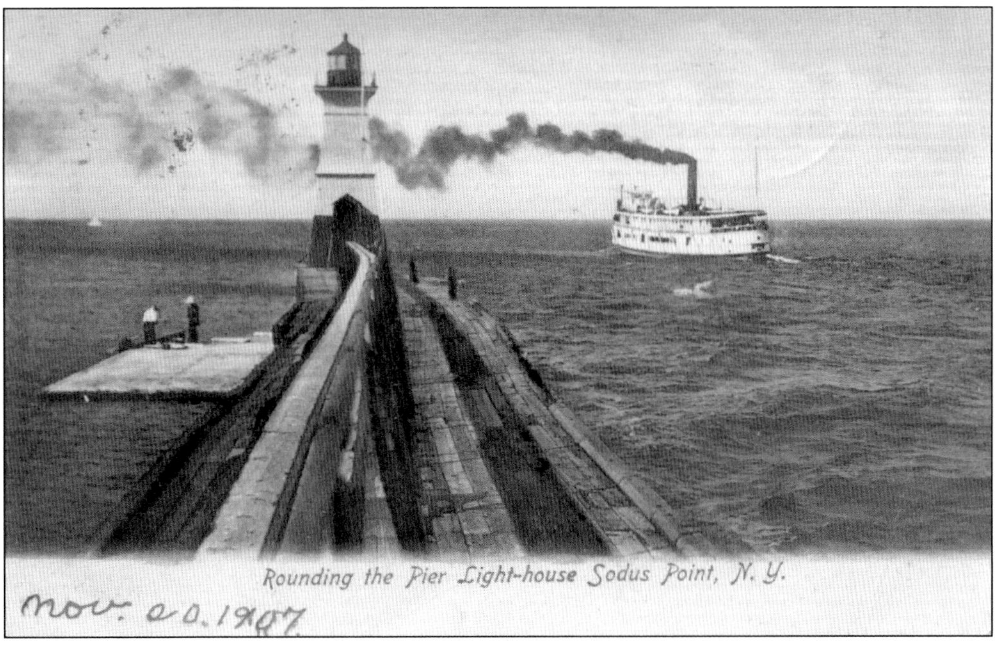

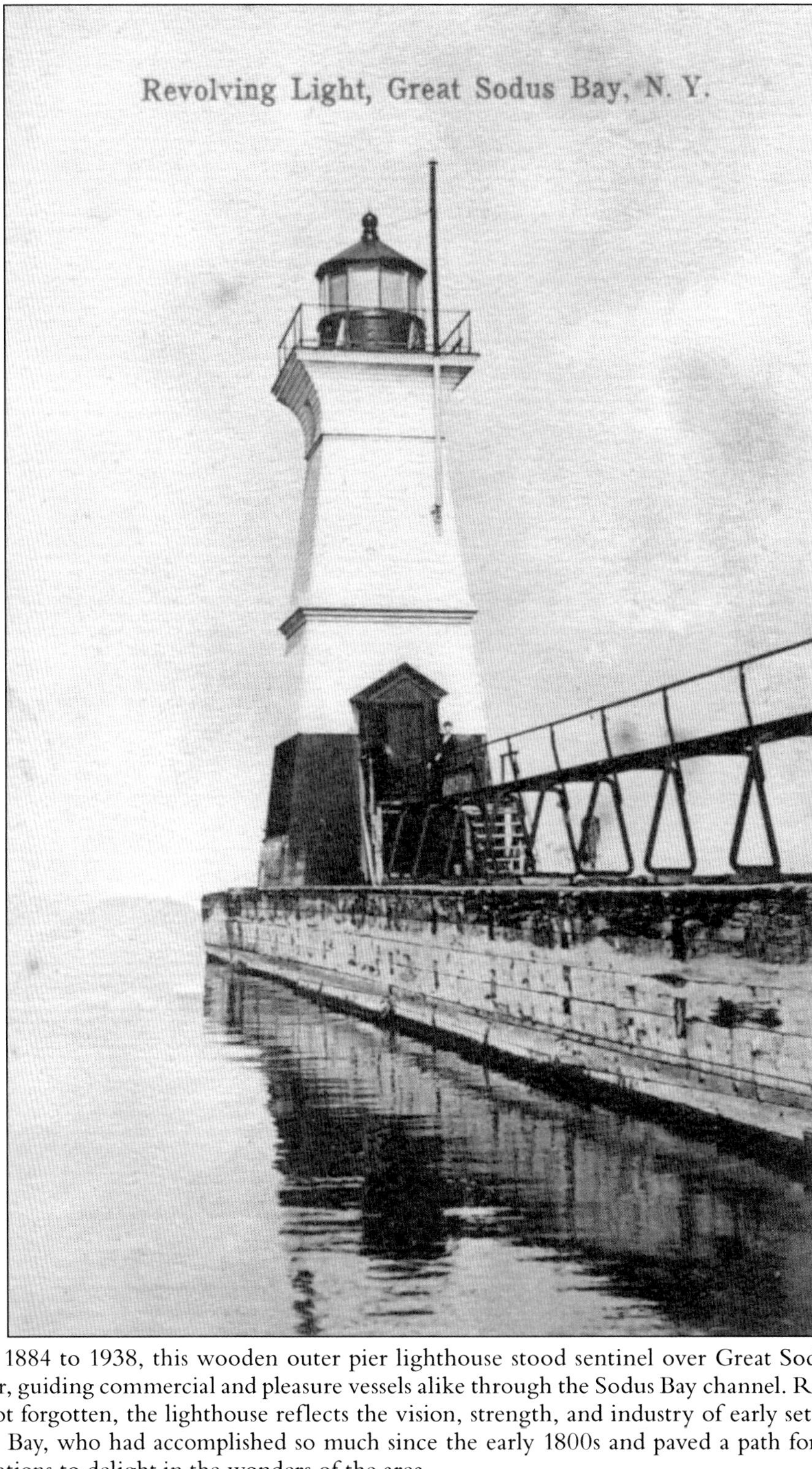


From 1884 to 1938, this wooden outer pier lighthouse stood sentinel over Great Sodus Bay harbor, guiding commercial and pleasure vessels alike through the Sodus Bay channel. Replaced but not forgotten, the lighthouse reflects the vision, strength, and industry of early settlers on Sodus Bay, who had accomplished so much since the early 1800s and paved a path for future generations to delight in the wonders of the area.

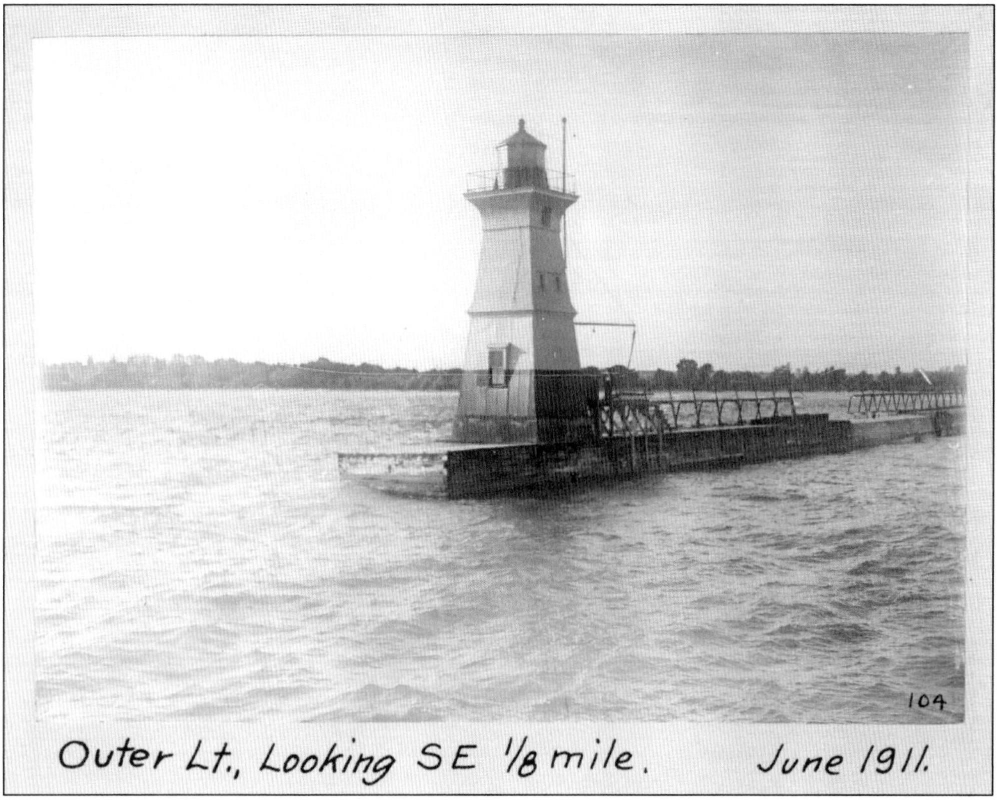


Looking south from Lake Ontario, through the channel toward the bay, the view in the 1911 photograph above shows the wood-cribbing pier. Some early concrete work appears to the right of the lighthouse. Assistant lighthouse keeper from 1923 to 1940, Charles A. Plummer took the photograph at right. A major change occurred when the outer pier wooden lighthouse was removed on August 23, 1938. (Both, US Coast Guard Historian's Office.)

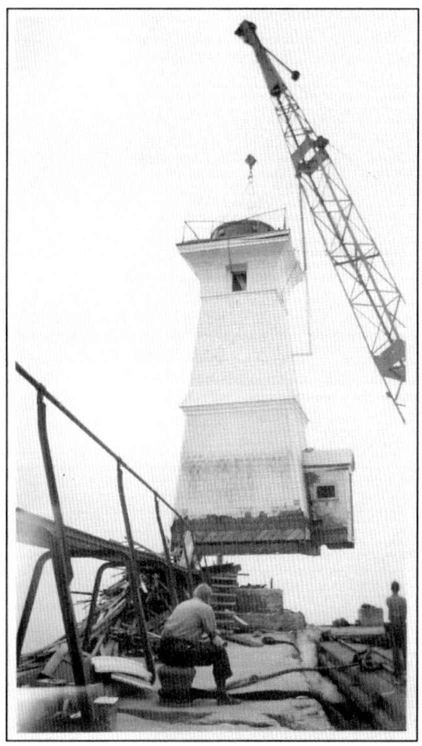

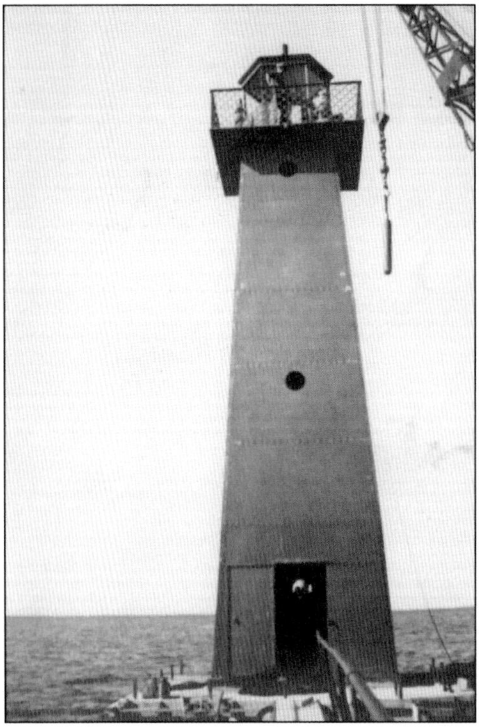

On September 2, 1938, a new steel lighthouse tower, delivered already assembled in four sections from Buffalo, was hoisted into place (left). Installation of this new lighthouse brought another change. Instead of kerosene to fuel the lamps, the operation converted to electricity for the light and foghorn. At the writing of this book, the 1938 lighthouse has been a guiding beacon for 77 years. It will likely continue its post for many more years to come. The aerial view below of the Great Sodus Bay outer pier lighthouse was taken in October 1955. (Both, US Coast Guard Historian's Office.)

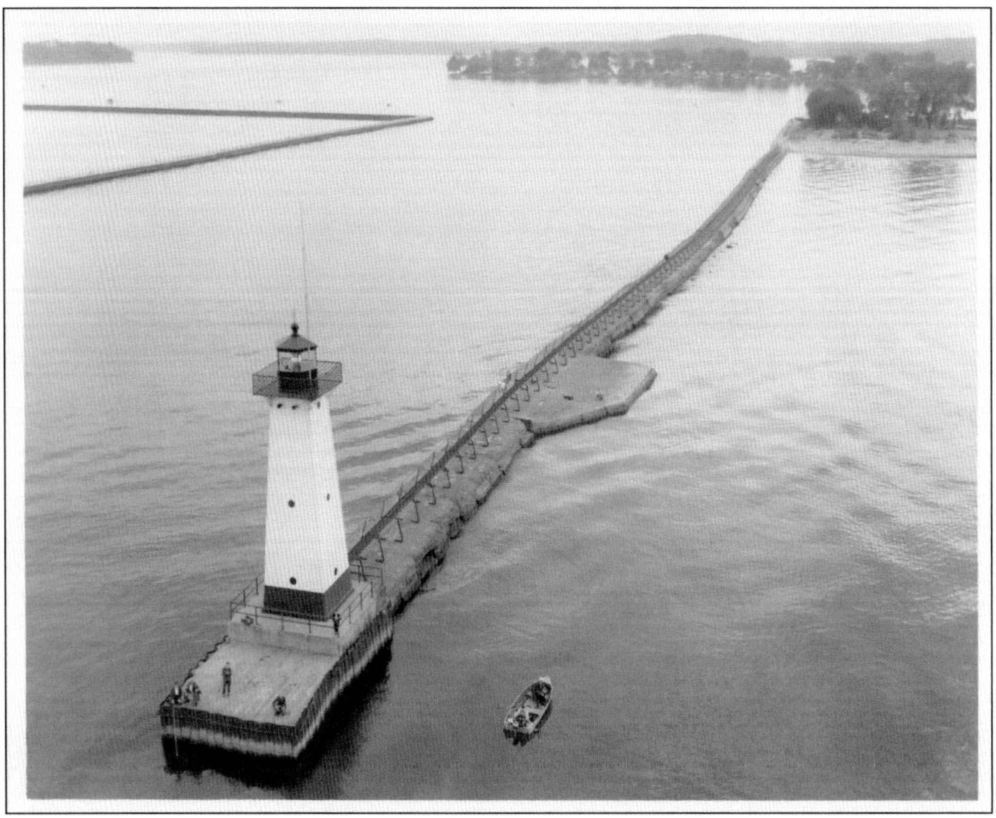

# *Nine*

# Boats about the Bay

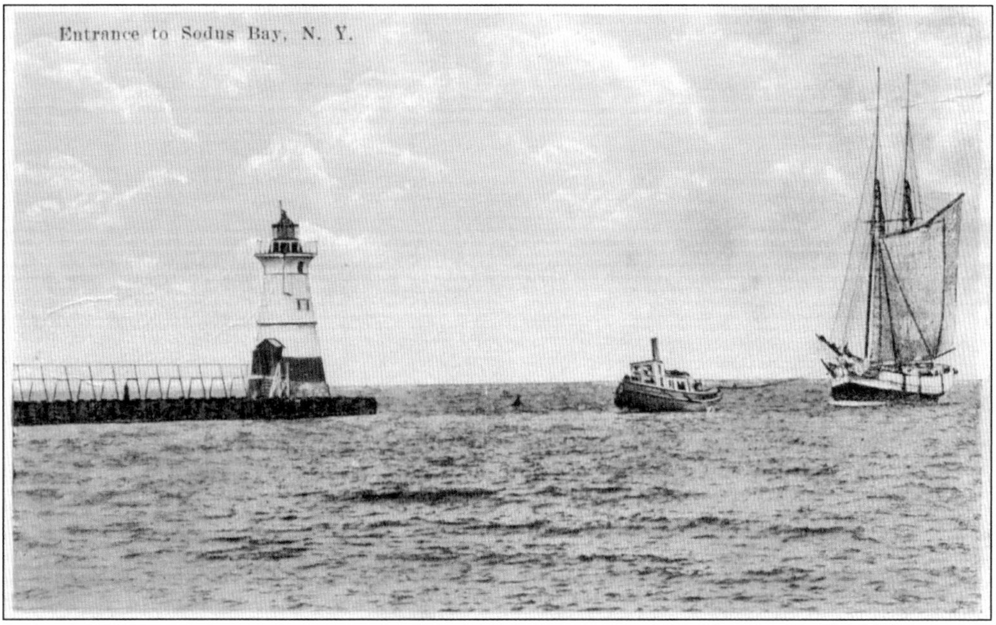


The Sodus Bay Lighthouse at the end of the west pier oversees a tugboat assisting a schooner through the Sodus Bay channel. Schooners made their way in and out of Sodus Bay harbor frequently in the early 1800s to pick up goods from Sodus Point (then Troupville) and other commercial docks around the bay. This schooner is likely arriving to take on a load of coal, shipments of which began at Sodus Point in the late 1800s.

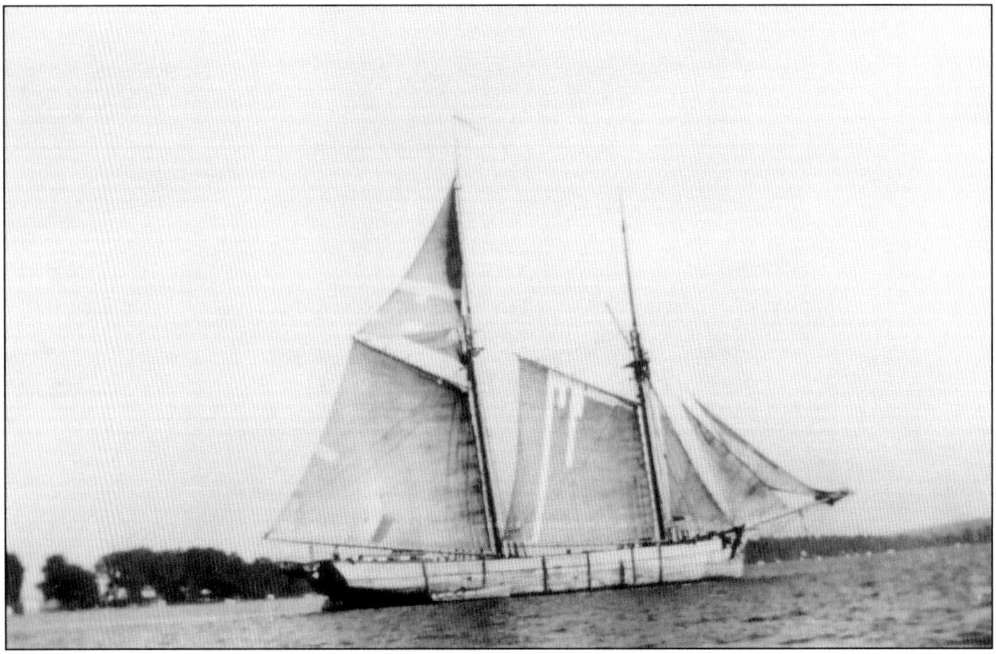

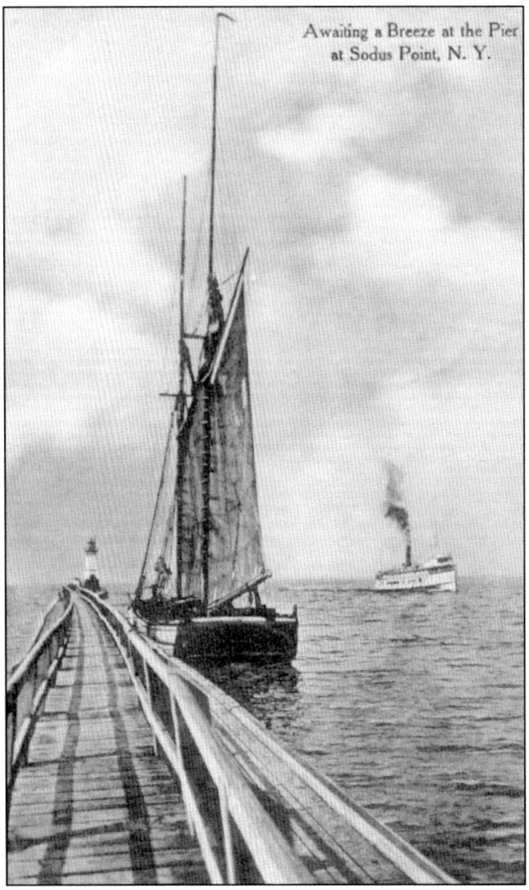


Coal schooners were rugged craft. This schooner, entering Sodus Bay harbor, rides high on the water headed for the coal trestle where its hold will be filled with coal. It will then set sail to deliver the coal to ports in Canada and elsewhere on the Great Lakes. Charles Point can be seen to the left in the background. (TOH.)

As the notation on the postcard reads, this coal schooner awaits a breeze before it can head out into Lake Ontario to deliver its shipment. In contrast to the sailing vessel, the steamer *Arundell*, a newer mode of transportation for the time, approaches the pier at Sodus Bay under steam power. *Arundell* is bringing summer visitors from Rochester to the bay and on to points farther east on the lakeshore.

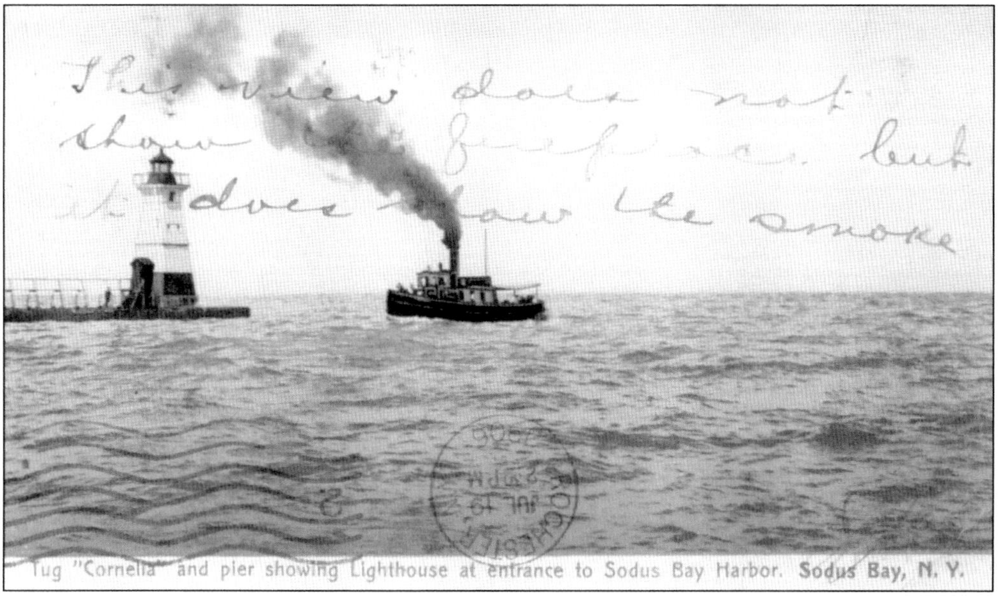


*Cornelia* was the official Sodus Bay harbor tugboat from 1882 until it was sold in 1916. Built by the Union Dry Dock Company of Buffalo, New York, in 1882, *Cornelia* was owned by S.B. Stewart of Sodus Point. At 61 feet in length, 16 feet abeam, and drawing 8 feet, *Cornelia* guided coal schooners and other sizable vessels. Last used in New York Harbor, *Cornelia* burned at Pier 2 on the North River on June 25, 1923.

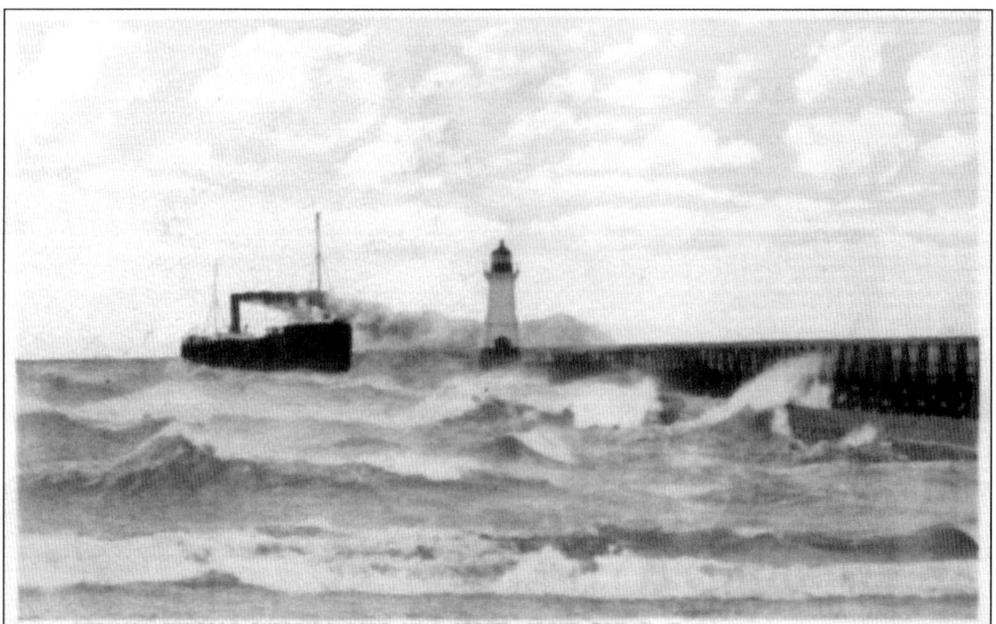


The Sodus Bay lighthouses have guided many a coal boat and other watercraft into Sodus Bay's harbor over the years. Here, the coal boat *Windsor* enters the channel. Ships like the *Fontana, Colfax*, and *Valley Forge* are just a few of the many vessels that navigated through the Sodus Bay channel to receive and transport shipments of coal from Sodus Point between 1873 and 1967.

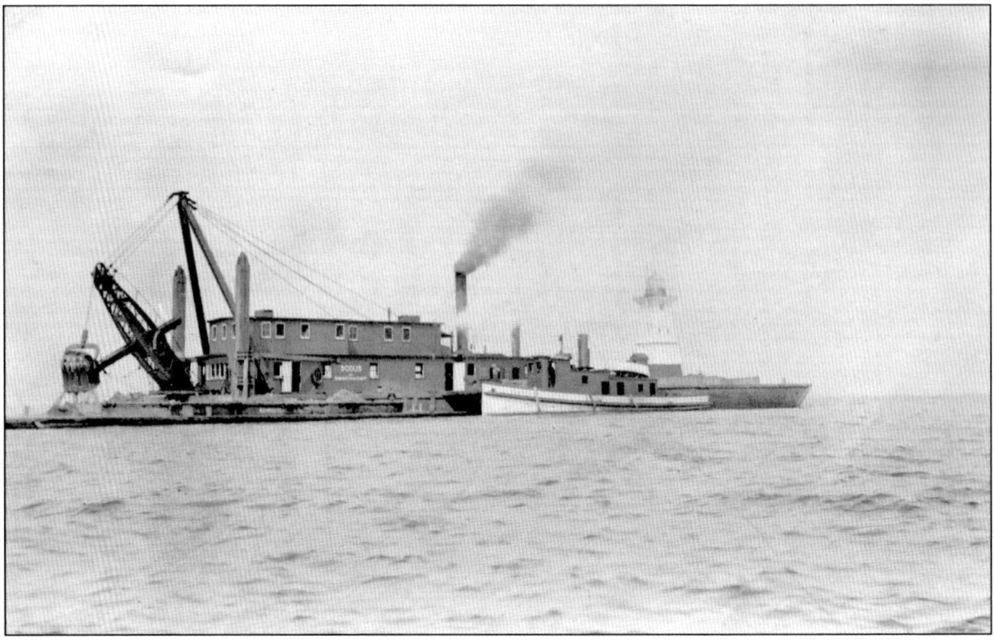

Wind and wave action deposit sand in the channel causing navigational problems. Newspaper records from the late 19th century report schooners going aground in the channel. In 1907, a report by the Army Corps of Engineers details that the channel was dredged to 14 feet at low water. When the deeper draft coal freighters began entering the bay around 1920, the channel was dredged to 22 feet. (SBHS.)

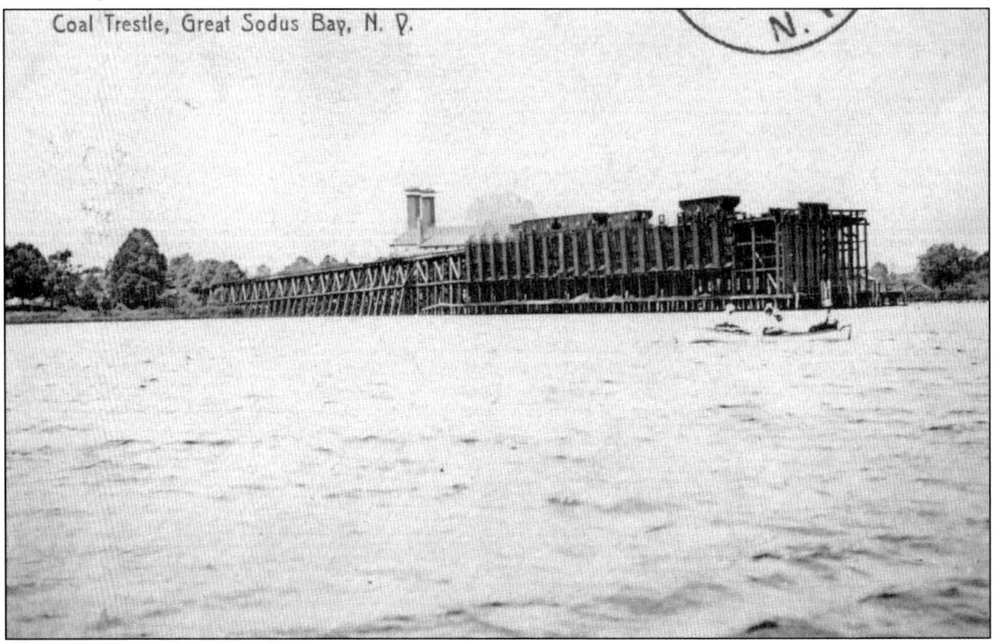


This postcard of the Sodus Bay coal trestle is postmarked 1912. The trestle in this picture would have been the first coal trestle at Sodus Point. Built in 1873, the structure was 400 feet long and rose 40 feet above the water. The second coal trestle, built in 1927, was 800 feet in length and 60 feet in height above the waterline.

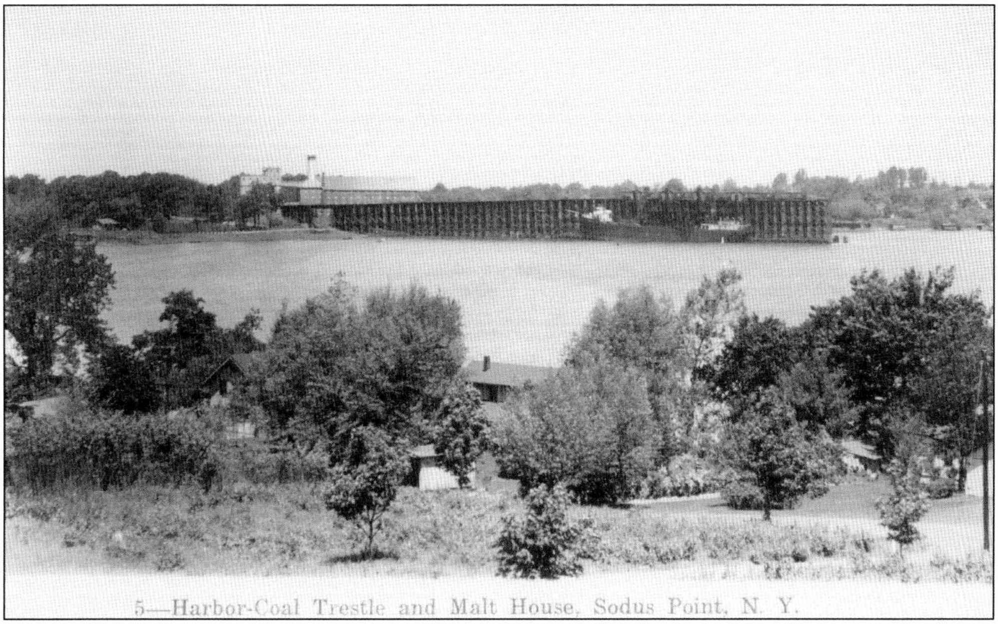


A great view from South Shore, looking across the cove near First Creek, shows the second coal trestle with the malt house behind. One of the larger coal freighters is at the coal dock. Barley was shipped by schooner to the malt house owned by Col. A.B. Parsons of Sodus Point. The Genesee Brewing Company purchased and renovated the malt house in 1936. The malt house closed in 1986. (SBHS.)

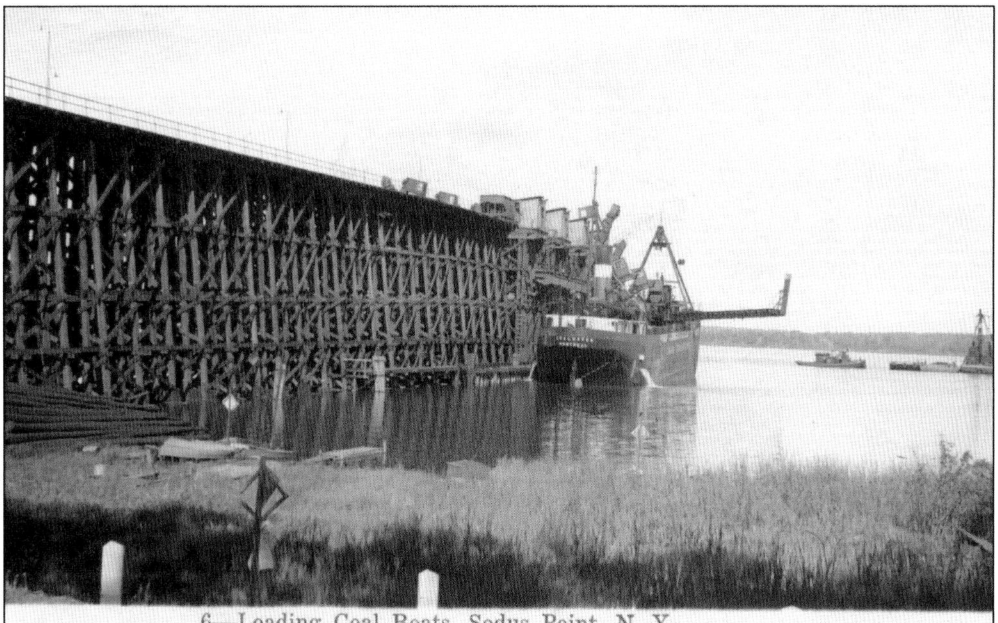


As seen from shore, the Canadian freighter *Coalhaven* sits at the trestle awaiting a shipment of coal to be loaded, after which it would deliver the shipment to ports in Canada. Built in 1928, *Coalhaven* measured 258 feet in length with a 43-foot beam and a 22-foot draft. *Coalhaven* was sold for scrap in 1968, one year after the closing of the Sodus Point coal trestle.

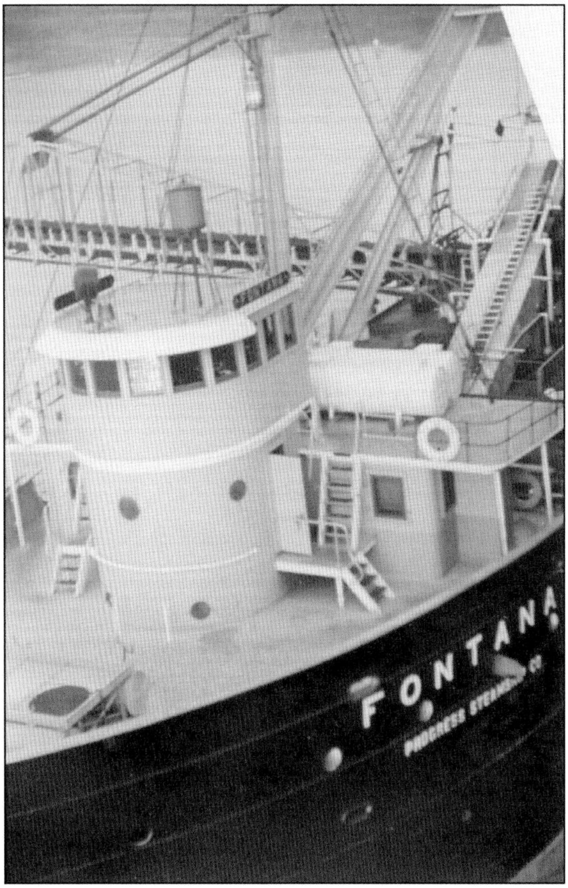


Paul Fox worked on the coal trestle as a teenager in the 1930s. Spending summers at Lake Bluff, Fox's mother would wake him when the coal boats arrived early in the morning. Paddling his canoe across the bay to the coal trestle at Sodus Point, Fox would join the team for a long and dirty day's work shoveling coal into the holds of the ships. Fox was an eager young photographer, and these photographs are from a collection of his. They were taken about 1937 and show men working at the top of the trestle and the boat being loaded on this day, the *Fontana*. Built in 1904, as the *R.W. England*, this freighter was 377 feet in length. With a varied history of ownership, it became the *Frank Seither* in 1919. The Progress S.S. Company bought the boat in 1923, naming it *Fontana*.

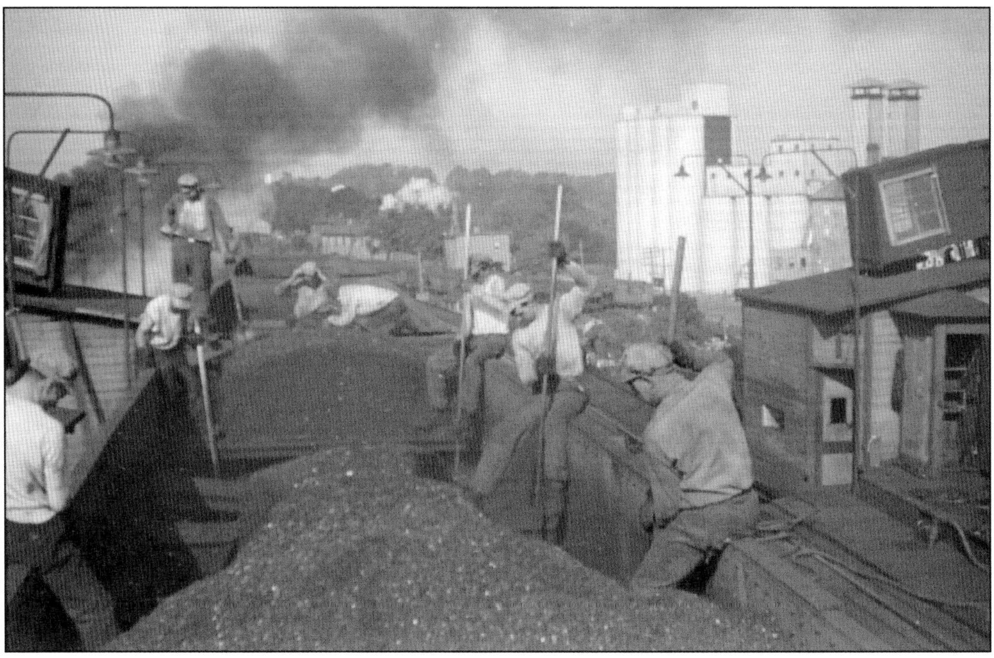

Young Paul Fox poses for a picture next to the railcars atop the coal trestle. The cars were driven out on tracks to the point where the men would shovel the coal into the hold of the ships. Shakers were added to the trestle around 1950. The shakers eliminated the dirty work the men had of shoveling the coal down chutes into the boat.

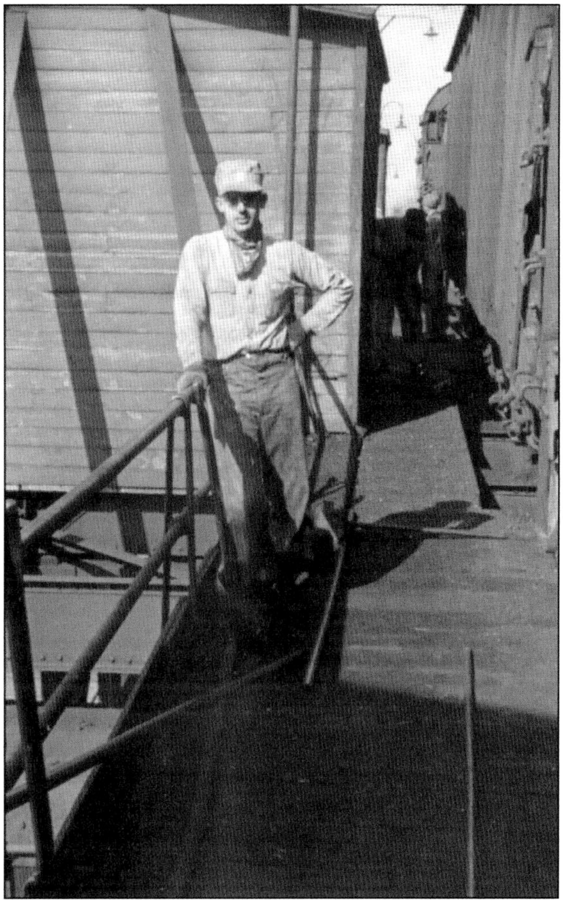

No, this is not a sunset, but a hazy Sodus Bay sunrise. Probably taking a break from shoveling, photographer Fox captured this early morning moment atop the coal trestle. The view looks east, between Sand Point in the foreground and the northern point of Newark Island on the right, toward Paul's homeland of Lake Bluff. The shipping of coal from Sodus Bay ceased in 1967. The trestle was destroyed by fire while being torn down in 1972.

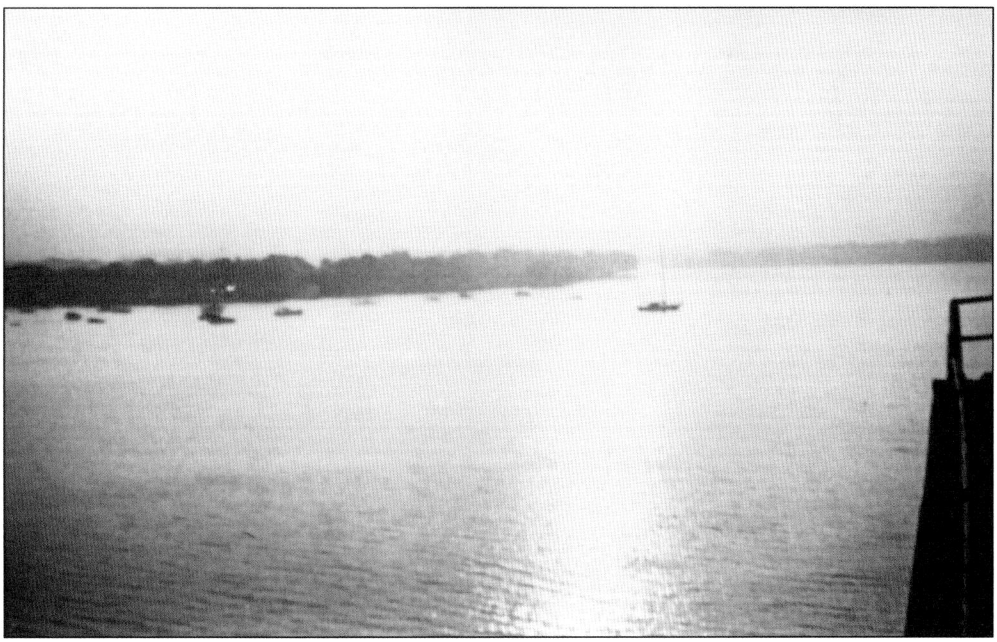

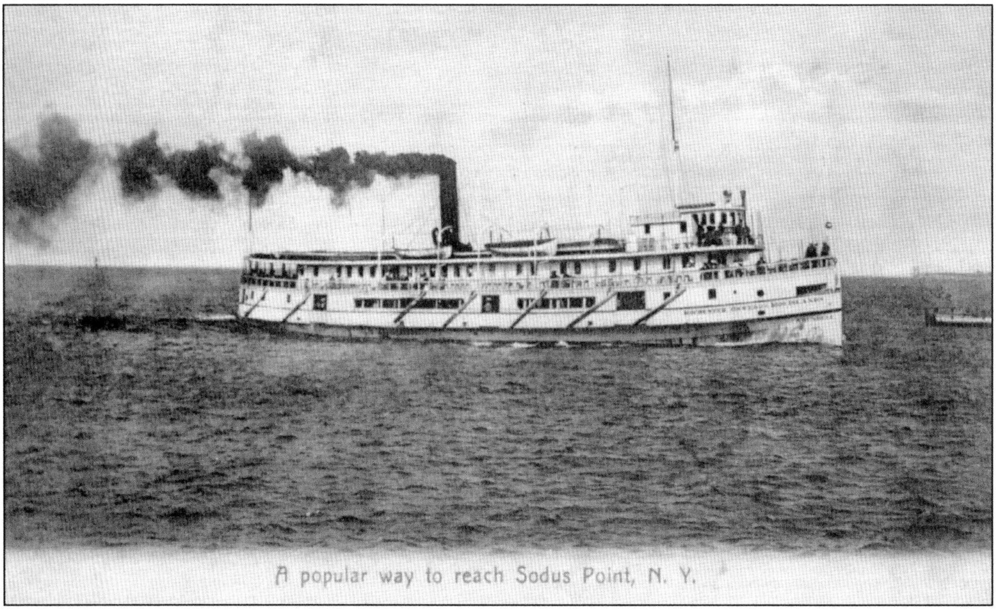


The *Arundell* enters Sodus Bay channel in the undivided back postcard above, dated May 11, 1907. Below, a stern view of the *Arundell*, postmarked 1905, reveals the first coal trestle with a coal schooner at dock. To *Arundell*'s starboard side, grain silos, a warehouse, and several smaller buildings are visible. Built of iron, *Arundell* was constructed in Buffalo by David Bell in 1878. The 306-ton boat was 136.6 feet long, with a 23.4-foot beam, and had an 11-foot draft. In 1892, it was lengthened to 166.6 feet with a 26.5-foot beam. *Arundell*'s history as a passenger steamer spanned across the Great Lakes until it burned at dock at Douglass, Michigan, in 1911. It was rebuilt as a barge, re-documented in 1916, and rechristened *Brewster* in 1921. In 1922, *Brewster* collided with a steamer and met its final resting place at the bottom of the James River in Virginia.

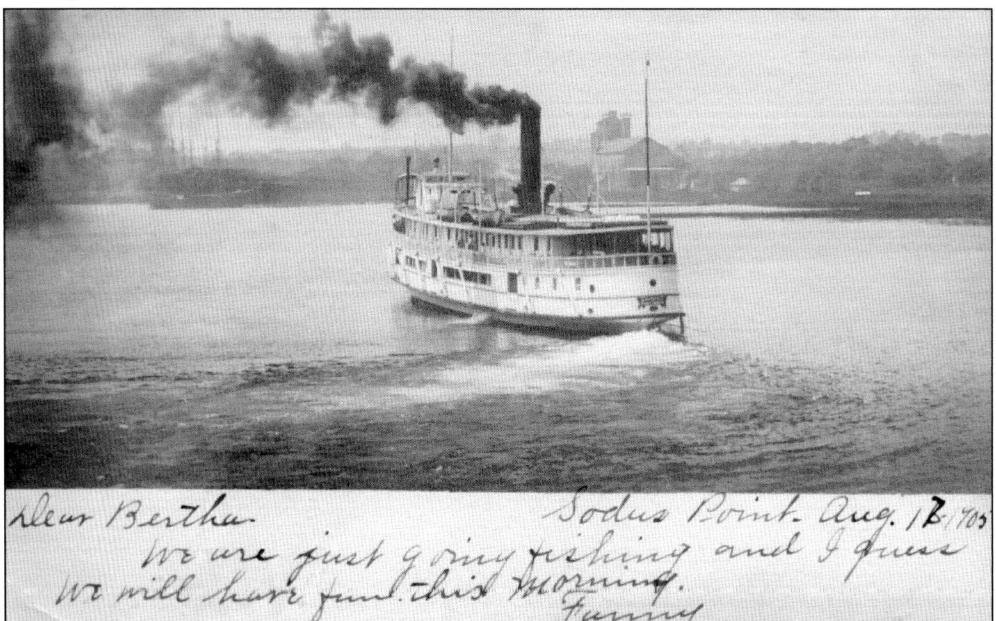

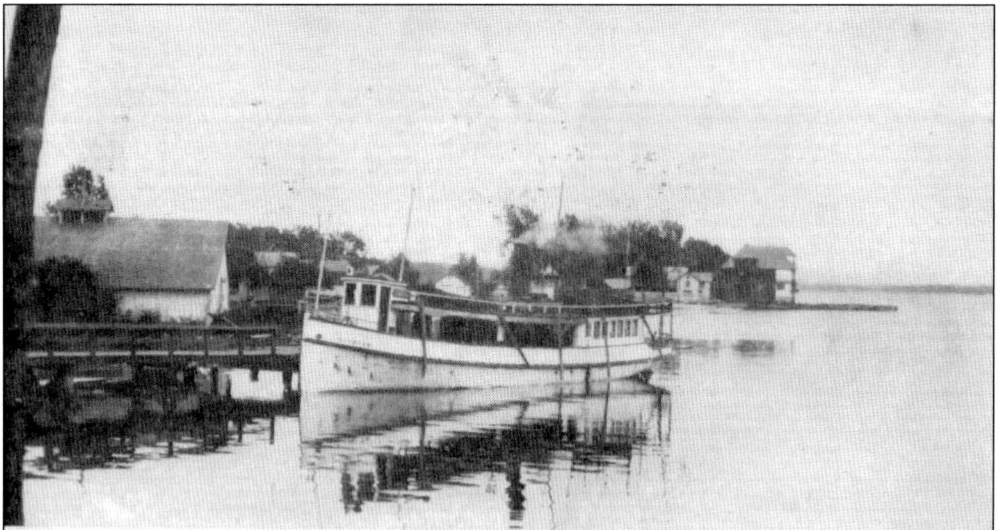

Boat Landing and Club House, Sodus Bay, N. Y.

Above, the steamer *Sunbeam* poses alone at the passenger dock located on the protected south shore of Sand Point. In the postcard below, *Sunbeam* sits at the end of the dock, and a twin steamer rests in the foreground. Between 1880 and 1910, steamers of all sizes traveled over the waters of Sodus Bay delivering mail and passengers to the bay's various resort areas. *Lizzie*, *Willie Poucher*, *Ideal*, *Algona*, *Glenn*, *Seabird*, and the *H.C. LeRoy* were familiar boats on the bay during this time of growth and popularity. Many passengers arrived at Sodus Point by train. Those vacationers with destinations elsewhere on the bay boarded one of the bay's steamers at this landing to continue their journeys. The Sodus Bay Yacht Club can be seen in the background on the left.

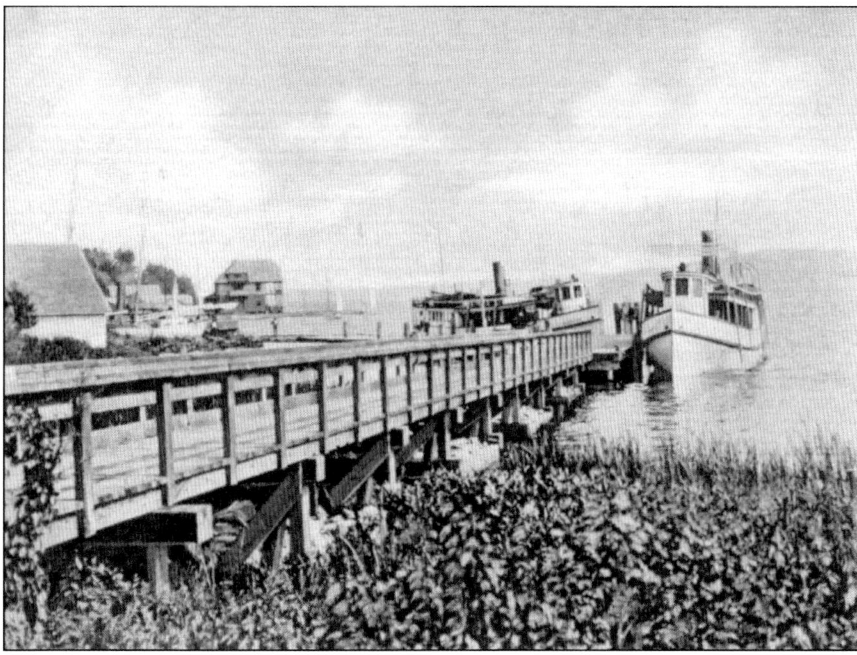

Steamer Landing and Yacht Club House at Sodus Point, N. Y.

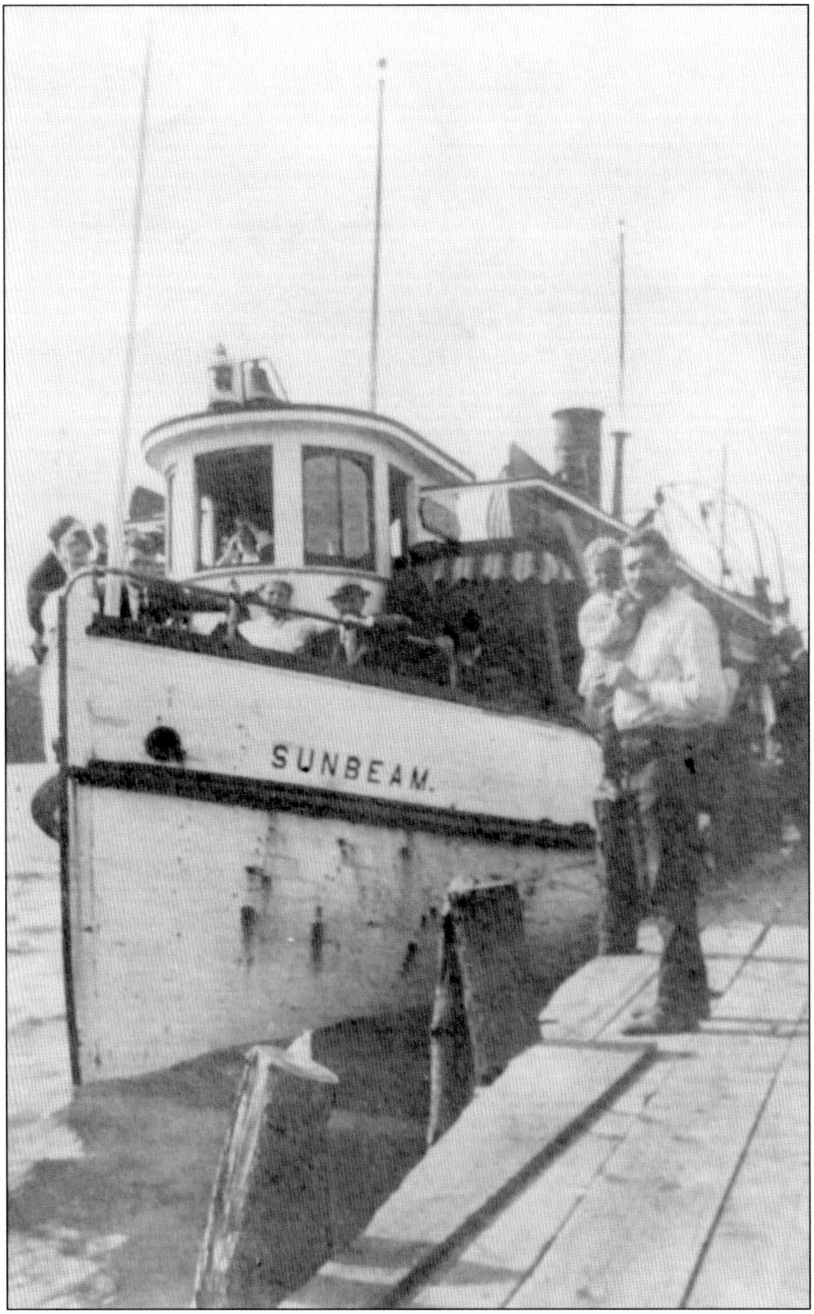


*Sunbeam* may well be the best-remembered, or at least the most talked about, of all the steamers on Sodus Bay. Built in 1888 in Buffalo, *Sunbeam* measured 64 feet long, 12.8 feet abeam, drew 5.8 feet, and had a gross tonnage of 52 tons. She ran the bay from 1890 to 1910 and was capable of carrying 110 passengers. Albert Benham, a longtime steamboat commander and fireman, wrote an article for the September 1955 *Steamboat Bill* magazine titled "Great Sodus Bay Steamboats from 1874 to 1910." Benham states that he decommissioned *Sunbeam* and *Glenn* at Resort on Sodus Bay. There, the two boats rested until they finally burned. Some say the smokestack of one of the steamers can still be seen to this day in its resting place near Resort. (TOH.)

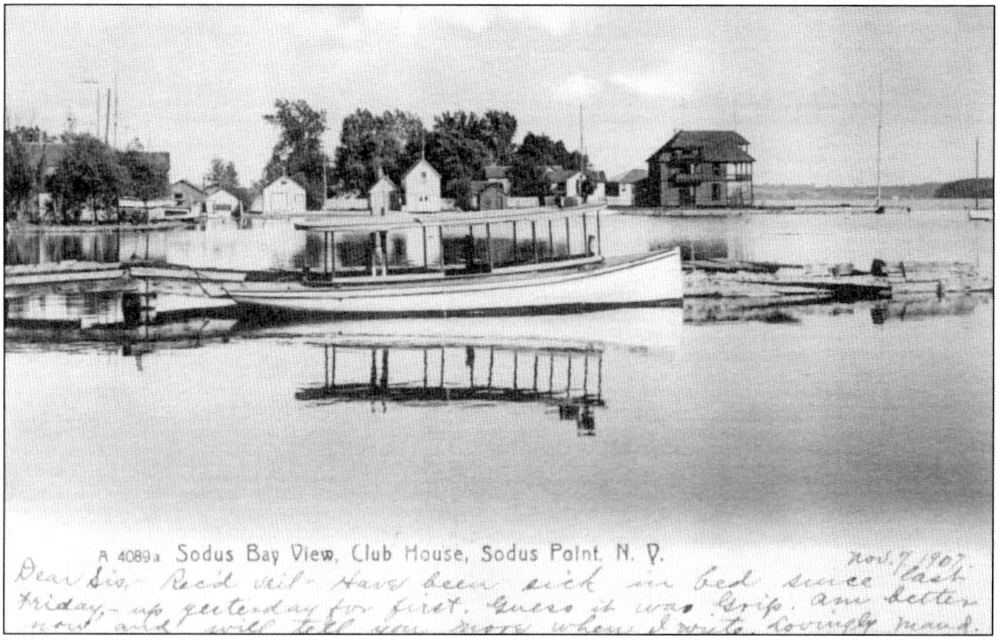


A small private launch sits at dock near the Sodus Bay Yacht Club (building in the top right). The Steamboat Act of 1852 required that all engineers and pilots of steam-driven vessels be licensed. Licensing required two years of formal training. People wanted to enjoy and control their own water travel, and so the naphtha launch became a popular alternative that was safe and easy to run.

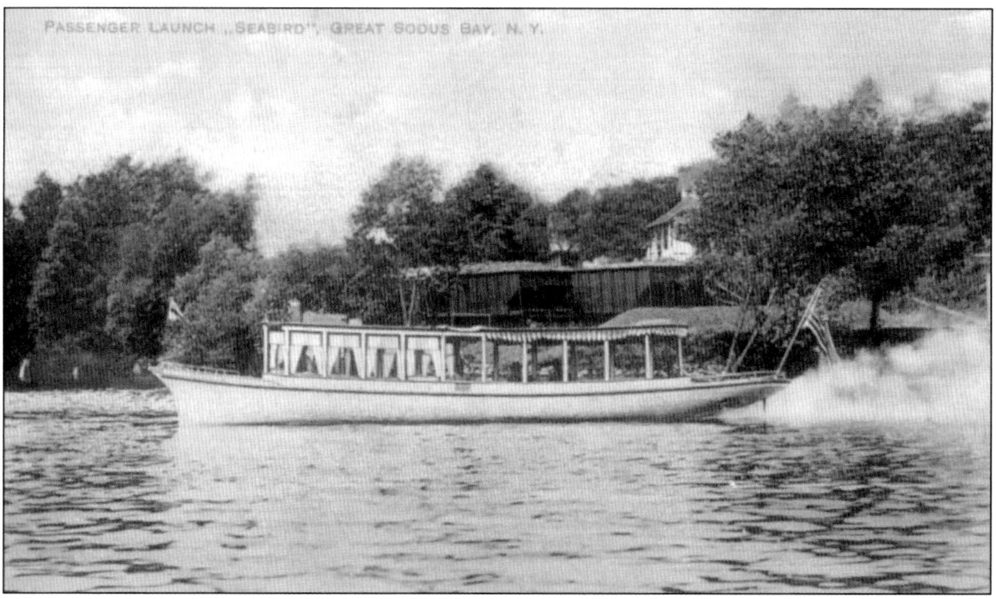


The passenger gasoline launch *Seabird* is seen here with railcars, probably coming from the ore dock, in the background at Sodus Point. Albert Benham, in his steamboat article in the September 1955 issue of *Steamboat Bill*, writes that it was around 1903 when gasoline boats began carrying passengers around Sodus Bay. *Seabird* was a familiar launch on the bay.

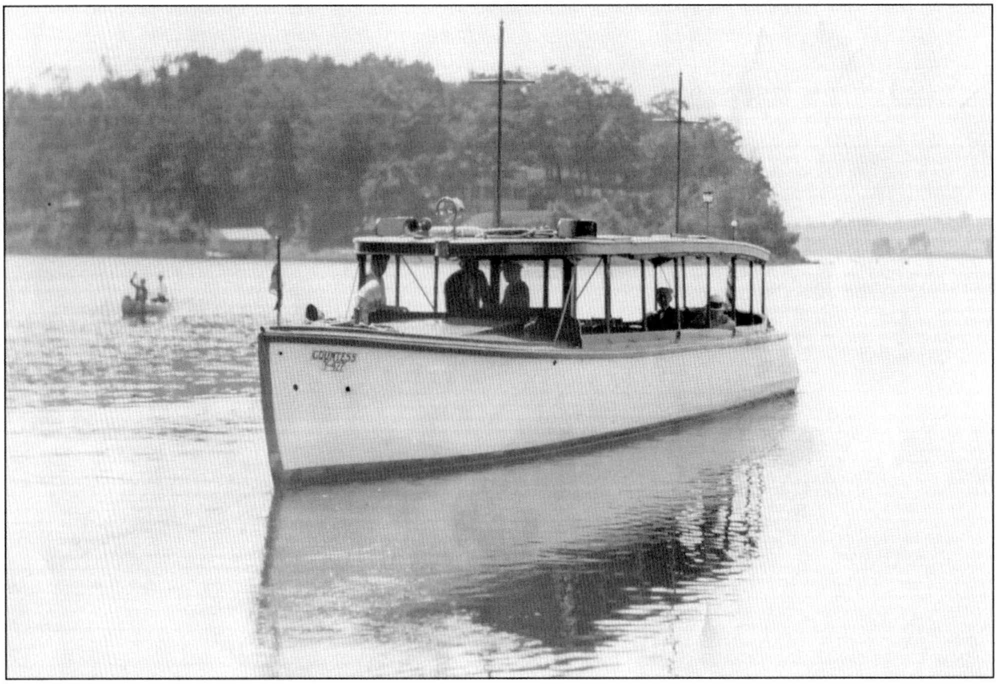

Many postcard images of boats were taken at Sodus Point or at the steamer landings around the bay. This wonderful 1930s-era photograph shows a gas launch, with a canoe to the starboard side, cruising along the waters between the north end of LeRoy Island, Crescent Beach, and Lake Bluff. Those familiar with cottages on LeRoy Island may recognize the lone cottage in this photograph. (SBHS.)

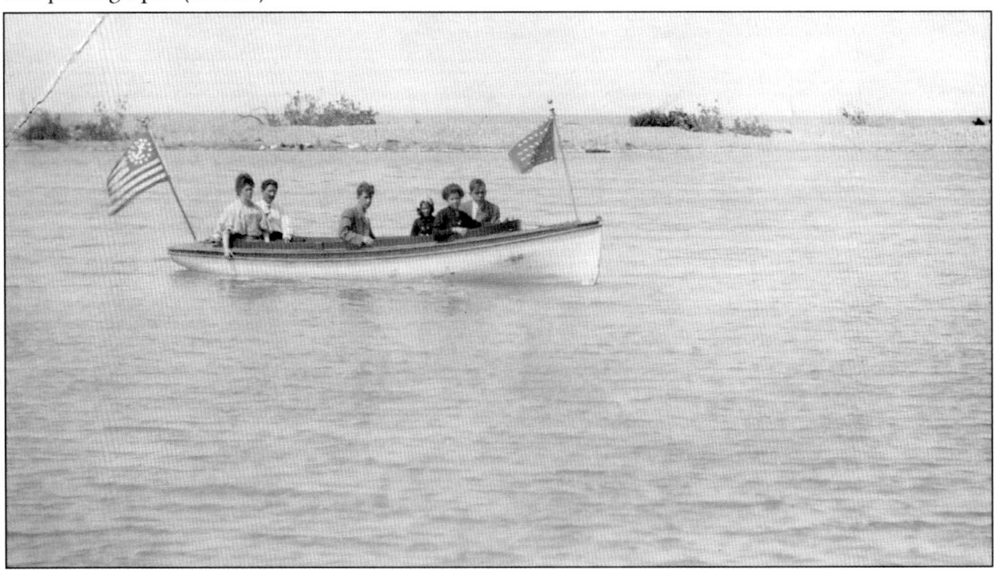

The people in this small gas launch are motoring in front of Crescent Beach. Lake Ontario can be easily seen on the other side of Crescent Beach. The US Yacht Ensign flag is flown at the stern. This flag was designed around 1840 and was used to designate that the yacht was registered and would not have to clear customs in traveling between ports. Flying on the bow is the US jack flag from 1908 to 1912. (TOH.)

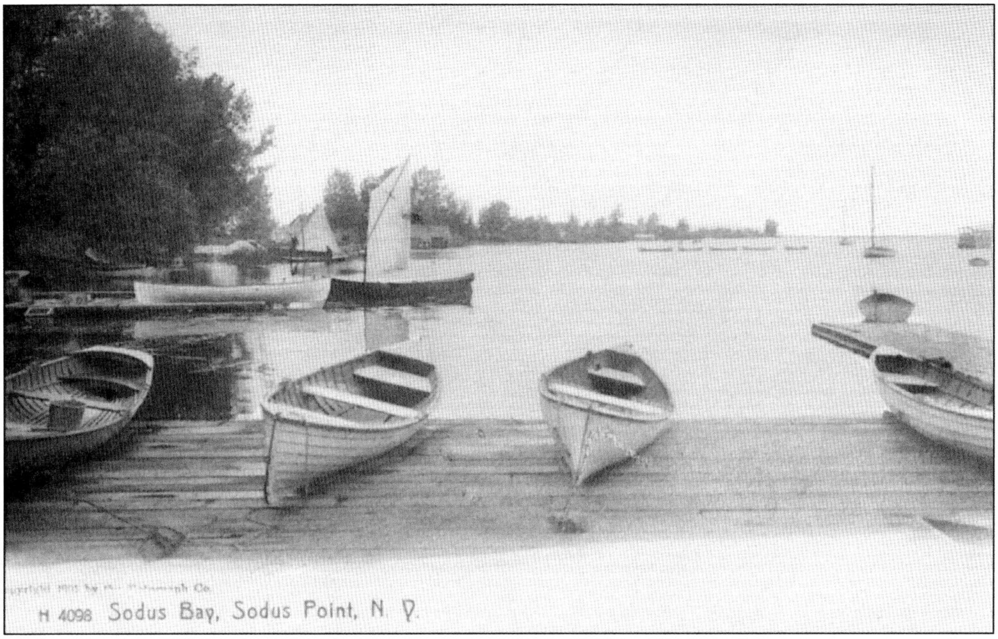


Rowing skiffs offered a safe, simple, and quiet form of moving about on the bay for fishing, visiting, or sightseeing. Many of the hotels and boat rental businesses kept a fleet of rowboats for loan to vacationers. The undivided back on the postcard above places the image as pre-1907. The view in the postcard above looks east toward the pier, with Lake Bluff in the right corner just above the covered launch. The view in the card below, with a 1911 postmark, was taken from a point a little farther east along Sand Point. Showing a similar view as the postcard above, the increasing busyness of the bay is apparent by growth of the number of boats in this shallow cove. A coal boat can be seen exiting the bay through the channel.

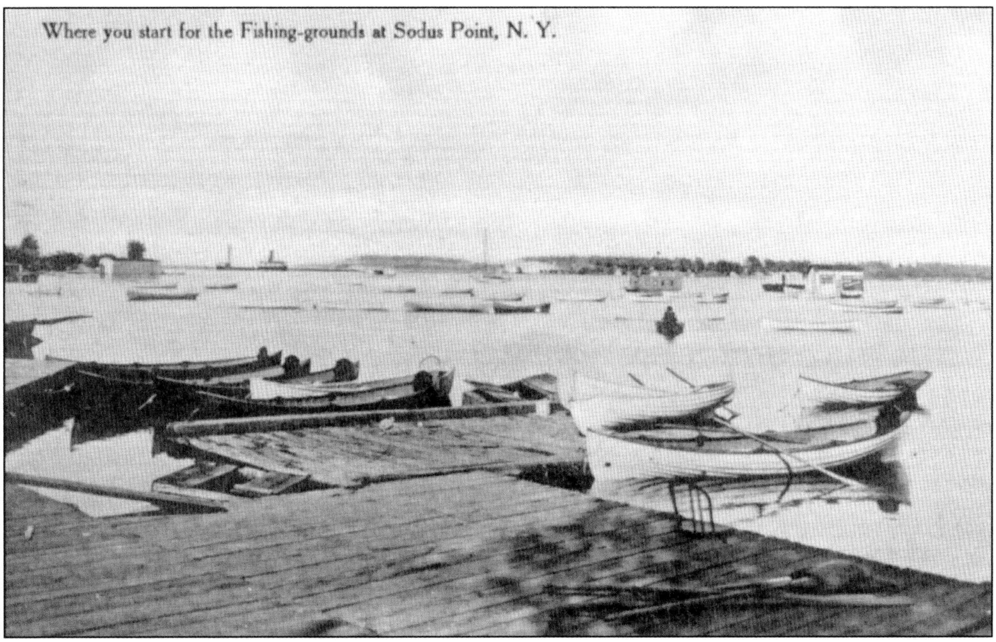

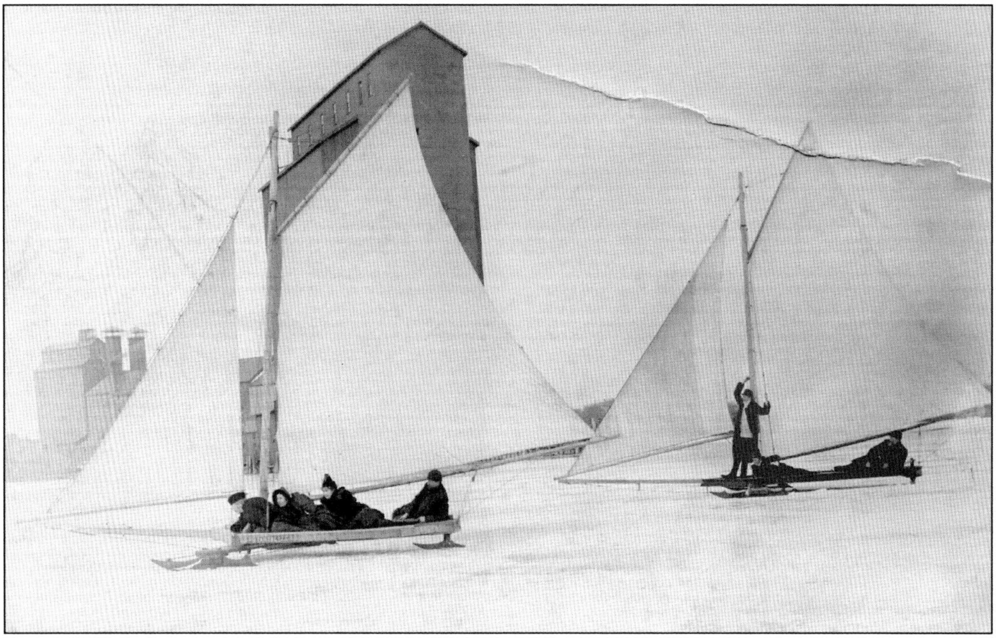

Water is not the only way to travel by boat. The smooth, hard surface of ice provides a speedy ride with very little resistance. With skis, iceboats allow the die-hard boater the possibility of "sailing" during the winter months. Iceboating has been a popular winter activity on Sodus Bay over the years. For some, it was a serious mode of transportation in the mid-1800s to get from one side of the bay to the other when the water was frozen. The photograph above shows iceboats in front of the grain elevators, north of the coal trestle, at Sodus Point. This has always been a well-liked spot for iceboating. In the photograph below, around 15 boats are lined up before the start of a race. The name of the lead iceboat in the above image is *Tantalizer.* (Both, SBHS.)

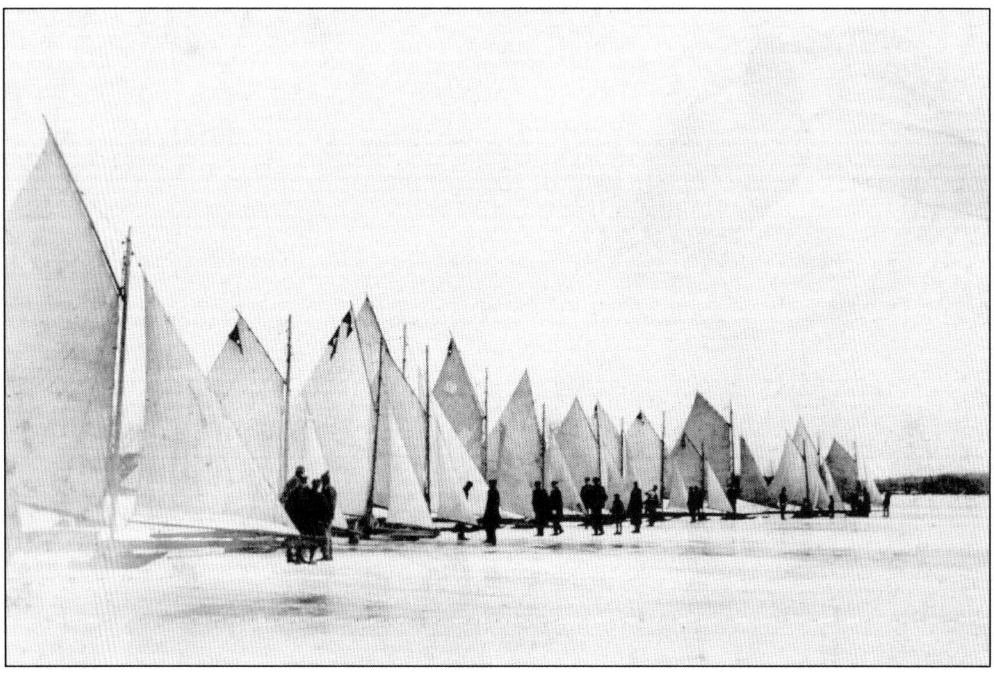

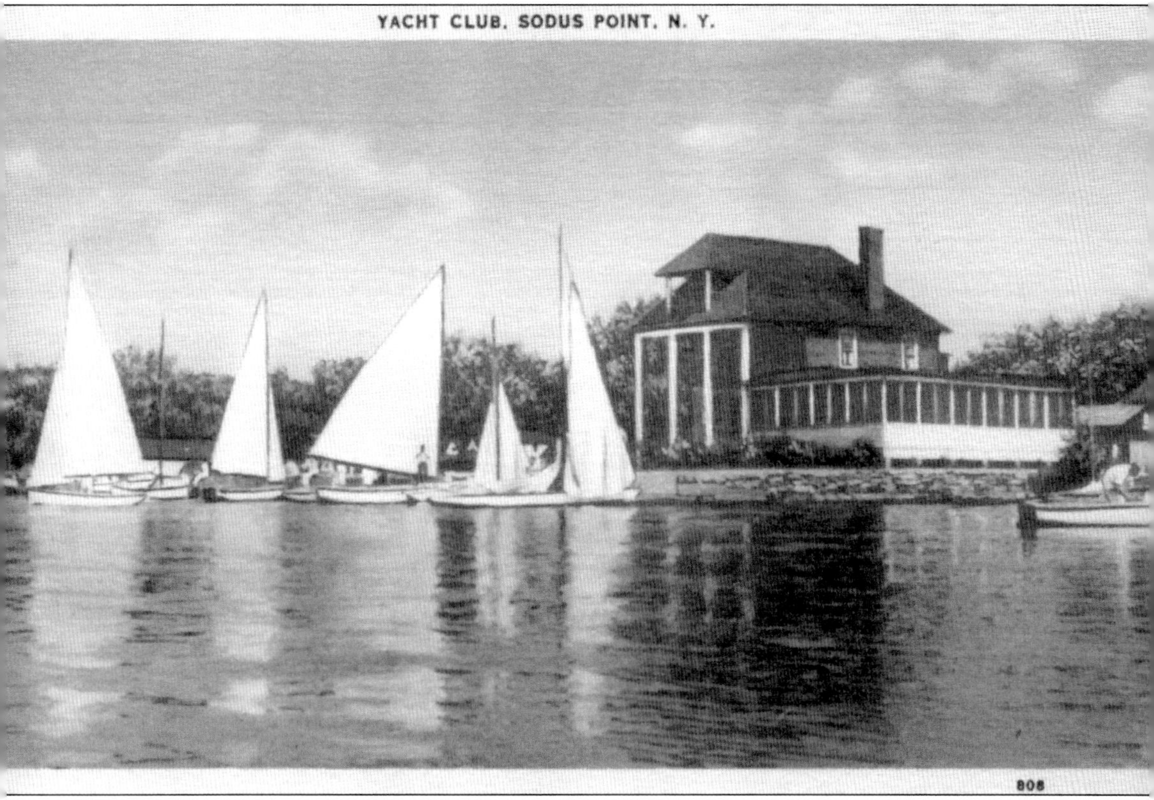


Some Sodus Point cottagers organized a sailing race on Sodus Bay to be held July 4, 1893. That race became inspiration for a challenge put forth by the *Newark Arcadian Gazette* newspaper to sponsor a series of races on Sodus Bay and present a trophy to the winner. Those 1893 races nurtured the creation of the Sodus Bay Yacht Club, which was formed later that summer and was incorporated on July 30, 1895. Land for the clubhouse was purchased for $400 from Charles Perkins of Newark in 1896. According to a lengthy article about the new clubhouse in the *Arcadian Weekly Gazette* dated September 22, 1897, construction of the building and docks was completed, and the club had its formal opening the week prior on September 16, 1897. Total cost for the clubhouse and docks was $2,200. The Sodus Bay Yacht Club has been the hub of sailing activity on the bay since. The postcard above shows the Sodus Bay Yacht Club house around 1913.

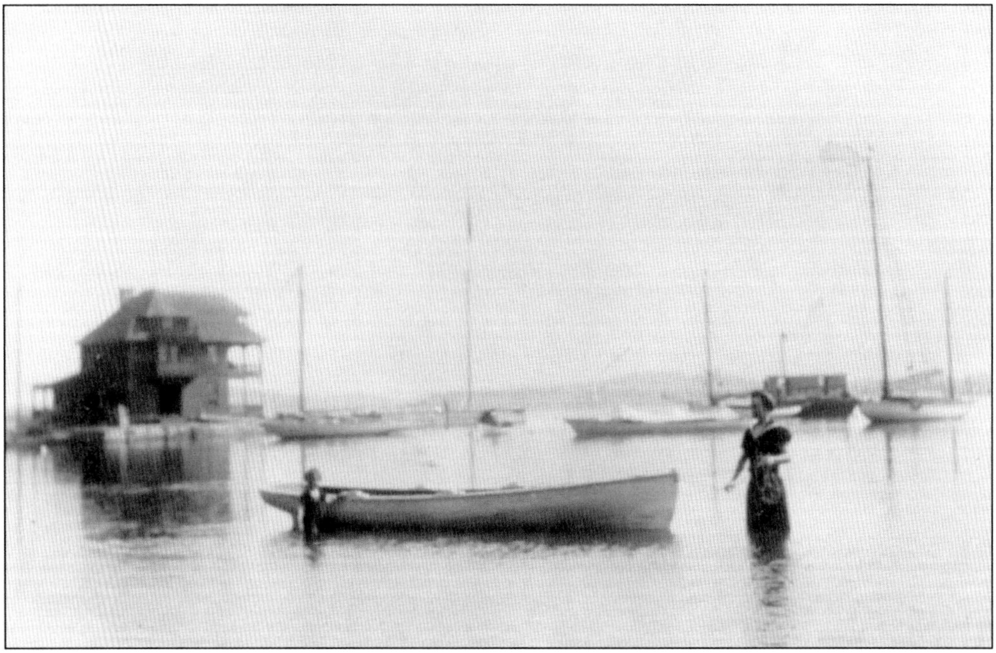

The images above, taken around 1900, and below, around 1915, show the change in the exterior of the Sodus Bay Yacht Club house in size, layout, and painting over the first two decades of the club's organization. By 1913, bathrooms and a kitchen were added to the clubhouse. Entertainment such as dances and dinner parties were frequent Saturday events. The yacht club was a place for everyone around Sodus Bay to gather for socialization, the pleasure of boating, and the thrill of racing. Racing events were not limited to sailboats and motorboats. Canoe, barrel tub, and swimming races were contests also organized by the yacht club. The yacht club's cove grew, as well, in the number and variety of boats occupying the club's moorings. (Above, Sodus Bay Yacht Club; below, SBHS.)

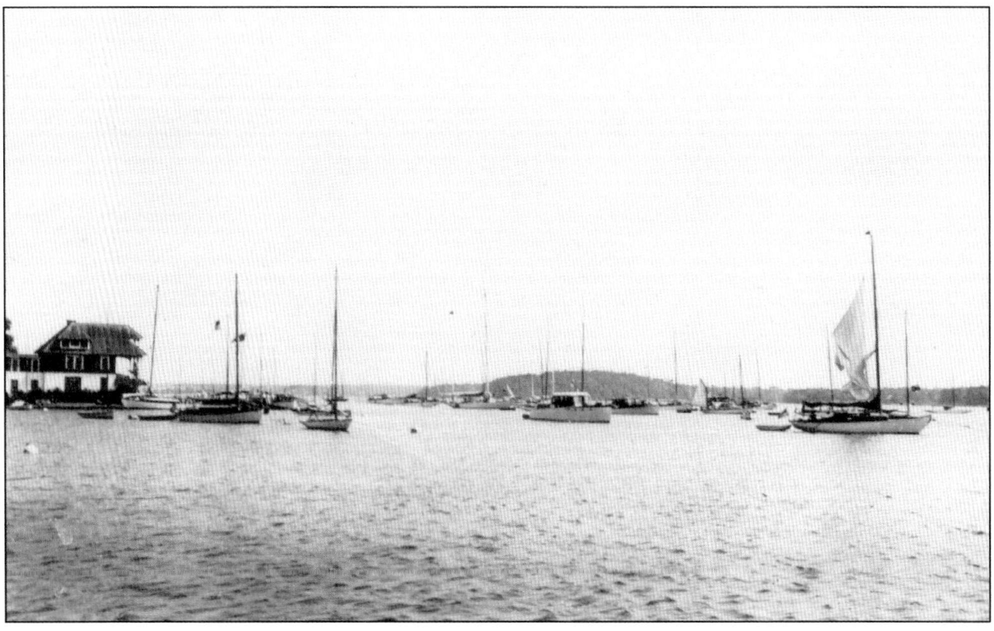

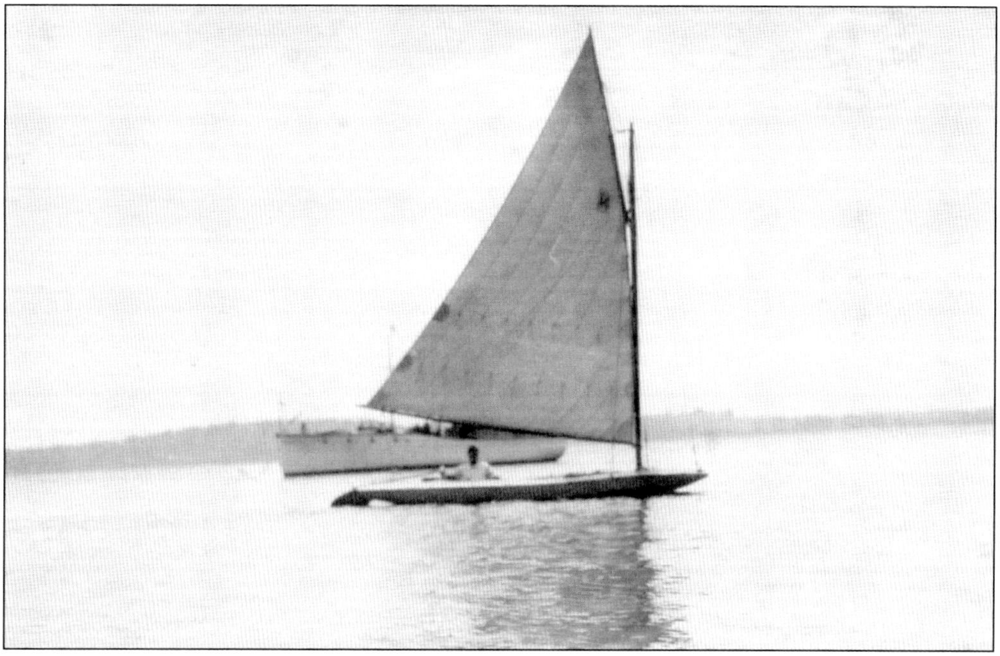

Pictured in the photographs on this page is a small sailboat known as a Lark. Also called "pumpkin seeds" and "skimming dishes," the small sailboats were 16 feet long, with a six-foot beam, had about six inches of freeboard, and hosted a single gaff-rigged sail. This little racer gained popularity in the early 1900s as the designer, C.G. Davis, published his plans for the sailboat in *Rudder* magazine, of which he was editor. From these plans, skilled boatbuilders as well as novices could now build the sailboat. Fleets of Larks popped up everywhere. They became a familiar sight on Sodus Bay and were a popular racing craft through the 1920s. (Above, SBHS; below, Sodus Bay Yacht Club.)

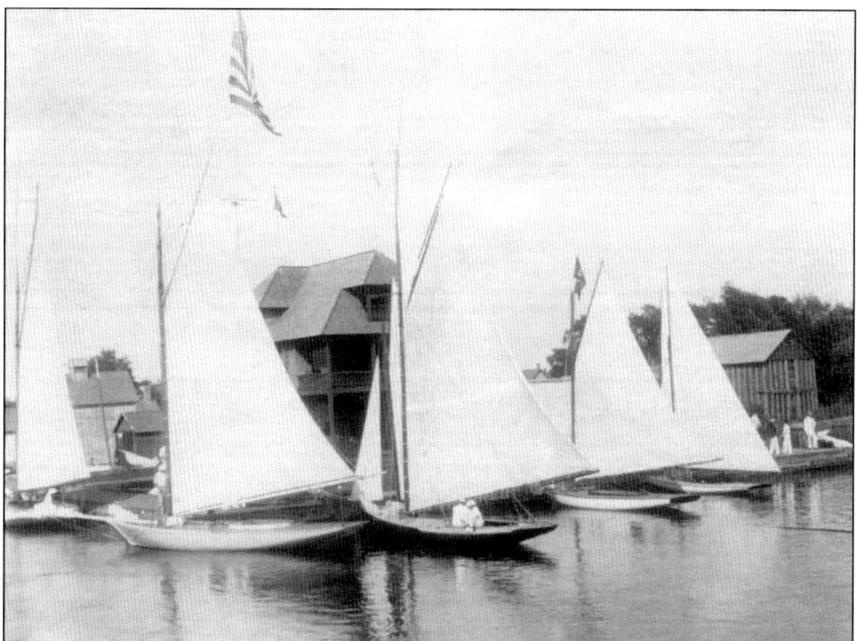

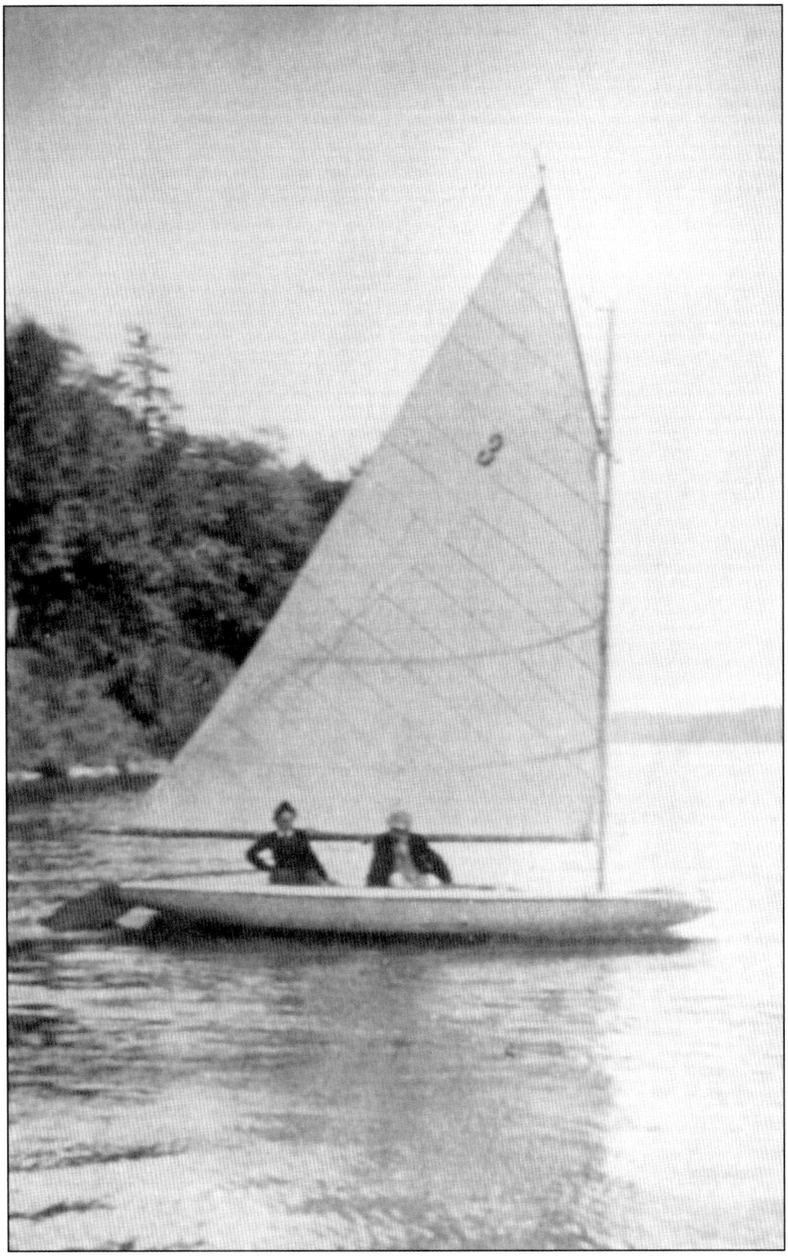

Women over the age of 21 were admitted to the Sodus Bay Yacht Club in 1905 as "associate members" with annual dues payment of $2. The decision to admit women may have been the result of Rose Williams's achievement in 1904 as the first woman to win a yacht race in central New York—racing a newly designed Lark. A Newark, New York, resident, Williams (1872–1967), pictured here with her sailboat, raced Larks on Sodus Bay, her summertime home. In 1905, she won the first Sodus Bay Yacht Club Lark Trophy. That trophy is now called the Old Timers Trophy. Williams won many other races with her No. 3 Lark during her highlighted racing career. Her obituary in the *Newark Courier-Gazette*, on July 6, 1967, reports that she was still racing in 1935, at the age of 63, and appropriately won the Old Timers Trophy "to prove she still knew her sailing and could still beat the boys." (Sodus Bay Yacht Club.)

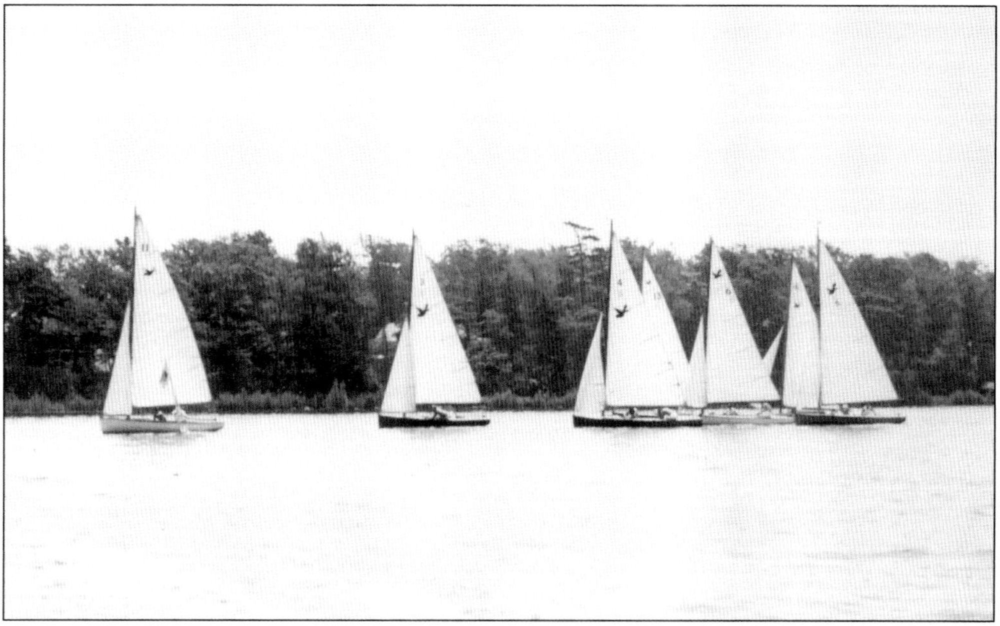

The Sodus Bay Yacht Club fell onto hard times and lost the clubhouse to foreclosure in 1920. It was reorganized in 1923, membership slowly regained its old level, and the club was able to repurchase the property in 1935. In an attempt to attract younger potential members during that period of rebuilding, Commodore Harrison Bloomer and other yacht club members asked retired naval architect Benjamin B. Wood to design a sailboat specifically for the wind and wave conditions of Sodus Bay. And thus, the Robin racing class was born, having the first official race in the summer of 1935. A centerboard boat, 17.5 feet long, with a 6-foot beam and two sails (a jib and a main), the Robin became a popular success in races that continued until the early 1950s. (Both, Sodus Bay Yacht Club.)

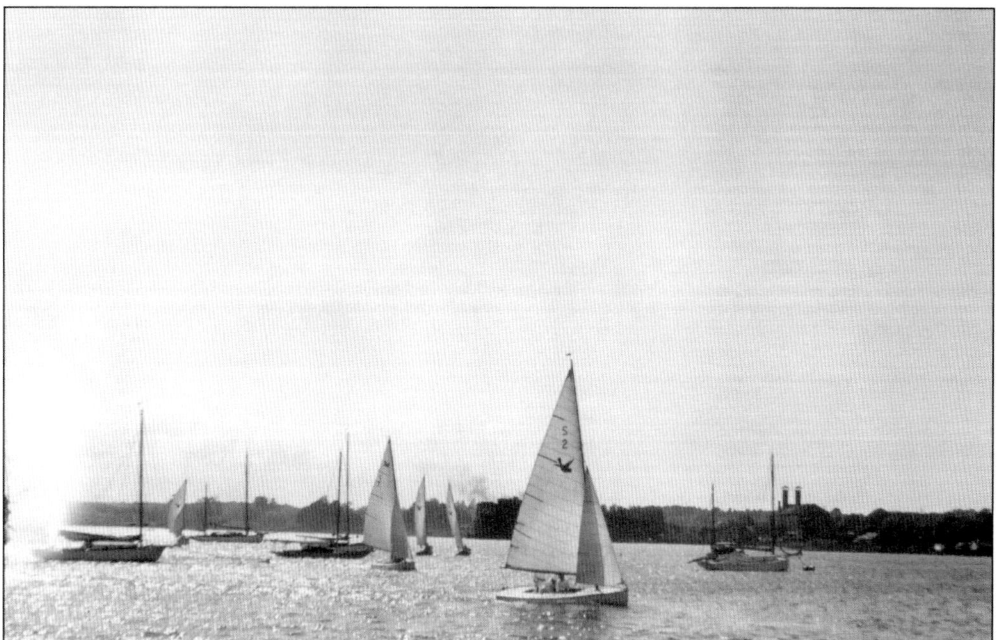

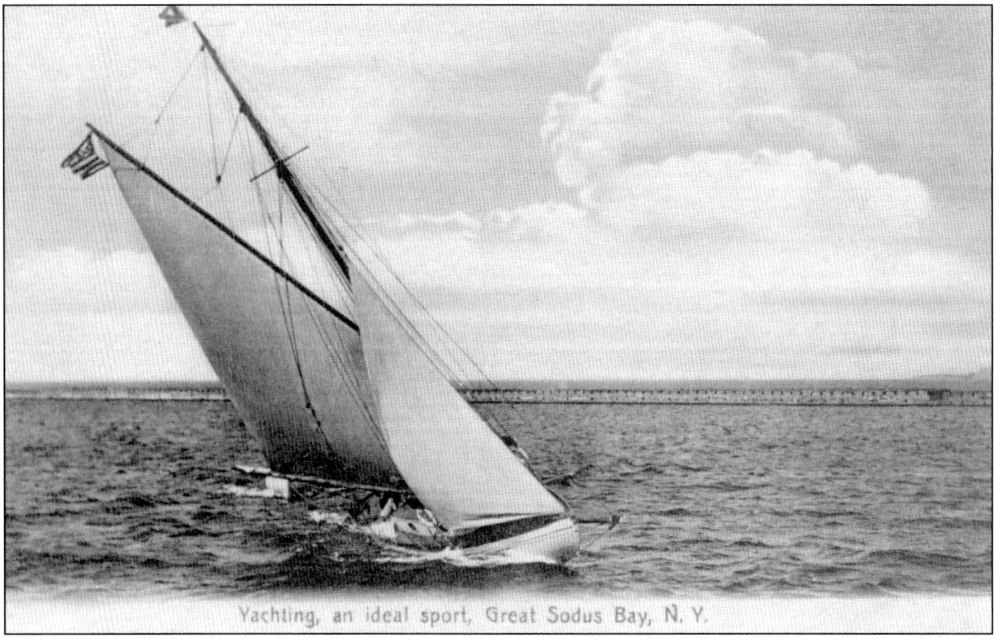


Tacking between the Sodus Bay channel piers can be a tricky maneuver even for the most-seasoned sailors. In days gone by, sailboats had no backup engines. To get through the channel in all sorts of winds, from all directions, timing of the tack was critical, or the boat might crash into the pier. Lake and Chimney Bluffs can be seen above the right side of the pier.

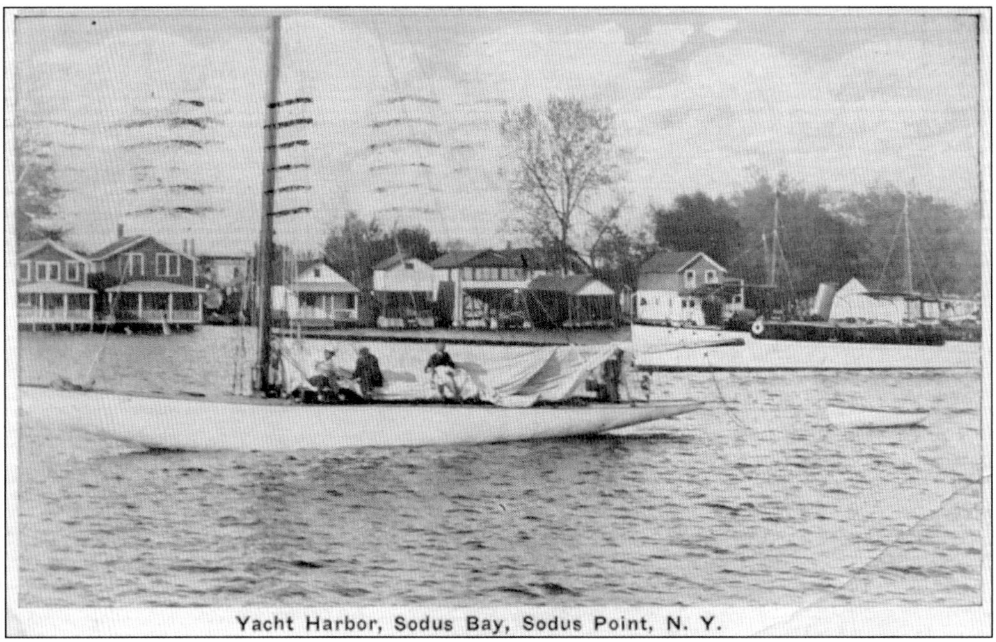


Sailing and motor yachts return to the Sodus Bay Yacht Club at the end of the day. In the foreground, with dingy in tow, the men on deck of this 40-foot sailboat take care of sails, storing them below, and making everything ready for the next day's pleasure sail or race. A motor launch moves along behind the sailboat. This image was taken just east of the yacht club.

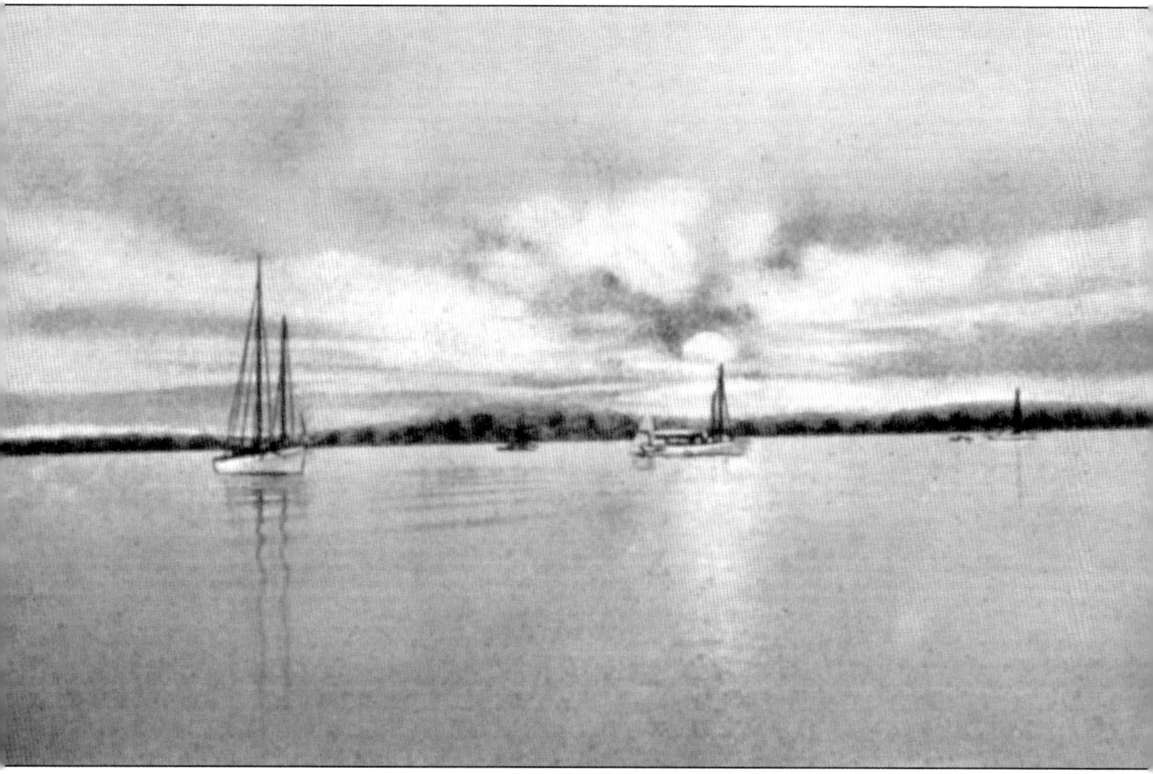

To conclude, a selected quote from James Sheffield's 1901 *Point Charles Sketches* best shares the sentiment of this postcard titled "Yachts at Sunset on Sodus Bay" and the period of time honored within this book: "Twilight is throwing its deep shadows on the distant landscape, and the gray mist is rising from the valleys; the various pleasures of the day are over, groups appear on the wide verandas, friends are hastening to meet incoming guests as the *Sunbeam* turns Sand Point and its whistle is heard, telling us 'someone is coming.' Others watch the little fleet of rowboats, one after another pulling out from Sodus Point, and with measured stroke of the oars, the tiny craft glide over the glassy waters, and friends slowly approach our green shores. And when the night covers us with its somber mantle, and the glittering stars, one after another appear in the heavens, the evening sports begin, and the children grow merry under the trees, and the older seek solace in friendly conversation." And so ends with the closing of the day and a tour around Great Sodus Bay!

# Bibliography


Becker, John C. *Hills Tumble Into Ontario: A History of Lake Bluff.* Private, New York, 1989.

Benham, Albert H. "Great Sodus Bay Steamboats from 1874 to 1910." *Steamboat Bill: Journal of the Steamship Historical Society of America.* September 1955.

Cook, A. Isabella. *Pioneer History of Sodus Point, N.Y.* Sodus Point, NY: Sodus Bay Historical Society, 1915 (1994).

"Historic Sodus Point." Historicsoduspoint.com. Bruce Farrington.

Green, Walter Henry. *Great Sodus Bay: History, Reminiscences, Anecdotes, and Legends.* Rochester, NY: Henderson-Mosher, 1947.

McNett, Mrs. D.F. *Great Sodus Bay: A Beautiful Historical Sketch of this Famous Resort.* Sodus Point, NY: Sodus Bay Improvement Association, 1912. Republished by Sodus Bay Historical Society, 1977.

Merrill, Arch. *The Ridge: Ontario's Blossom Country.* Rochester, NY: Louis Heindl and Son, 1944.

Northern New York Library Network. New York State Historic Newspapers Project. nyhistoricnewspapers.org.

Sheffield, James Cory. *Point Charles Sketch.* Private, 1901.

"Sodus Bay, NY." lighthousefriends.com. Kraig Anderson. October 4, 2014. Web. October 8, 2015.

Sodus Bay Yacht Club. *Sodus Bay Yacht Club: The Centennial History 1893–1993.* Sodus Point, NY: Sodus Bay Yacht Club, 1993.

# About the Sodus Bay Historical Society

The Sodus Bay Historical Society (SBHS) was founded in 1972. The mission of the society is to collect, preserve, and exhibit records, writings, historical items, and artifacts pertinent to the history of the Great Sodus Bay area. The society works to serve the educational and cultural needs of the Sodus Bay community and surrounding area. Free summertime lecture and concert series are local events SBHS provides to inform and enhance the lives of both community members and summer visitors to the Sodus Bay region.

The preservation of historic structures, sites, and monuments is an important component of the mission of SBHS. The group has been instrumental in getting several buildings listed in the National Register of Historic Places, including the Sodus Bay Lighthouse, located on Lake Ontario in the village of Sodus Point.

Since July 4, 1985, SBHS has operated a museum, which is located in the old lighthouse and focuses on local and maritime history, and maintains beautiful gardens surrounding this historic 1870 structure, located at 7606 North Ontario Street in the village of Sodus Point.

For additional information, please visit www.sodusbaylighthouse.org.